PEN PORTRAITS AND REVIEWS

LONDON

PUBLISHED BY

Constable and Company Ltd.

10-12 Orange Street, W.C.2

PEN PORTRAITS AND REVIEWS BY BERNARD SHAW

LONDON

CONSTABLE AND COMPANY

LIMITED

Published in the Limited Collected Edition 1931
Revised and reprinted for this Standard Edition 1932
Reprinted 1949
Reprinted 1963

PRINTED IN GREAT BRITAIN
BY R. & R. CLARK, LIMITED, EDINBURGH

CONTENTS

CONTENTS

PEN PORTRAITS AND REVIEWS

HOW WILLIAM ARCHER IMPRESSED BERNARD SHAW

From a volume entitled Three Plays, by William Archer
(Constable & Co., 1927)

WILLIAM ARCHER, though the most lucid and unequivocal of writers, was in person and manner probably the most deceptive man of his time. Nobody could have been less of an impostor in character; yet he took in all his contemporaries, even those who were fairly intimate with him. One of the cleverest of our younger essayists has described him as a dour Scot, without the slightest sense of humor, hard, logical, with an ability that was always in cold storage. This was not a stranger's deduction from his writings. It was a personal impression so strong that no study of his writings could quite dispel it. Not until the last London journalist who has met him has perished will William Archer be judged by his writings; and even in them there is an emotional reticence that will leave an incomplete picture of the man, though they will do him more justice than he ever did to himself. For the present, there is a fabulous Archer who is extremely unlike the real Archer, and much less amiable.

Had the fabulous Archer been the real one, our long friendship would have been impossible: indeed any friendship with him would have been impossible. Fortunately the real Archer was, like myself, the victim of an unsleeping and incorrigible sense of humor: the very quality (or fault) which the fabulous Archer utterly lacked. No doubt when we first met as young men of the same age some forty-five years ago, I interested him as a person free from certain superstitions that had been oppressive to him; but I interested him still more by being so laughably free, not only from superstitions recognized by him as such, but from many conventions which he had never dreamt of challenging, that I appealed irresistibly to him as an incarnate joke. The

Shavianismus tickled him enormously; and he was never tired of quoting not only my jokes, but my heresies and paradoxes, many of which have by this time become platitudes. The way to get on with Archer was to amuse him: to argue with him was dangerous. The invaluable precept of Robert Owen: "Never argue: repeat your assertion," established me with Archer on the footing of a privileged lunatic, and made quarrels impossible.

Archer had the air of a stoic: he was really a humorist to whom a jest was worth more than most of the things common men prize. For instance, he was unlucky enough to have trouble with one of his eyes. He went to an oculist, and returned so radiant that I concluded that the oculist had cured him. On the contrary, the oculist had diagnosed amblyopia. "What is amblyopia?" said Archer. "Well," said the oculist, "the eye is quite perfect. There is no lesion or defect of any sort. A first-class eye. Only, it does not see anything." Archer found this so funny that he thought half his sight well lost for the fun of repeating it to me and everyone else.

Another instance, in which money was at stake. Though a thoroughbred Scot, he was usually so indifferent to it, so untouched by vulgar ambition or by the least taint of snobbery, so sensibly unpretentious in his habits, so content to go to the pit when he paid to enter a theatre or even in the steerage when he made a long voyage, that nothing but a stroke of luck could ever have made him rich; but when he got married he conscientiously set to work to accumulate savings; and by doing too much journalism he succeeded in making some provision for family contingencies. Unfortunately, on the best advice, he invested it all in Australian banks; and Australian banks presently went smash. I have known men reduced to fury and despair by less serious losses. Archer was sustained and even elated by our friend John Mackinnon Robertson. Robertson, not at that time the Right Honorable (he had not yet entered on the distinguished parliamentary career which he managed to combine so oddly with an equally distinguished literary activity), had just written an economic treatise entitled The Fallacy of Saving. He sent a copy to

Archer; and it arrived simultaneously with the bad news from Australia. Archer at once sat down and wrote, "My dear Robertson: I am already completely convinced of the fallacy of saving, thank you." He came to me to tell me the story, chuckling with the enjoyment of a man who had just heard that his uncle had died in Australia and left him a million. Had he been a giggling fribble, incapable of his own distress, I should have had no patience with him. But, as I shall presently shew, never was there a man less a trifler than William Archer. He laughed at his misfortunes because things of the mind were important to him (humor is purely mental), and things of the body and of the pocket, as long as they stopped short of disablement and painful privation, relatively trivial. The sight of one eye did not matter provided he could see with the other; and he, who set very little store by what people call good living, could hardly be expected to feel much concern about savings whilst he could pay his way with earnings: a comic speech consoled him for both losses.

Why was it, then, that he produced so strong an impression of dourness, unbending Puritan rigidity, and total lack of humor?

The explanation is that in spite of his lifelong preoccupation with the theatre, he was not a dramatic, self-expressive person. Physically he was a tall upstanding well-built good-looking Scot, keeping his figure and bearing to the last. He had an agreeable voice and unaffected manners, and no touch of malice in him. But nobody could tell from any external sign what he was thinking about, or how he felt. The amblyopic eye may have contributed to this air of powerful reserve; but the reserve was real: it was a habit that had become first nature to him. In modern psycho-pathological terms it was a repression that had become a complex. Accustomed as I was to this, he amazed even me once. He had just completed his translation of Ibsen's Little Eyolf; and he read it to two or three friends of whom I was one. His reading was clear, intelligent, cold, without a trace of emotion, and rather wooden in the more moving passages. When he came to the last pages he suddenly handed me the book, and said, formally and with a marked access of woodenness, "Shaw: I must ask you to finish the reading for me. My feelings will not allow me to proceed." The contrast between the matter and the manner of this speech would have been irresistibly comic had any doubt of the sincerity of his distress been possible. I took the proof-sheets in silence, and finished the reading as desired. We were face to face with a man in whom dissimulation had become so instinctive that it had become his natural form of emotional expression. No wonder he seemed a monster of insensibility to those who did not know him very intimately.

To explain this, I must cast back to the year 1730 as a date in religious history. In that year, just before Wesley began Methodism in England, a Scots minister named John Glas was cast out by the General Assembly of the Kirk in Scotland as a Congregationalist heretic. Glas thought this was so much the worse for the Kirk in Scotland. Bible in hand, and strong in the Protestant right to private judgment, he founded one of the innumerable Separatist sects that arose in the eighteenth century. Shakespear would have called him a Brownist. He maintained that any group of persons organized according to the instructions of St Paul to Timothy, and qualified as godly according to the prescription of Matthew, was independent of any Kirk or General Assembly or ecclesiastical authority whatsoever, and was answerable to God alone. The aim of his own group was the realization of Christ's kingdom as defined in the famous reply to Pilate, "My kingdom is not of this world." Glas's son-in-law, Sandeman, carried this doctrine to England, where the groups became known as Sandemanians.

Now of Separation there is no end until every human being is a Separate Church, for which there is much to be said. The Separatists continue to separate. In 1804 John Walker, Bachelor of Divinity (for so I construe the letters B.D.) and Fellow of Trinity College, Dublin, separated himself from the Episcopal Church of Ireland, and founded a sect called by him The Church of God, and by the profane The Walkerites. Its tenets resembled those of the Glasites so closely that there was talk of an amalgamation; but the Glasites were Sabbatarians; the Walkerites held that Christ had discarded the Sabbath; and so they could not agree. Anyhow Walkerism was superfluous in Scotland, where its numbers were often so small that worship among them was a family affair conducted by the head of the household, assisted by such male members of the sect as happened to be present. As the Glasites had flourishing congregations in many centres, Walkerite children would be sent to a Glasite Meeting when there was no Walkerite Meeting to send them to.

In the second generation of Walkerites, a Miss Walker married a Mr Archer. And one of their sons complicated the faith by marrying a daughter of James Morison, one of the shining lights of Glasism. From that exogamous alliance William Archer sprang. If ever there was a doubly predestined heir of grace, William, one would think, was he. And, on the whole, he lived up to his antecedents. But God fulfils Himself in many ways, and often in extremely unexpected ones. As William grew up, he felt obliged to pursue his hereditary Separatism to the point of separating himself not only from the Separatists, but from the curious fetish worship of the Bible, and the idolization of Christ, with which all the sects and Churches were still saturated.

This looks like a complete explanation of the reserve that was a second nature with him. But, if you are an English reader, do not infer too much from your ignorance of Scoto-Norwegian Separatism. Long before Archer's views had formed themselves sufficiently to threaten a schism in the family if he gave voice to them, he had profited, without the smallest friction, by the fact that both Walkerites and Glasites regarded religion as too sacred to be made a subject of private conversation. They actually barred private prayer, and not only neither asked their children controversial questions nor permitted them to put any, but would not allow even a catechism to come between them and their God. In their view, you were either damned or saved by your own nature and the act of God; and any attempt to force God's hand in the transaction was sedition in His kingdom. Thus William was never driven to lie about his beliefs or about the family beliefs. He was simply not allowed to talk about either. He was, however, expected to go to Meeting when there was a meeting (Walkerite or Glasite) within reach, and not to laugh when his sense of humour got the better of the solemnity of the occasion. In the latter observance the Archer children were by no means uniformly successful. In William as in Mark Twain, the meetings had a marked homeopathic effect.

Another feature of Separatism which favored his freedom of thought was its anti-clericalism. The common English association of clericalism with piety is often misleading. The revolt against institutional religion which moved George Fox to regard a priest of any denomination as Mr Winston Churchill regards a Bolshevist, and to revile a church as a steeple house, has produced all the Separatist sects, and has in our day invaded even the Church of England in the person of the most intellectually eminent of its dignitaries. William Archer's father would have been surprised if anyone had called him an anti-clerical; but he had the Separatist habit of assuming that parsons are inadmissible acquaintances. The family atmosphere, if not explicitly anti-clerical, was, to say the least, not prelatical.

Archer's brother and collaborator in their translation of Peer Gynt tells me that he never heard his father say a word of any kind on any religious subject. This gives in a single sentence a vision of the extraordinary reserve imposed by the Separatism of Glas and Walker, surviving as a habit long after the original impulse had lost its fervor, and had even provoked a reaction. The reaction in William Archer carried him to a Modernism which would have been taken by Glas and Walker as unmistakeable evidence of his predestined damnation; but the habit of reserve remained.

It was reinforced as he grew older by the clash of his political opinions with those of the Glasites, who interpreted Christ's declaration that His kingdom was not of this world as implying a duty of unquestioning submission to all duly constituted secular authority. This view had settled down into simple political Conservatism; and when Archer's inner light led him to a vigorous Radicalism, it became necessary for him to extend his reserve from religion to politics, or else grieve his people very sorely, a cruelty of which he was quite incapable. He was hereditarily affectionate, and even suffered from a family inability to control his diaphragm (I borrow this quaint diagnosis from an expert) which made it impossible for him to command his voice when he was deeply moved, which explains both why he could not finish reading Little Eyolf and why up to the moment of relinquishing the attempt he had had to constrain himself so rigidly as to seem a wooden image rather than a very emotional man.

He was not himself conscious of the extent to which the Glasite diathesis influenced him. I do not believe that he knew or cared anything about the constitution or origin of Glasism: all he could tell me to satisfy my curiosity as a connoisseur in religious beliefs was that the performance, as he called it, consisted mainly in his grandfather reading the Bible phrase by phrase, and extracting from every phrase some not immediately obvious significance, the more far-fetched and fantastic the better. The grandson was interested neither in Kirk nor Conventicle, but in the theatre. He was prepared to attend to Shakespear, but not to Glasite hermeneutics. He had a certain admiration for his grandfather's ingenuity as an exegete, and was rather proud of him; but he soon learnt to defend himself from his expositions by an acquirement that often stood him in good stead in the theatre later on. He could slip his finger under the next page of his open Bible; go fast asleep; and turn the page without waking up when the rustling of all the other Bibles as their readers turned over struck on his sleeping ear and started a reflex action.

If I had known this when I attempted to read my first play to him I might not have abandoned it for years as an unfinished failure. He was utterly contemptuous of its construction; but this I did not mind, as I classed constructed plays with artificial flowers, clockwork mice, and the like. Unfortunately, when I came to the second act, something—possibly something exegetic in my tone—revived the old protective habit. He fell into a deep slumber; and I softly put the manuscript away and let him have his sleep out. When I mentioned this to our friend Henry Arthur

7

Jones he reminded me of a member of the *Comédie Française*, who, on being remonstrated with for sleeping whilst an author was reading a play, said "Sleep is a criticism." This was my own view of the case; and I might never have meddled with the stage again had not Archer unconsciously discounted the incident one day by telling me the tale of his famous grandfather.

Thus he never came to know what his grandfather's religion was. He dismissed it, and most of Scriptural theology with it, as flat nonsense. And from this estimate he never to the end of his days retreated. It may seem strange that a man whose literary bent was so strong that he made literature his profession, whose ear was so musical that he could write excellent verse, and whose judgment was so respected that he was accepted as the most serious critic of his day, should be able to read the dregs of Elizabethan drama and not to read the Bible; but the fact remains that when I was writing my preface on Christianity (to Androcles and the Lion) and, having just read the New Testament through, asked him whether he had read the Gospels lately, and what he made of them, he replied that he had tried, but "could not stick it." The doctrine was nonsense to him; and he had no patience with it because he took no interest in it. I pleaded that though Matthew had muddled his gospel by stringing sayings together in the wrong order, a more intelligible arrangement of them could be discovered by reading the other evangelists; but this produced no impression on him: the subject simply bored him; and he rather resented any attempt on my part to give the slightest importance to it. This was a very natural consequence of dosing a clever child prematurely with mental food that Ecumenical Councils have before now failed to digest; and parents and school committees will do well to make a careful note of it; but in Archer's case the intolerance it produced became a quality, as his book on India proves. There was no morbid nonsense about understanding everything and pardoning everything in the Archer family. The glimpses I had of them were quite convincing as to their being healthy-minded sensible open-air colonially rejuvenated people who, having to keep an inherited form of worship from making social life impossible, instinctively avoided sophistry and speculation, and took their intellectual course simply and downrightly. When, in what was then called The Conflict Between Religion and Science, William Archer took the side of Science, he broke away as cleanly and confidently as Glas had broken away from the Assembly or Walker from the Church of Ireland. He expressly denied having ever had any internal struggle or qualm. His only difficulty was to maintain his convictions without making his parents unhappy; and the Separatist reserve made it quite easy to do this whilst he lived with them.

When he came to London and began to write for the Secularist press, thus breaking the Separatist silence, he resorted to a *nom de plume*, for which, in those days, there were other reasons than family ones. A then future president of the National Secular Society had been actually imprisoned for a year for publishing in The Freethinker, his weekly journal, a picture of Samuel anointing Saul, in which the costumes and accessories were those of a modern hairdresser's shop; and until the expiration of the sentence Archer had to help with a monthly review which the victim of persecution edited for his more scholarly and fastidious followers. The leaders of the Secularist movement, including at that time Mrs Besant, were delighted to welcome Archer as a brilliant young recruit, and were somewhat taken aback when he would not enter into intimate social relations with them lest they should meet his parents, and quite simply told them so in his most expressionless manner. But for the strained relations which ensued, and for his preoccupation with the theatre, he might, like Robertson, have become a familiar figure in the pulpit of South Place Chapel, and been as definitely associated with Rationalism as Mr Edward Clodd. As it was, his position was sufficiently affirmed to make me ask him one day what his parents had to say about it. His reply was that the subject was never mentioned between them, but that he supposed they must have noticed that he did not attend any place of worship. Clearly there was no bitterness nor bigotry in the matter; and the fact that there was no resistance to break down made it impossible for a man of

Archer's affectionate sensitiveness not to shield his father and mother from every contact with his heresy and its associations that could possibly be avoided without a sacrifice of his convictions.

Presently another interest came into his life. One showery day I was in New Oxford Street, probably going to or from the British Museum reading room, when I saw Archer coming towards me past Mudie's, looking much more momentous than usual. He seemed eight feet high; and his aspect was stern and even threatening, as if he were defying all Oxford Street, buses and all, to take the smallest liberty with him. His air of formidable height was partly due, perhaps, to his having draped himself in a buff-colored mackintosh which descended to his calves. But it was quaintly aided by the contrast of his inches with those of a lady who clung to his arm to keep pace with his unmerciful strides. She had a small head and a proportionately small comely face, winsome and ready to smile when not actually smiling. I had never seen Archer with a woman on his arm before, nor indeed concerning himself with one in any way; and, as the future author of Man and Superman, I feared the worst. And, sure enough, I was immediately introduced to the lady as his selection for the destiny of being Mrs Archer.

The marriage seemed a great success. Mrs Archer fitted herself into the simple and frugal life of her husband quite naturally, caring no more for fashion or manufactured pleasures and luxuries than he did. There came a wonderful son: he who figures in the correspondence of Robert Louis Stevenson as Tomarcher. Mrs Archer found the world paradise enough first with her Willie, and then with her man and her boy. She tolerated me and indulged me as an incarnate joke because he did; and I saw rather more of him after his marriage than before it, instead of less: a rare privilege for a bachelor friend.

But the more Archer's slender means obliged him to put Mrs Archer and the boy first, and literature comparatively nowhere, the more I, having among my budget of novels that nobody would publish a book called The Irrational Knot (meaning the marriage tie), began to doubt whether domesticity was good for his career. At last I read an anonymous article on one of Archer's subjects which seemed to me a poor one. I was on the point of abusing it roundly to him one day when, to my consternation, he said, just in time, that he had written it. My concern was not because I thought the article unsatisfactory: every writer produces unsatisfactory articles occasionally. But that, good or bad, I had not recognized it as his: a failure unprecedented so far, proved to me that he had lost some of the brilliancy and unmistakeable individuality of style which had attracted me in his articles in The London Figaro long before I made his acquaintance. I knew that the way to make money in journalism is to turn out rapidly great quantities of undistinguished stuff; and I knew also that when a man marries he gives up his right to put quality of work first, and income second. I did not conceive it possible at that time that I should ever become a married man myself. With an artistic recklessness which shocks me in retrospect I told Archer that Mrs Archer was spoiling him, and that he would be a lost man unless he broke loose. He said, with that wooden formality which was the surest sign that he was deeply moved, that he must ask me not to visit his house whilst I held opinions so disparaging to Mrs Archer.

I was not in the least offended. Indeed I never was offended by anything Archer ever said to me or wrote about me, though he sometimes expressed a quite unnecessary remorse for speeches or articles which he supposed must have been painful to me. For some time I remained under his interdict, and saw nothing of Mrs Archer. Then the unexpected happened. Archer did not break loose; but Mrs Archer did. Let me not be misunderstood. There was no gentleman in the case. It was much more interesting than that.

I forget how long Mrs Archer remained a dropped subject between us; but it was Archer himself who resumed it. I found him in a state of frank anxiety which in him indicated considerable distress of mind; and he told me that Mrs Archer fancied that there was something the matter with her, though she was, as he believed, in perfect health. Now Mrs Archer, like her husband, was not at all the sort of person her appearance suggested. She seemed dainty, unassuming, clinging. Really, she was a woman of independent character, great decision and pertinacity, and considerable physical hardihood. This I had half guessed that day in Oxford Street, but I kept the guess to myself, as it might have been taken as a wanton paradox until the sequel bore it out. When Archer told me of his perplexity I shared it, and could think of nothing to suggest.

To the rescue of this male helplessness came a remarkable lady from America, Miss Annie Payson Call, authoress of a book entitled Power through Repose, and of a system, partly manipulative, partly sympathetic, of straightening out tangled nerves. Miss Call had the same sort of amiability as Mrs Archer, and the same overflow of energy for which selfishness was not enough. She tackled Mrs Archer; she tackled me; she tackled everybody; and as she was a charming person, nobody objected. But she found in Mrs Archer something more than the passive subject of a cure. She found a pupil, a disciple, and finally an apostle in England. Mrs Archer's vocation also was for healing sore minds and wandering wits. With what seems to me in retrospect a staggering suddenness, though in fact she had to see Tom through to his independent manhood first, she created the nerve training institution at King's Langley which survives her. Literary people in the eighteen-nineties used to write futile sequels to Ibsen's Doll's House: Mrs Archer found a real and perfectly satisfactory sequel. She became an independent professional woman most affectionately married to an independent professional man, the two complementing instead of hampering each other; for in practical matters he was full of inhibitions and diffidences from which she was vigorously free. Incidentally I ceased to be one of Willie's bachelor encumbrances. Mrs Archer, having developed considerably more practical initiative and ability than ever I possessed, took me in hand fearlessly on her new footing, and admitted me, I think, to as much of her friendship as I deserved.

Thus Archer's domesticity ceased to be a problem; and you may set him down for good and all as fortunate in his marriage. But to suggest all that his marriage meant for him I must return to the child Tom Archer. The extraordinary companionship which Archer found in his little son could not have existed but for a double bond between them. First, Archer had retained much more of his own childhood than even his most intimate friends suspected. He must have been a very imaginative child; and he had retained so much of a child's imagination and fun that it was for some time a puzzle to me that he could be so completely fascinated as he was by Ibsen's imagination, and that yet, when I produced my Quintessence of Ibsenism, he dismissed much of the specifically adult and worldly part of it precisely as he had dismissed the Scriptural exegetics of his grandfather. This devoted Ibsenite, who translated the Master's works so forcibly and vividly, was never in the least an Ibsenist: he delighted in Ibsen's plays just as a child delights in The Arabian Nights without taking in anything of the passages which Captain Burton left unexpurgated. It was this innocence that limited his own excursions into dramatic literature; he could not see that the life around him, including his own, was teeming with dramatic material, and persisted in looking for his subjects either in literature or in fairyland.

Now it happened that Tom Archer, though so entirely his mother's son in most respects that, save for an occasional fleeting revelation in his expression, he was not a bit like Archer, had a prodigious imagination. Having no derisive brothers and sisters to make him sensitive and secretive about it, but, on the contrary, a father who took it with the tenderest seriousness, and in fact became an accomplice in all its extravagances, Tom was able to let himself go gloriously. He invented a *pays de Cocagne* which he called Peona, which went far beyond the garret-forest in The Wild Duck, as it had no contact with limited mechanical realities. I heard much of Peona and its inhabitants at second hand, and even a little at first hand, on which occasions I swallowed every adventure with a gravity not surpassed by Archer's own. I am sure that Archer, whose youth as one of a large and robust family enjoyed no such protection, could never have felt this delicacy had he not remembered his own youth, and recognized his own imagination in his son's.

There was another experience from which he was determined to protect Tom; and that was the British boarding school, or boy farm, as William Morris called it. It was useless to romance to him about the character-forming virtues and historic glories of Eton and Harrow, Winchester and Rugby and Marlborough: he anticipated the opinions of Sanderson of Oundle, who heartily agreed with me when I expressed my opinion that these places should be razed to the ground, and their foundations sown with salt. Archer had taken his own schooling as a dayboy, and was convinced, with good reason, that this arrangement, however inconvenient for the parents, was much more wholesome for the child. Accordingly, Tom spent his childish schooldays with his people in a Surrey cottage on the façade of which Mr Edward Rimbault Dibdin inscribed the name Walden (a compliment to Thoreau) in highly artistic lettering. When he outgrew the educational resources of that primitive neighborhood the family moved to Dulwich and sent him to the college there.

Meanwhile my comment on Tom was that he was a second Rudyard Kipling; for, as I happened to know from William Morris, Mr Kipling had been a great Peoneer in his nonage. The years in which Archer and Tom explored Peona together passed as fast as real years in a real country until at last the once inexhaustible subject of Tom dropped so completely that I actually had to ask Archer about him. To my amazement he conveyed to me, with a manner that would have done credit to a piece of mahogany, that the firm of Archer & Son of Peona had dissolved partnership. Tom, he explained, had been ill; and Archer opined that the illness had affected his character, which, he said, was totally changed. This theory of the alleged change was too summary and too surgical to convince me. But I forbore to probe; and the truth came out gradually. The child Tom, developing into the incipient man, emerged from Peona a most unnatural

WILLIAM ARCHER

son. He was as keen about the glories of public schools as if he were indeed the author of Stalky and Co. He distinguished himself at Dulwich by the facility with which he turned out Latin verses, becoming Captain of the Classical Side. He joined the Officers' Training Corps, and actually made his father enlist in the Inns of Court Volunteers, a trial which Archer supported because, being a private, and having to salute Tom, who was an officer, the situation appealed to his sense of humor as well as to his conscientious public spirit. In short, he dragged Archer out of Peona with him, and imposed public schools ideals on him. Military romance alone survived from fairyland; and even that took the fashionable imperialist shape.

Up to this time Archer had, without knowing it, been a true Glasite in the essential sense. His kingdom had not been of this world. But now, what with the son grasping with all his imaginative power at conventional military ideals, and this world beginning to treat the father with more and more of the distinguished consideration which his work earned and his unworldly character commanded, Archer had to adapt himself as far as he could to the responsibilities of his celebrity, and to set himself to make the best of convention instead of criticizing it with the independence of a young and comparatively unknown man. Every free-lance who makes a reputation has to go through this phase; but Archer was under the special emotional pressure of having to adapt himself to Tom's Kiplingesque war mentality in and out of season. He became as conventional as it was in his nature to be, and indeed, for Tom's sake, perhaps a little more, though the public school had taken away his playmate.

Presently Tom's boyhood passed like his childhood, and left him a young man, still his mother's son in respect of being under average military size and considerably over average military vigor of mind and practical initiative. Oxford, where he had expected to distinguish himself because he had done so at Dulwich, did not suit him. True, his aptitude for classical exercises did not desert him. He took honors in law, and was in no sense a failure. But Oxford was something of a failure for him. The

15

struggle for life was not real enough there for a youth who had a passion for the military realism of soldiering. When he left Oxford to begin adult life, he worked as a solicitor for a couple of years in London. Then an opening in America, with a promise of a speedy return to rejoin his family at home, took him across the Atlantic.

Two months later the gulf of war opened at the feet of our young men. Tom rushed back to hurl himself into it. Amid the volcanoes of Messines he was serving as a lance-corporal in "the dear old G Company" of the London Scottish. Invalided home, he accepted a commission, and for a year was able to do no more than sit on the brink of the gulf in the Ordnance until his strength returned, when he volunteered afresh for the firing line as lieutenant in the King's Own Scottish Borderers. In February 1918 he married Alys Morty, cousin to a comrade-at-arms fallen at Messines, and had a deliriously happy honeymoon in Ireland. Then, the war still dragging on, he hurled himself into the gulf again; and this time, at Mount Kemmel, it closed on him, and his father saw him no more. He left his young widow to take his place in his parents' affections, the newly found beloved daughter succeeding to the newly lost beloved son. Yet Archer was loth to let the son go. He renewed an old interest in super-rational research; investigated dreams and the new psycho-analysis; and even experimented unsuccessfully in those posthumous conversations in which so many of the bereaved found comfort. And so, between daughter and son, the adventure of parentage never ended for Archer.

When the war broke out he was past military age, and had to confine his part in it to countering the German propaganda service and doing some of our own, an employment in which his knowledge of languages stood him in good stead. When the Armistice made an end of that, his own bent reasserted itself and took him back to the theatre, and (save where his memories of Tom were concerned) to militant Rationalism.

His great work of translating Ibsen had by this time been brought to an end by Ibsen's death. I am myself a much-translated author; and I know how hard the lot of a translator is if he is sensitive to frantic abuse both by rival or would-be rival translators, and by literary men inflamed by an enthusiasm for the author (gained from the translations they abuse) which convinces them that his opinions are their own, and that the translator, not seeing this, has missed the whole point of the work. I use the word frantic advisedly: the lengths to which these attacks go are incredible. At one time it was the fashion in the literary cliques to dismiss Archer's translations as impossible. I told them it was no use: that Archer-Ibsen had seized the public imagination as it had seized theirs, and would beat any other brand of Ibsen in English. And it was so. Whenever a translation was produced without the peculiar character that Archer gave to his, it had no character at all, no challenge, at best only a drawing room elegance that was a drawback rather than an advantage. When Mr Anstey burlesqued Ibsen in Punch, he did it by burlesquing Archer: without Archer the plays would not have bitten deep enough to be burlesqued. Even in the case of Peer Gynt, which moved several enthusiasts to attempt translations following the rhymes and metres of the original (I began one myself, with our friend Braekstad translating for me literally, line by line, and got as far as a couple of pages or so), the unrhymed translation by Archer and his brother Colonel Charles Archer held its own against the most ingenious and elaborate rival versions. Whenever Peer Gynt was quoted it was always in the Archer version. I have already given the explanation. Archer understood and cared for Ibsen's imagination. For his sociological views he cared so little that he regarded them mostly as aberrations when he was conscious of them. Thus, undistracted by Ibsen's discussions, he went straight for his poetry, and reproduced every stroke of imagination in a phraseology that invented itself *ad hoc* in his hands. As nothing else really mattered, the critics who could not see this, and would have it that everything else mattered, neither made nor deserved to make any permanent impression. Besides, the air of Norway breathed through his versions. He had breathed it himself from his childhood during his frequent visits, beginning at the age of three, to the Norwegian home of his grandparents, where he had two unmarried aunts who exercised his tenderness and powers of admiration very beneficently. As to the few lyrics which occur in Ibsen's plays, and which would have baffled a prosaic translator, they gave Archer no trouble at all: he was at his best in them. If it had been possible for the father of a family to live by writing verse in the nineteenth century, Archer would probably have done more in that manner on his own account.

How far he sacrificed a career as an original playwright to putting the English-speaking peoples in possession of Ibsen is an open question. In my opinion he instinctively chose the better part, because the theatre was not to him a workshop but part of his fairyland. He never really got behind the scenes, and never wanted to. The illusion that had charmed his youth was so strong and lasting that not even fifty years of professional theatre-going in London could dispel it. Inevitably then he liked the theatre as he found it at first: the theatre of the French "well-made play." But the attraction of this school of theatrical art for him did not lie in its ingenuities and neatnesses of construction, though he sometimes wrote as if it did. He liked it because it also lived in fairyland. Sophisticated as it was, yet was its kingdom not of this world. Archer, though he approached it as a reformer, did not want to reform it out of existence: he wanted to strengthen it by giving some sort of subsistence to its make-believe, which had worn thin and stale, ignorant and incredible. He did not want to drag the heroine from her fairyland; but how could he believe in her if she had an obviously impossible solicitor and butler and lady's maid? If she lived in a world totally exhausted of ideas, created by authors who, outside their little theatrical clique, knew nothing of their country, and conceived it as a complete vacuum in respect of the things it had most at heart: business, sport, politics, and religion, how could a man of any strength of mind or sense of verisimilitude take her seriously? That was why Archer cried out in one breath for naturalness in the theatre and for artifice in dramatic authorship. In the novel, which raises no question of technique, he welcomed the most uncompromising naturalness, making me read De Maupassant's Une Vie, applauding Zola, and coming into my rooms one day full of his discovery of a new novelist of our own, who had burst on the world with a naturalistic novel entitled A Mummer's Wife. I was so impressed with his account of it that I eagerly asked the name of the author; but when he told me it was George Moore I burst into irreverent laughter, knowing the said George personally as an inveterate romancer, whose crimson inventions, so far delivered orally for private circulation only, suggested that he had been brought into the world by a union of Victor Hugo with Ouida. But Archer insisted on my reading the book, as he had insisted on my reading Une Vie; and I stood rebuked for my incredulity.

I never read Archer's one novel, a youthful exploit called The Doom of the Destroyed, which had been published serially in a Scottish newspaper, and was one of his favorite jokes. I gathered that in point of romance it left George Moore's unpublished *quasi* autobiographical tales of adventure nowhere; but it is certain that Archer's adult taste in novels was for merciless realism. Therefore when one day he proposed that we two should collaborate in writing a play, he to supply the constructional scaffolding or scenario, and I to fill in the dialogue, I assumed that I might be as realistic as Zola or De Maupassant with his entire sympathy. But he was always upsetting my assumptions as to his sympathies; and he did so signally on this occasion.

It happened in this way. Archer had planned for two heroines, a rich one and a poor one. The hero was to prefer the poor one to the rich one; and in the end his disinterestedness was to be rewarded by the lucrative discovery that the poor one was really the rich one. When I came to fill in this scheme I compressed the two heroines into one; but I made up the one out of two models, whom I will now describe.

Once, when I was walking homewards at midnight through Wigmore Street, taking advantage of its stillness and loneliness at that hour to contemplate, like Kant, the starry heaven above me, the solitude was harshly broken by the voices of two young women who came out of Mandeville Place on the other side of the street a couple of hundred yards behind me. The dominant one of the pair was in a black rage: the other was feebly trying to quiet her. The strained strong voice and the whimpering remonstrant one went on for some time. Then came the explosion. The angry one fell on the other, buffeting her, tearing at her hair, grasping at her neck. The victim, evidently used to it, cowered against the railings, covering herself as best she could, and imploring and remonstrating in a carefully subdued tone, dreading a police rescue more than the other's violence. Presently the fit passed, and the two came on their way, the lioness silent, and the lamb reproachful and rather emboldened by her sense of injury. The scene stuck in my memory, to be used in due time.

Also I had about this time a friendship with a young independent professional woman, who enjoyed, as such, an exceptional freedom of social intercourse in artistic circles in London. As she was clever, goodnatured, and very goodlooking, all her men friends fell in love with her. This had occurred so often that she had lost all patience with the hesitating preliminaries of her less practised adorers. Accordingly, when they clearly longed to kiss her, and she did not dislike them sufficiently to make their gratification too great a strain on her excessive goodnature, she would seize the stammering suitor firmly by the wrists, bring him into her arms by a smart pull, and saying "Let's get it over," allow the startled gentleman to have his kiss, and then proceed to converse with him at her ease on subjects of more general interest.

I provided Archer with a heroine by inventing a young woman who developed from my obliging but impatient friend in the first act to the fury of Wigmore Street in the second: such a heroine as had not been seen on the London stage since Shakespear's Taming of the Shrew. And my shrew was never tamed.

Now Archer was not such a simpleton as to be unaware that some women are vulgar, violent, and immodest according to Victorian conceptions of modesty. He would probably have assented to the proposition that as vulgarity, violence, and immodesty are elements in human nature, it is absurd to think of them as unwomanly, unmanly, or unnatural. But he also knew that a character practically free from these three vices could be put on the stage without any departure from nature, for the excellent reason that his own character was most unusually free from them, even his strong Scottish sense of humor being, like his conversation, entirely clean. Why, then, impose them wantonly on his charming and refined heroine? He repudiated all complicity in such an outrage. He reproached me for my apparent obsession with abominably ill-tempered characters, oversexed to saturation. My way in the theatre was evidently not his way; and it was not until, at my third attempt as a playwright, I achieved a play (Mrs Warren's Profession) which appealed to his sense of Zolaistic naturalism, that he ceased to dissuade me from pursuing the occupation into which he had innocently tempted me.

I must mention that his decisive and indignant retirement from the collaboration occurred whilst the play was still in shorthand, and therefore quite illegible by him, and not legible enough by myself to admit of my reading it aloud to him tolerably. But I had made demands on him which betrayed my deliberate and unconscionable disregard of his rules of the art of play construction. His scenario had been communicated to me *viva voce*; and when I told him I had finished the first act, and had not yet come to his plot, asking him to refresh my memory about it, he felt as the architect of a cathedral might if the builder had remarked one day that he had finished the nave and transepts according to his own fancy, and, having lost the architect's plans, would like to have another copy of them before he tackled the tower, the choir, and the lady chapel. I managed to appease my architect by arguing that it was not until the second act that a well-made play came to business seriously, and that meanwhile I had fulfilled his design by making the river Rhine the scene of the meeting of the lovers in the first act. But when, having written some pages of the second act, I said I had used up all his plot and wanted some more to go on with, he retired peremptorily from the firm. He was of course quite right: I was transmogrifying not only his design but the whole British drama of that day so recklessly that my privilege as a paradoxical lunatic broke down under the strain; and he could no longer with any self-respect allow me to play the fool with his scenario. For it was not a question of this particular scenario only. He did not agree with me that the form of drama which had been perfected in the middle of the nineteenth century in the French theatre was essentially mechanistic and therefore incapable of producing vital drama. That it was exhausted and, for the moment, sterile, was too obvious to escape an observer of his intelligence; but he saw nothing fundamentally wrong with it, and to the end of his life maintained that it was indispensable as a form for sound theatrical work, needing only to be brought into contact with life by having new ideas poured into it. I held, on the contrary, that a play is a vital growth and not a mechanical construction; that a plot is the ruin of a story and therefore of a play, which is essentially a story; that Shakespear's plays and Dickens's novels, though redeemed by their authors' genius, were as ridiculous in their plots as Goldsmith's hopelessly spoilt Goodnatured Man: in short, that a play should never have a plot, because, if it has any natural life in it, it will construct itself, like a flowering plant, far more wonderfully than its author can consciously construct it.

On such terms collaboration between us was impossible: indeed my view practically excludes collaboration. His view does not; and we shall presently see him returning to it after an interval of many years, during which I had become an established playwright, possibly wrong in my theory, but beyond all question successful in my practice.

He had already written plays single-handed. I remember a one-act play called Clive, dealing with the failure of that hero's attempt at suicide, and his conclusion that Heaven had other views for him. As this has disappeared, he may have destroyed it as puerile; but I thought it promising, and more alive than a play about a prima donna who lost her voice, a theme frankly taken from George Eliot's Armgart. George Eliot's reputation was then enormous, in spite of the protests of Ruskin, and of the alliterative vituperations of Swinburne; and it was very far from being undeserved. When I read Middlemarch in my teens I was impressed by it as by a masterpiece of a new order; and I have no doubt that Archer was equally impressed, though I do not remember discussing George Eliot with him. But the impression she made was not encouraging. The effect of the fatalistic determinism into which the scientific thought of that day had driven her was distinctly depressing and laming. Her characters seemed the helpless victims of their environment and inherited dispositions, contributing nothing except a few follies and weaknesses to the evolutionary struggle, if the word struggle can be used where there is no real resistance to what Darwin called natural selection. Now a fatalist, as George Eliot proved, can write so well that a capable man of letters like the late Lord Bryce, in a public eulogy of Tolstoy, could think of nothing more complimentary to say of him than that as a novelist he was second only to George Eliot. But, for all that, she discouraged many noble spirits; and I think she disabled Archer to some extent, directly or indirectly. The last drop of dramatic vitality in her school was drained by Ibsen; and when Archer had translated Ibsen there was nothing left for the translator.

Archer had various theories as to this disablement: as, for instance, that he could not write dialogue, which was nonsense; but the fact was that a George Eliotish philosophy of life, and a mechanistic limitation of the possibilities of the theatre, combined with his natural and very amiable diffidence and his unconsciously Glasite unworldliness, kept him back from the newly broken and rather unsightly ground in which alone a new drama could germinate.

At last, quite late in life, he had a dream; and the dream was a good story about an Asiatic Rajah made cynical by a Western education, and a Green Goddess who had to be propitiated by blood sacrifices, some English captives becoming available for that purpose. The result proved that the complexes which inhibited him from writing effective plays when he was awake, did not operate when he was asleep. When he turned his dream into a play it was prodigiously successful, first in America and then in England; and Archer ceased at last to be a much underpaid man. I had urged at every opportunity that the great national services he had done by his Englishing of Ibsen should be acknowledged by a pension (a title without one is only a source of expense); but I was always met with the difficulty that in this Philistine country parliamentary grants are made only to generals, pro-consuls, and Polar explorers. Literature and art have nothing to look for but an occasional knighthood or a civil list pension; and to obtain the pension it is necessary to assert that the postulant is in straitened circumstances. For Ashton Ellis, the translator of Richard Wagner's voluminous prose works, it had been possible, when he was almost destitute, to obtain a wretched pittance of £80 a year; but Archer was at no time at a loss for his livelihood. After the success of The Green Goddess a pension was more than ever out of the question; and Archer never had any official recognition of his public service, out of which, by the way, he steadfastly refused to make money through translator's performing fees, lest he should compromise his disinterestedness as a critic.

Here let me say, parenthetically, that Archer was incorruptible as a critic. In his day there were various methods of amiable corruption in vogue. One was called simply Chicken & Champagne, which explains itself. It includes various degrees of blandishment; and some of them were tried on Archer; but they were hopelessly thrown away on him, because he never had the least suspicion of their nature, and either accepted them in unconquerable innocence at their face value, or declined them because they bored him. Another way was available if the critic was known to have written a play. The manager asked for it; put it on the shelf; promised production at some future unspecified time; and offered an advance on account of author's fees. A third method was almost a routine. An actor-manager would write to a critic to say that he wanted to consult him as an expert. An interview would follow. The manager would explain that he had acquired the performing right of some foreign play, and was thinking of attempting a part in it. Would the critic advise him about the translation? Would he care to undertake the translation? If so, would he sell a six months' option on the translation for, say, £50? If the critic was amenable, the £50 changed hands; and nothing more was heard of the play or the translation. If not, he recommended another translator; the manager shrugged his shoulders; and the two parted smiling. The managers did this, I believe, rather because it was the fashion, and almost the due of a leading critic, than with any sense that the proposal was in any way improper. Certainly the actor-managers who made it to me when I was a critic thought no worse of it than of tipping a waiter, and probably considered it rather unsocial on my part to evade the transaction.

Notwithstanding Archer's reputation as a translator, no such proposals were made, as far as I know, to him. His integrity was unassailed because it was so obviously impregnable. I doubt if he even knew the game as a usage, though he must have been aware of instances in which dealings in options had been followed by marked accesses of eulogy. After all, the instances were exceptional; besides, he went his own way so completely as a matter of course that he passed through the theatrical world without noticing all its aberrations, as indeed he passed through the kingdom of this world in general. He was much too scrupulous in the matter of the Ibsen translations; but the position of a critic who is also a proprietor of performing rights of any kind is certainly a very delicate one; and it was characteristic of Archer to carry his delicacy too far rather than accept a commercial interest in the plays of an author whom his critical conscience obliged him to recommend with all his might.

Diffident to the last, Archer had no sooner constructed The Green Goddess according to rule, and finished the two main acts, than he lost self-confidence, and perhaps patience, over the dénouement in the third act, and asked me to finish the play for him on the old ground that he could not write dialogue. I overwhelmed him with denunciations of his laziness; told him he could finish it perfectly well for himself if he chose to; and

C

threatened that if I did the work I would make the lady get the better of the wicked Rajah in the vein of Captain Brassbound's Conversion. This threat was effectual; and he turned to Arthur Pinero to finish the play for him. Pinero, with great tact, made an alternative suggestion which opened Archer's eyes to the fact that if it was not worth his while to write the last act because it was to be hack work, he should offer it to a hack writer. Archer thereupon finished the play himself, and was, I hope, delivered by the result from all further misgivings as to his own competence. But it was too late in the day to begin life anew as a fashionable playwright; and The Green Goddess stands, by no means as the crown of his career, but rather as a proof that the inhibitions which prevented him from achieving this sort of worldly success earlier were not due, as he himself feared, to lack of faculty, but to Providence, which had other fish for him to fry.

In his predestined work I do not include the whole of his huge output of notices of theatrical performances, nor even the plans for a national theatre, which he prepared in collaboration with Harley Granville-Barker, then the most wonderful of the younger generation knocking at our doors. Journalistic criticism, after the first years, becomes necessarily for the most part repetitive breadwinning; and the theatre planning was rather like building sand castles in the face of a flood tide, a pastime to which Granville-Barker was much addicted as a refuge from his proper business of writing plays. Archer's essays on the censorship, on Diderot's Paradox (Masks or Faces?), and on Macready, with his reprints of the theatrical criticisms of Lewes and Forster, are all valuable and readable; but they lay in his path as a professional critic of the theatre, and are therefore not so significant as the excursions to which his spirit drove him.

In 1906 a Spanish educationalist and philanthropist who was also strongly anti-clerical (meaning really anti-obscurantist), and was therefore supposed by the officers of the Spanish army to be in his nature essentially diabolical, and in his habits an assassin of all royal persons, had the misfortune to fall into the hands of a court-martial in Barcelona, where he was shamefully ill-used whilst in custody, and finally shot. It was a monstrous case of class ignorance and vindictive bigotry; and Archer willingly accepted a journalistic commission to visit Spain and investigate it. He exposed it so effectually that the biographical dictionaries and encyclopædias now refer to him as their authority for their accounts of the martyrdom—for that is what it came to —of Ferrer.

His subsequent visit to India, though it had no such sensational provocation, produced his remarkable book on the subject. At that time it was the fashion for literary European travellers returning from Asia to display their susceptibilities to the call of the East by depicting an India of boundless and magical fascination, lit up with Bengal lights, saturated with the charm of Pierre Loti's romances, adorned with the temples of a living religion more profound than our own, and inhabited by Rabindranath Tagores and dark-eyed enchantresses, with Mahatmas in the mountain background. These enthusiasts were more Indian than any Indian; and their readers, who had never been in India, began where they left off, and went much further into an imaginary East. Archer went to see for himself, and instantly and uncompromisingly denounced the temples as the shambles of a barbarous ritual of blood sacrifice, and the people as idolaters with repulsive rings through their noses. He refused to accept the interest of Indian art and the fictions of Indian romance as excuses. He remained invincibly faithful to Western civilization, and told the Indians flatly what a civilized Western gentleman must think of them and feel about some of their customs. Had he been able to get behind the scenes of Indian domestic life as Katherine Mayo did some years later, his book might have made as great a sensation as hers.

In writing thus he did India the only service in his power. If Western civilization is not more enlightened than Eastern we have clearly no right to be in India. When once the British conqueror and master of India comes to think that suttee is a touching and beautiful act of wifely sacrifice, he had better abdicate, come home, and introduce suttee in England. When he ceases to treat the car of Juggernaut precisely as he would treat a motor-bus driven to the public danger, his mission in India is over. What we owe to the Roman occupation of Britain we do not know: in fact there is too much ground for Mr George Trevelyan's conclusion that we relapsed the moment the Romans left us to ourselves; but we should certainly owe nothing at all if the Romans had had the slightest doubt that the augur represented a less grossly superstitious religion than the Druid, and that Roman law and Roman civilization were higher than British. They may have been as hasty and superficial as Sir John Wood-roffe declares Archer to have been; but they did not think so; and anyhow the sole justification of their conquest and occupation was that they were right. We shall have to clear out of India some day as the Romans had to clear out of Britain: perhaps the sooner the better for both parties. But it is certain that if, after that happens, the Indians are ever to say "It was a good thing for us that the westerners came and taught us something," it will be because the English criticism of India was Archer's criticism, and not that of the occidental renegades who swell the heads of our Indian students by assuring them that we are crude barbarians compared to them. Archer would have been the last man to deny that we are shocking barbarians according to our own standards; that white women with small earrings cannot logically despise brown women with large noserings; and that the Fundamentalist who prosecutes a school teacher for refusing to bow the knee to the god to whom Jephthah sacrificed his daughter can hardly hope to impose himself on an educated Hindu as a pioneer of thought. All the same, the Fundamentalist does not sacrifice his daughter or even his calf, and would send anyone who did to the electric chair or the lunatic asylum; and the Eastern toleration of nose-rings is not justified by the Western toleration of earrings. People who make the one an excuse for the other will never do anything to lighten the load of human superstition; and as this was really Archer's appointed task in life he wrote one of the most useful because one of the most resolutely unsympathetic books on India produced in his generation. It is not all unsympathetic or anti-

Indian: very far from it. But it was the unsympathetic part that was needed and effective. If you like, he wrote about the Indians as John Glas would have written about the heathen. But why not rather put it that he wrote about the Indians as Dickens wrote about the Americans? And does anyone now doubt that Dickens told the Americans what they needed to be told, and that his honesty did not prevent his becoming more popular with them than any of their romantic flatterers?

I have no more to say about William Archer that matters enough to be printed. Looking back as far as the days when, finding me full of literary ability but ridiculously incapable of obtaining literary employment and desperately in need of it, he set me on my feet as a critical journalist by simply handing me over a share of his own work, and making excuses for having deputed it until the Pall Mall Gazette and The World, then in the van of fashionable journalism, accepted the deputy as a principal, I am conscious that many of our contemporaries must have seen him much oftener than I, and that this sketch of him must be incomplete and perhaps in some points misleading. And there is the other possibility: that I may have been too close to him, and known him too early, to realize his full stature. But I am sure that I never could get him to think as well of himself as I thought of him. I leave it to others to compose a proper full-dress literary portrait of him: all I have tried to do here is to give some sort of life to a sketch of a friend of whom, after more than forty years, I have not a single unpleasant recollection, and whom I was never sorry to see or unready to talk to.

One day I received from him the following letter:

27, FITZROY SQUARE, W.1.
17th December 1924.

MY DEAR G. B. S.

Since I wrote you, I have learnt that I shall have to undergo an operation one of these days—I go into a nursing home tomorrow. I don't know that the operation is a very serious one, and as a matter of fact I feel as fit as a fiddle, so I suppose my chances are pretty good. Still, accidents will happen; and this episode gives me an excuse for saying, what I hope you don't doubt—namely, that though I may sometimes have played the part of all-too candid mentor, I have never wavered in my admiration and affection for you, or ceased to feel that the Fates had treated me kindly in making me your contemporary and friend. I thank you from my heart for forty years of good comradeship.

Whatever happens, let it never be said that I did not move in good society—I lunched today with the King of Norway and Prince Olaf.

Very kind regards to Mrs Shaw, and all good wishes for 1925.
—Ever yours,   W. A.

I was not seriously alarmed, and presently sailed for Madeira. On landing there, the first words that caught my eye on the news bulletin in the hall of Reid's Hotel were "Death of Mr William Archer." They threw me into a transport of fury. The operation had killed him. I am unfashionable enough to hold that an operation which does not justify itself by its promised results should always be the subject of a stringent inquest; for I have never been able to regard a death caused by an operation as a natural death. My rage may have been unjust to the surgeons; but it carried me over my first sense of bereavement. When I returned to an Archer-less London it seemed to me that the place had entered on a new age in which I was lagging superfluous.

I still feel that when he went he took a piece of me with him.

BEETHOVEN'S CENTENARY
From the Radio Times, 18 March 1927

A HUNDRED years ago a crusty old bachelor of fifty-seven, so deaf that he could not hear his own music played by a full orchestra, yet still able to hear thunder, shook his fist at the roaring heavens for the last time, and died as he had lived, challenging God and defying the universe. He was Defiance Incarnate: he could not even meet a Grand Duke and his court in the street without jamming his hat tight down on his head and striding through the very middle of them. He had the manners of a disobliging steam-roller (most steamrollers are abjectly obliging and conciliatory); and he was rather less particular about his dress than a scarecrow: in fact he was once arrested as a tramp because the police refused to believe that such a tatterdemalion could be a famous composer, much less a temple of the most turbulent spirit that ever found expression in pure sound. It was indeed a mighty spirit; but if I had written the mightiest, which would mean mightier than the spirit of Handel, Beethoven himself would have rebuked me; and what mortal man could pretend to a spirit mightier than Bach's? But that Beethoven's spirit was the most turbulent is beyond all question. The impetuous fury of his strength, which he could quite easily contain and control, but often would not, and the uproariousness of his fun, go beyond anything of the kind to be found in the works of other composers. Greenhorns write of syncopation now as if it were a new way of giving the utmost impetus to a musical measure; but the rowdiest jazz sounds like The Maiden's Prayer after Beethoven's third Leonora overture; and certainly no negro corobbery that I ever heard could inspire the blackest dancer with such *diable au corps* as the last movement of the Seventh Symphony. And no other com-poser has ever melted his hearers into complete sentimentality by the tender beauty of his music, and then suddenly turned on them and mocked them with derisive trumpet blasts for being such fools. Nobody but Beethoven could govern Beethoven; and when, as happened when the fit was on him, he deliberately re-fused to govern himself, he was ungovernable.

It was this turbulence, this deliberate disorder, this mockery, this reckless and triumphant disregard of conventional manners, that set Beethoven apart from the musical geniuses of the cere-monious seventeenth and eighteenth centuries. He was a giant wave in that storm of the human spirit which produced the French Revolution. He called no man master. Mozart, his great-est predecessor in his own department, had from his childhood been washed, combed, splendidly dressed, and beautifully be-haved in the presence of royal personages and peers. His childish outburst at the Pompadour, "Who is this woman who does not kiss me? The Queen kisses me," would be incredible of Beethoven, who was still an unlicked cub even when he had grown into a very grizzly bear. Mozart had the refinement of convention and society as well as the refinement of nature and of the solitudes of the soul. Mozart and Gluck are refined as the court of Louis XIV was refined: Haydn is refined as the most cultivated country gentlemen of his day were refined: compared to them socially Beethoven was an obstreperous Bohemian: a man of the people. Haydn, so superior to envy that he declared his junior, Mozart, to be the greatest composer that ever lived, could not stand Beethoven: Mozart, more farseeing, listened to his playing, and said "You will hear of him some day"; but the two would never have hit it off together had Mozart lived long enough to try. Beethoven had a moral horror of Mozart, who in Don Giovanni had thrown a halo of enchantment round an aristocratic blackguard, and then, with the unscrupulous moral versatility of a born dramatist, turned round to cast a halo of divinity round Sarastro, setting his words to the only music yet written that would not sound out of place in the mouth of God.

Beethoven was no dramatist: moral versatility was to him revolting cynicism. Mozart was still to him the master of masters (this is not an empty eulogistic superlative: it means literally that Mozart is a composer's composer much more than he has ever been a really popular composer); but he was a court flunkey in breeches whilst Beethoven was a Sansculotte; and Haydn also was a flunkey in the old livery: the Revolution stood between them as it stood between the eighteenth and nineteenth centuries. But to Beethoven Mozart was worse than Haydn because he trifled with morality by setting vice to music as magically as virtue. The Puritan who is in every true Sansculotte rose up against him in Beethoven, though Mozart had shewn him all the possibilities of nineteenth-century music. So Beethoven cast back for a hero to Handel, another crusty old bachelor of his own kidney, who despised Mozart's hero Gluck, though the pastoral symphony in The Messiah is the nearest thing in music to the scenes in which Gluck, in his Orfeo, opened to us the plains of Heaven.

Thanks to broadcasting, millions of musical novices will hear the music of Beethoven this anniversary year for the first time with their expectations raised to an extraordinary pitch by hundreds of newspaper articles piling up all the conventional eulogies that are applied indiscriminately to all the great composers. And like his contemporaries they will be puzzled by getting from him not merely a music that they did not expect, but often an orchestral hurlyburly that they may not recognize as what they call music at all, though they can appreciate Gluck and Haydn and Mozart quite well. The explanation is simple enough. The music of the eighteenth century is all dance music. A dance is a symmetrical pattern of steps that are pleasant to move to; and its music is a symmetrical pattern of sound that is pleasant to listen to even when you are not dancing to it. Consequently the sound patterns, though they begin by being as simple as chessboards, get lengthened and elaborated and enriched with harmonies until they are more like Persian carpets; and the composers who design these patterns no longer expect people to dance to them. Only a whirling Dervish could dance a Mozart symphony: indeed, I have reduced two young and practised dancers to exhaustion by making them dance a Mozart overture. The very names of the dances are dropped: instead of suites consisting of sarabands, pavanes, gavottes, and jigs, the designs are presented as sonatas and symphonies consisting of sections called simply movements, and labelled according to their speed (in Italian) as allegros, adagios, scherzos, and prestos. But all the time, from Bach's preludes to Mozart's Jupiter Symphony, the music makes a symmetrical sound pattern, and gives us the dancer's pleasure always as the form and foundation of the piece.

Music, however, can do more than make beautiful sound patterns. It can express emotion. You can look at a Persian carpet and listen to a Bach prelude with a delicious admiration that goes no further than itself; but you cannot listen to the overture to Don Giovanni without being thrown into a complicated mood which prepares you for a tragedy of some terrible doom over-shadowing an exquisite but Satanic gaiety. If you listen to the last movement of Mozart's Jupiter Symphony, you hear that it is as much a riotous corobbery as the last movement of Beethoven's Seventh Symphony: it is an orgy of ranting drumming tow-row-row, made poignant by an opening strain of strange and painful beauty which is woven through the pattern all through. And yet the movement is a masterpiece of pattern designing all the time.

Now what Beethoven did, and what made some of his greatest contemporaries give him up as a madman with lucid intervals of clowning and bad taste, was that he used music altogether as a means of expressing moods, and completely threw over pattern designing as an end in itself. It is true that he used the old patterns all his life with dogged conservatism (another Sansculotte characteristic, by the way); but he imposed on them such an over-whelming charge of human energy and passion, including that highest passion which accompanies thought, and reduces the passion of the physical appetites to mere animalism, that he not only played Old Harry with their symmetry but often made it impossible to notice that there was any pattern at all beneath the storm of emotion. The Eroica Symphony begins by a pattern (borrowed from an overture which Mozart wrote when he was a boy), followed by a couple more very pretty patterns; but they are tremendously energized, and in the middle of the movement the patterns are torn up savagely; and Beethoven, from the point of view of the mere pattern musician, goes raving mad, hurling out terrible chords in which all the notes of the scale are sounded simultaneously, just because he feels like that, and wants you to feel like it.

And there you have the whole secret of Beethoven. He could design patterns with the best of them; he could write music whose beauty will last you all your life; he could take the driest sticks of themes and work them up so interestingly that you find something new in them at the hundredth hearing: in short, you can say of him all that you can say of the greatest pattern composers; but his diagnostic, the thing that marks him out from all the others, is his disturbing quality, his power of unsettling us and imposing his giant moods on us. Berlioz was very angry with an old French composer who expressed the discomfort Beethoven gave him by saying "*J'aime la musique qui me berce*," "I like music that lulls me." Beethoven's is music that wakes you up; and the one mood in which you shrink from it is the mood in which you want to be let alone.

When you understand this you will advance beyond the eighteenth century and the old-fashioned dance band (jazz, by the way, is the old dance band Beethovenized), and understand not only Beethoven's music, but what is deepest in post-Beethoven music as well.

HOW FREE IS THE PRESS?

THE FREE PRESS. By Hilaire Belloc. (Allen & Unwin.)

From The Nation, 9 February 1918

"To release the truth against whatever odds, even if so doing can no longer help the Commonwealth, is a necessity for the soul," says Mr Belloc. And again, "Those who prefer to sell themselves or to be cowed, gain as a rule, not even that ephemeral security for which they betrayed their fellows; meanwhile they leave to us [journalists] the only permanent form of power, which is the gift of mastery through persuasion."

Now it is more than forty years since my first contribution to the press appeared in print; and I am not sure that this necessity of the soul to which Mr Belloc testifies, thereby echoing Jeremiah (a Jew, I regret to say) who declared that the word was in his heart as a burning fire shut up in his bones, and he was weary with forbearing and could not stay, is really a necessity of *the* soul. I must ask whose soul? Certainly not that of your average journalist or of the man who swallows his articles as soothing syrup. The first necessity of such souls when truth is about, as it always is, is camouflage, or, better still, complete cover. I, like Mr Belloc, and those heroes of the free press whom he celebrates in this book: Mr Orage, the Chestertons, and himself, have conducted truth raids, and seen all England rush to the cellars every time. It takes a very hardy constitution to stand the truth. Is an evening with Ibsen as popular as an evening with Mary Pickford at the movies? A simple No is hardly emphatic enough. One feels the need of the French *Point!* so useful in similar emergencies to Molière.

Before I forget it—for I am going to wander considerably—let me say that Mr Belloc's pamphlet is true enough within its own express limitations. It serves the press right, the parliament right, and our plutocratic humbugs right. But I think he lets the public off too easily; and as for the free press, by which he means specifically The New Age, The New Witness, and in general the coterie press, he is a bit of a flatterer. An amiable weakness; but still, a weakness.

The coterie press is no doubt a free press in a sense; and I have often availed myself of its freedom to say things I should not have been allowed to say elsewhere. When I want somebody to throw a stone at the Lord Mayor, or the Lord Chamberlain, or any other panjandrum, I do not offer six-and-eightpence to my solicitor to do it: I offer a shilling to a tramp. The tramp is free to throw the stone: the respectable solicitor is not. Similarly, when the missile is a literary one, I do not send it to The Times, I offer it to a coterie editor. He has the tramp's freedom. He is not afraid of the advertisers, because he has no advertisements. He is not afraid of the plutocrats, because he has no rich backers. He is not afraid of the lawyers, because he is not worth powder and shot. He is not afraid of losing his social position, because he is not in smart society, and would rather die than get into it. Sometimes he is not afraid of anything, because he has no sense.

In short, Mr Belloc will say with some impatience, the coterie editor is free; and I do not alter that fact by explaining why he is free. *Parfaitement, cher Hilaire* (which I may translate as "Who deniges of it, Betsy?"); but does this freedom, this irresponsibility, carry with it any guarantee of liberality or veracity? Clearly not: all that it does is, within certain limits, to allow the coterie paper to be liberal and veracious if it likes. But if you come to that, do not Lord Northcliffe's millions set him free to attack and destroy people who could crush a coterie paper by a libel action or by setting Dora at it, if Lord Northcliffe liked? Let us not deceive ourselves: we are between the nether millstone of the press that is too poor to tell the truth and the upper one of the press that is too rich. Mr Belloc says that the falsehood of the press operates more by suppression of truth than assertion of lies. Well, I am prepared to maintain that every coterie editor in the world suppresses more truth, according to his lights, than Lord Northcliffe. He perceives more. My fellow countryman, Lord Northcliffe, whom I do not know personally (otherwise how could I be free to be uncivil to him?) is not, for an Irishman, conspicuously intellectual, though he may pass in England; and it must be plain to everyone that his brother was far more completely and unreservedly sincere in his denunciation of the Germans as police-court murderers for actually killing Englishmen in war, and in his conception of the British Museum as a comfortable place for his armchair and Turkey carpet, than any coterie paper has ever dared to be in any single sentence it has published. What happens is not that a certain born liar named Harmsworth publishes a paper to tell his lies in, and that a child of integrity named Belloc or Shaw publishes another to tell the utter truth. It is simply that Belloc and Harmsworth publish papers to say what they sincerely want to have said as far as the police will let them. Their success is according to the number of people who agree with them. Consequently, as Harmsworth's tastes are widespread, his paper catches on; the public rallies to him; he is made a peer; he makes and unmakes ministers and commanders as Warwick made and unmade kings; and he establishes his brother, in the middle of an epoch-making war, as chief of a national service on which our fate in the war will probably depend, without having to offer the public the smallest evidence that the said brother is capable of conducting a whelk-stall successfully. Belloc, on the other hand, having very select intellectual tastes, has presently to sell his paper as a coterie paper, and set up as a war prophet in the columns of the sort of paper he denounces as corrupt, in which employment his gains are like the stripes of Autolycus, mighty ones and millions.

That both Northcliffe and the coterie editor immediately find themselves entangled in the coils of their own circulation, and obliged, on pain of being unable to meet their engagements, to consult their readers' opinions as well as their own, does not leave the coterie editor with any advantage. I have belonged to too many coteries to have any illusions on this point. My correspondents frequently appeal to me to intervene in some public question on the ground that I am a fearless champion of the truth and have never hesitated to say what I think. I reply always, "Heaven save your innocence! If you only knew all the things I think and dare not say!"

Let us have a look at the general ethical character of Mr Belloc's free press. His favorite example is The New Witness, *cidevant* The Eye-Witness, founded by himself, and now edited by Mr Gilbert K. Chesterton as *locum tenens* for Mr Cecil Chesterton, who is in arms in defence of his country. Well, The New Witness is easily the wickedest paper in the world as far as my knowledge goes. G. K. C. as Antichrist has achieved a diabolical enormity which goes to the very verge of breaking down through overacting. His policy is that of Count Reventlow (with the boot on the other leg, of course); but although Reventlow has a much stronger historical case (for what are the trumpery exploits of the new toy soldiers of the new toy kings of Prussia beside our terrific record of invasion, piracy, plunder, conquest, and arrogant claim to rule the waves as well as make Governor Generalships of all the earth for our younger sons?) he cannot touch Mr Chesterton in skill as a pleader, or ferocity as a crusader. There is no "Vengeance is mine, saith the Lord" nonsense about Mr Chesterton. For him, vengeance is the Napoleon of Notting Hill's. He calls on Kensington and Croydon and Tooting and Balham to wipe out the accursed races of Central Europe; to bind their kings in chains; to cast them into the abyss as holy Michael cast Lucifer from Heaven. Not one chivalrous word escapes him when the Hun is his theme. We are to curse the Germans when they are up and kick them when they are down. To turn the page from Mr Chesterton preaching hate against the Prussians to Mr Ernest Newman extolling Beethoven and Bach is to turn from the blasphemies of a stage demon to the judgments of sanity and civilization.

Dare I ask Mr Belloc why Mr Chesterton tolerates Mr Newman? He has almost boasted of his ignorance of and indifference to music. I have no inside knowledge of the matter; but I strongly suspect that The New Witness is as much in the hands of a moneyed interest as the Cocoa Press or the Northcliffe Press or any of the other journalistic ventures that grind the axes of the rich.

Let me hasten to add that, if my suspicion is well founded, the particular interest which supports Mr Chesterton is as gloriously indifferent to his patriotic views on the war as he himself is to Mr Newman's unpatriotic preference of Handel to Dr Arne and of Mozart to Sir Henry Bishop. In fact, I drag the matter in expressly to shew that Mr Chesterton, by an extraordinary piece of luck, is really free to say what he likes about everything except music (which he does not want to say anything about); and this he would not be if the money behind the paper were political money or smart society money or commercial money. Therefore the diabolical element in Mr Chesterton's gospel of murderous hate on a basis of our heavenly nature as opposed to the hellish nature of the Prussian, is quite wanton: he is as free to be bravely magnanimous, chivalrous, Christian, fair and reasonable before Europe, and contrite before history and Heaven, as he is to be just the opposite. Otherwise he would chuck The New Witness as he chucked The Daily News. What makes his choice frightfully wicked to me is that it is not natural choice but artistic virtuosity. He is not really a devil. He can no more hate the Kaiser than Shakespear could hate Iago or Richard. Mr Belloc is a good hater: the proof is that though he is a humorist, there is not in this little book of his, launched as a torpedo at poor Northcliffe, a single conscious joke. There are two unconscious ones. He speaks of "two dots arranged in a spiral" (let him arrange two dots in a spiral if he can); and he says that a newspaper report is less truthful than the thousand tongues of rumor because it tells the same thing simultaneously to a million people in the same words. And this is not a joke at all, because when all the witnesses tell the story in the same words, the case is sure to be a conspiracy. But Mr Chesterton, in his wildest hymns of hate, will break into a joke on his top note, preferably some outrageous pun. He has actually written during the war a book called The Crimes of England, putting Reventlow's case ten times better than Reventlow could put it himself; and no Sinn Feiner alive can write on the oppression of Ireland as he does. Talk of his handling of the violated treaty of 1839, the scrap of paper! You should hear him on the Treaty of Limerick. To put it in the Irish way, his war articles are not devilry: they are pure devilment. To put it in the English way, they are art for art's sake: the political variety of Whistlerism.

So much for your free press at its freest. As Napoleon made war because he could do it so well, the brothers Chesterton write invective because they do it so well. Betrayed as they are at every step to connoisseurs, Gilbert by his humor, and Cecil by his good humor (his smile becomes sunnier at every epithet), they are taken at their word by readers who are not connoisseurs (if any such can read really artistic writing) and play The Corsican Brothers in the costume of The Christian Brothers. And in the strangest way, having no Northcliffe to forge chains for them, they forge chains for themselves, making rules for their artistic and intellectual games which finally leave them speechless on the most vital issues of the day. Take for example the case of the new Bishop of Hereford. Everybody knows the bishop's views on the Virgin Birth and the Resurrection. Everyone chuckled cynically over the solemn assurance of his ecclesiastical superior that there was no evidence that the postulant held any such views. Granted that "the capitalist press" had to allow its readers to gather the truth between the lines, still, it was bolder than The New Witness, which dared not print any lines to read between.

The New Witness may not allude to Evolution, to the Virgin Birth, to the Resurrection, or even to the Garden of Eden, lest it should have to choose between modernism and patent bosh. It has laid on itself the fantastic bond that it must believe what Buffalmacco believed when he painted the walls of the Campo Santo in Pisa, and must forget what has been learnt since. When we are threatened, and indeed already oppressed, by a tyranny of pseudo-science worse than even the tyranny of pseudo-education, The New Witness must take the Inquisition's view of eugenics and welfare work, and dares not venture into argument because it would have to refer to later authorities than Aristotle and Thomas Aquinas, and thus get ahead of Buffalmacco. It has forbidden itself to talk a word of sense about Mr Herbert Samuel, because Mr Samuel is a Jew, and Buffalmacco must place him with Judas Iscariot in hell. The consequence is that it has to live on Buffalmacco's fat, so to speak, to an extent that may eventually make even the Chestertons unreadable. It is hard enough to keep up the interest of a journal even by the freest play upon the actual events of the current week in every department. But if you must ignore not only the current week, but the last three or four centuries, and dare not hint that the earth may be round, you are committing yourself to a literary *tour de force* which begins by being impossible and must end by being ridiculous.

The New Age, Mr Belloc's other example of the free press, may be compared to the venture of a too clever painter who, finding the Academy and all the regular galleries closed to him, opens a Salon of the Rejected to provide an exhibition for himself. The experiment has been remarkably successful: Mr Orage has secured a free pulpit for himself; and his contributors are often as readable as he. Even when he has to fill up with trash, it is not really worse than the average "middles" of his contemporaries, though it may be less plausible and trade-finished. But outside Mr Orage's own notes the paper has no policy and no character. It is a hotch-potch, stimulating thought in general, but not prompting opinion like The Nation or The New Statesman, nor reflecting it like The Spectator. It cannot get things done any more than Notes and Queries can: it is probable that politicians pay much more attention to John Bull. Its freedom is the freedom of the explosive which is not confined in a cannon, spending itself incalculably in all directions.

Organized capital and Judaism do not trouble themselves much with The Freethinker, the organ of the atheists, or The War Cry, the organ of the Salvation Army. Yet the late editor of The Freethinker was not the same man in his private correspondence with Meredith as in his editorial columns. He knew quite well that the sort of atheist who called the Bethlehem stable The Pig and Whistle, not merely to change the atmosphere of the discussion, but with the quaintly snobbish notion that nothing miraculous could happen in a vulgar public-house, was a danger to Secularism; yet he was not free to say so: too many of his subscribers would have suspected him of superstition, if not of downright Christianity, and abandoned him. The leaders of the Salvation Army know as well as old General Booth did that religion does not stand or fall with belief in the adventure of Jonah and the great fish, nor consist of a race for the prize of Heaven; but they dare not say so: they would be cast out as atheists by "some of our old folk." Those who pay the piper call the tune, unless the piper is a veritable Pied Piper whose tune no one can resist.

And here, I think, is the factor to which Mr Belloc gives too little space in his book. There are no irresistible Pied Pipers; but the skill of the piper counts for what it is worth. No release from the pressure of capitalism can make an editor free if he lacks character and judgment. If he has them, he can make a capitalist paper as free as a coterie paper. When The Times makes a series of *gaffes* culminating in the rejection of the Lansdowne letter, it is not because advertisers or proprietors have dictated them, but because the editor, though he may be stuffed with all sorts of excellent qualities, does not know what to put in and what to leave out in his correspondence columns. Mr Massingham, in the teeth of his proprietors and of all the vested interests, political and commercial, which controlled the daily papers he edited, succeeded in changing the politics and outlook of The Star and

The Chronicle from the Whig-ridden Socialist Radicalism of the 'eighties to the Collectivist Progressivism of the 'nineties. Capital has neither a body to be kicked nor a soul to be damned: advertisers are only a mob, without sense enough, as Mr Belloc points out, to use the opportunities offered them by the highly specialized coterie papers. An editor is a man: something much more formidable. Mr Belloc himself has achieved the astounding and hardly sane feat of establishing, with other people's capital, a press organ of the Holy Roman Empire in London in the twentieth century. He is driven to conclude that the able-minded editor with convictions will finally beat the whole field, and destroy the forces that now make his strife so inhumanly hazardous.

My own most polemical writings are to be found in the files of The Times, The Morning Post, The Daily Express, The World, and The Saturday Review. I found out early in my career that a Conservative paper may steal a horse when a Radical paper dare not look over a hedge, and that the rich, though very determined that the poor shall read nothing unconventional, are equally determined to be preached at themselves. In short, I found that only for the classes would I be allowed, and indeed tacitly required, to write on revolutionary assumptions. I filled their columns with sedition; and they filled my pockets (not very deep ones then) with money. In the press as in other departments the greatest freedom may be found where there is least talk about it.

MR ARNOLD BENNETT THINKS PLAY-WRITING EASIER THAN NOVEL WRITING

THE AUTHOR'S CRAFT. By Arnold Bennett. (Hodder & Stoughton.)

From The Nation, 11 March 1916

I DID not at first understand why the Editor of The Nation sent me Mr Bennett's book as one which I might like to review. Mr Bennett talks shop and debits harmless tosh about technique for the entertainment of literary amateurs in a very agreeable and suggestive manner, as he has every right to do, being so distinguished a master of the craft. But why on earth should I join in the conversation and snatch a professional job from some young reviewer whose week's board and lodging it would provide?

I found the solution of the enigma on page 76, which begins with the words, "One reason why a play is easier to write than a novel." That fetched me. I did not want to know "one reason" for so outrageous a stroke of novelist's bluff. But the impetus of my reading carried me on, in spite of the shock; and so I learnt that this one reason is "that a play is shorter than a novel." It is; and so is the Bible shorter than the London Directory. "Excuse the length of my letter," said Pascal: "I had no time to write a short one."

Now, I am not going to argue. I never do. I will simply take one of the shortest, most intense, and most famous scenes in English dramatic literature, and rewrite it as a chapter in a novel in the style of my friends Bennett and Galsworthy when they are too lazy to write plays:

MACBETH

A Play. By William Shakespear. *Act V. Scene 8*

The precinct of Macbeth's Castle on Dunsinane Hill

Enter Macbeth

MACB. Why should I play the Roman fool, and die
On mine own sword? Whiles I see lives, the gashes
Do better upon *them*.

Enter Macduff

MACD.   Turn, hell-hound, turn.

MACB. Of all men else I have avoided thee;
But get thee back: my soul is too much charg'd
With blood of thine already.

MACD.   I have no words,
My voice is in my sword, thou bloodier villain
Than terms can give thee out! (*They fight.*)

MACB.   Thou losest labor.
As easy may'st thou the intrenchant air
With thy keen sword impress, as make me bleed.
Let fall thy blade on vulnerable crests:
I bear a charmed life, which must not yield
To one of woman born.

MACD.   Despair thy charm;
And let the angel whom thou still hast serv'd
Tell thee, Macduff was from his mother's womb
Untimely ripp'd.

MACB. Accurséd be that tongue that tells me so;
For it hath cow'd my better part of man.
And be these juggling fiends no more believ'd
That palter with us in a double sense;
That keep the word of promise to our ear,
And break it to our hope. I'll not fight with thee.

MACD. Then yield thee, coward;
And live to be the show and gaze o' the time.
We'll have thee, as our rarer monsters are,
Painted upon a pole; and, underwrit,
"Here may you see the tyrant."

MACB.   I'll not yield,
To kiss the ground before young Malcolm's feet,
And to be baited with the rabble's curse.
Though Birnam wood *be* come to Dunsinane,
And thou oppos'd, being of no woman born,
Yet I will try the last: before my body
I throw my warlike shield. Lay on, Macduff;
And damn'd be him that first cries, "Hold! Enough!"
                              (*Exeunt fighting.*)

MACBETH

A NOVEL. By Arnold Bennett, John Galsworthy, or
Anybody. The Last Chapter

He was to fail, after all, then. The day was going against him.
His men were not really fighting. They had conveyed to Old

Siward that they were open to an offer of quarter; and the hint had not been lost on that ancient campaigner, whose son he had just slain.

What was the use of killing? Duncan, Banquo, the Macduff people: he had waded through their blood; and how much better would it not be if it were all a dream and they were alive and kind to him?

How the martins were singing! Banquo, always a bit of a fool, had been sentimental about the martins. Gruach, the dear dead wife whom the southrons persisted in calling Lady Macbeth, had argued with Banquo about them, telling him that their habits were insanitary, and that they were infested with small bugs which got into the castle, already too rich in insect life. But Duncan had agreed with Banquo; and when Gruach became queen she would not let the martins' nests be broken down, being anxious to copy Duncan's tastes in every way, lest anyone should say that the Macbeths did not know how kings lived. And so the martins were singing, singing, always singing when they were not fly-catching.

It came to him, with a twist at the heart, that he had never told Gruach the truth about Banquo. He had left her to believe that he had killed him because the witches had foretold that his posterity should be kings. But the real reason was that Banquo had given himself moral airs. That is hard to bear at any time; but when you are within ten minutes of committing a murder, it is insufferable. Morality is easy for a man who does not intend to do anything; but a man of action cannot stand on scruples. These idle thanes who sat down on their little patrimonies and had no ambition: they had invented this moral twaddle to excuse their laziness.

What an exquisite morning it was! Was there anything so blue as a blue sky, anything so white as a white cloud, any gold so golden as the gold of the gorse? From the summit of Dunsinane he could see almost to the Roman wall on the south and to the Forth Bridge on the north. The wind had backed a little to the north: perhaps it would rain later. But no such foreboding troubled the wood pigeon that now called to him, "Tak two coos, Taffy: tak two coos, Taffy." He smiled grimly. He had taken from first to last not less than a thousand coos; and this funny bird kept on exhorting him to take two. And yet he did not throw a stone at it as he once would have done. It seemed all so useless. You strove and strove, and killed and killed, and made journeys to consult witches; and at the end of it all the wood pigeon had no more to say to you than before; and the sky was no bluer, the cloud no whiter, the whins no yellower. Curse the sky! Curse the whins! Doubly damn the wood pigeon! Why not make an end of it, like the Roman fool at Philippi? He stood his claymore on its hilt on the flags and bent over the point. Just to lean on it, and let it go through him: then the wood pigeon might coo itself black in the face: Macbeth would be at rest with Duncan. Where had he heard about Philippi? It seemed unlikely that he could have learned Roman history; and yet he found that he did know. Do men know everything before death? He shuddered. Strange, that he, who rather enjoyed killing other people, should feel an intense repugnance to kill himself! Yet there was one canny thing about killing yourself: it relieved you of all concern for the future. You could kill as many other people as you liked first without considering the consequences. He would, please God, spit a few more of his enemies on that sword before his own turn came. He tossed it into the air by the point, and caught the hilt as it came down. He no longer heard the wood pigeon.

And yet, what was that? Had the wood pigeon called him a hell-hound? He turned, and saw Macduff there, between him and the sun, glaring at him. If the sun had been in his eyes, he could not have glared. It was clever of him to come that way and get the advantage of the sun.

Macduff! Yes, Macduff: the man of whom the spirit called up by the witches had bade him beware. The man whose wife and child he had slaughtered. Could he blame him for glaring? Would not any man glare after such an experience? Banquo had glared even after his death, but with no speculation in his eyes. There was speculation enough in Macduff's: he was speculating on the sun being in the eyes of his adversary.

How the martins were singing! How fresh the air tasted! How good life was! How many pleasant paths there were on those hillsides, paths that had led his feet and Macduff's to this one spot of all spots in the world! Well, if Macduff had not come by one path he would have come by another. That was life, always inscrutable, sometimes a little ironical. The wind dropped: the banner had ceased to flap, and hung inert. A number of birds and crickets, no longer scared into silence by its flapping, joined the concert of the martins. Again came the wood pigeon's incitement, "Tak two coos, Taffy: tak——" What was that? A sharp, rasping sound called Macbeth from the landscape. He looked again at the man against whom he had been warned.

Macduff had stooped to sharpen his claymore on the flags. He was squatting down in an attitude which brought his boney knees into prominence just below his kilt, and drawing his blade to and fro with a harsh, rhythmical grating on the granite. By the mere instinct of imitation, Macbeth did the same. His knees were fleshier; and it was harder for him to stoop; but he did it. It is never easy for a king to stoop; but Fate will have it so sometimes. Now there were two blades scraping. The birds stopped singing, and listened in astonished suspicious silence. Only a jay laughed.

Macbeth heard it. Something stirred in him, and distorted his lips into a grin. It seemed to him that he suddenly opened a book that had always been sealed to him. When Gruach was dying he had asked the doctor for some physic for the mind; and the doctor had failed him. Then he had asked the porter, because he had noticed that the porter, alone among all the men of his acquaintance, was light-hearted, and would laugh, even when nobody was being hurt or ridiculed, and seemed to despise ambition. And the porter had told him that life is not so bad if you can see the fun of it. Old Siward had nailed the porter to the door that morning because he refused to open it to the enemy. Did he see the fun of that, Macbeth wondered? Yet here, as he squatted before Macduff, and they both sharpened their blades on the flags, a dim sense of something laughable in the situation

48

ARNOLD BENNETT

touched him, though, God knows, there was nothing to laugh at if the warning of the witches were trustworthy. The spirits had said that no man born of woman should harm Macbeth. That seemed pretty conclusive. But they had also said that he would not be vanquished until Birnam Wood came to Dunsinane. That also seemed conclusive; yet the thing had happened: he had seen the wood walking.

He decided to give Macduff a chance. He was tired of killing people named Macduff. He said so. He advised Macduff to go away.

Macduff tried to speak; gulped; and came on. His voice was in his sword.

Macbeth was not afraid, though he knew he was not the man he had been. He had drunk heavily since he seized the throne: the Scots expected that from a king. But he could fight as well as ever for forty-five seconds; and then he could clinch, and try to get in his dirk somewhere. After all, Macduff was no teetotaller, if one might judge by his nose, which was red and swollen. Only, the doubt came: was the redness and the swelling from drink, or from weeping over his slaughtered family? With that thought came Macduff's first blow: a feint, followed by a vicious thrust at the groin.

Macbeth was quick enough to drop his targe and stop the thrust, even while he guarded the blow that did not come. That reassured him, and took some of the bounce out of Macduff. He was equally successful the next time, and the next. He became elated. At last his pride in his charmed life got the better of his prudence. He told Macduff that he was losing his labor, and told him why.

The effect was exactly the contrary of what he had anticipated. A gleam of savage delight came into Macduff's eyes.

What did it mean?

Macbeth was not left long in doubt. He stood petrified, whilst a tale poured from Macduff's lips such as had never before blasted the ears of mortal man. It cannot be repeated here: there is such a thing as the library censorship. Let it suffice that it was a tale of

49

the rude but efficient obstetric surgery of those ancient times, and that it established beyond all question the fact that Macduff had never been born.

After that, Macbeth felt that he simply could not fight with him. It was not that he was afraid, even now. Nor was it that he was utterly disgusted at the way the witches had let him down again. He just could not bring himself to hack at a man who was not natural. It was like trying to eat a cat. He flatly refused further combat.

Of course, Macduff called him Coward. He did not mind that so much; for he had given his proofs, and nobody would believe Macduff; nor, indeed, would any reasonable Scot expect him to fight an unborn adversary. But Macduff hinted at unbearable things: at defeat, disgrace, the pillory even.

There was a lark singing now. Far down the hillside, where the rugged road wound up to the barbican, the last of Birnam Wood was still on the march. A hawk hovered motionless over a walking oak: he could see the glint of the sun on its brown back. The oak's legs must be those of an old soldier, he thought, who had cunningly taken the heaviest tree so that he might be late for the fighting. But, old or young, the soldier was now anxious lest he should be late for the plunder and the other sequels to the sack of a castle; for the oak was coming up at a rattling pace. There were nests in it, too. Curious, to wonder how those nesting pairs took their moving!

A surge of wrath went through Macbeth. He was, above all things, a country gentleman; and that another country gentleman should move his timber without acquiring any rights infuriated him. He became reckless. Birnam Wood—*his* wood—had been taken to Dunsinane: was that a thing he could be expected to stand? What though Macduff had not been properly born: was it not all the more likely that he had a weak constitution and could not stick it out if he were pressed hard in the fight? Anyhow, Macbeth would try. He braced himself; grasped his claymore powerfully; thrust his shield under the chin of his adversary; and cried, "Lay on, Macduff."

He could not have chosen a more unfortunate form of defiance. When the news had come to Macduff of the slaughter of his wife and boy, he had astonished the messenger by exclaiming, "What! All my pretty chickens and their dam at one fell swoop!" Accustomed from his earliest youth to deal with horses, he knew hardly anything of poultry, which was a woman's business. When he applied the word dam, properly applicable only to a mare, to a hen, Malcolm, though deeply moved by his distress, had a narrow escape of a fit of hysterics; for the innocent blunder gave him an impulse of untimely laughter. The story had been repeated; and something of it had come to Macduff's ears. He was a highly-strung man, exquisitely sensitive to ridicule. Since that time the slightest allusion to chickens had driven him to transports of fury. At the words "Lay on," he saw red. Macbeth, from the instant those fatal words passed his lips, had not a dog's chance.

In any case, he would not have been ready to meet a sudden attack. All his life he had been subject to a strange discursiveness which sent his mind wandering to the landscape, and to the fauna and flora of the district, at the most exciting crises of his fate. When he meant to tell Gruach that he had arranged to have Banquo killed, he had said to her, instead, "Light thickens; and the crow makes wing to the rooky wood." His attention had already strayed to the wood pigeon when Macduff's yell of fury split his ears; and at the same moment he felt his foe's teeth snap through his nose and his foe's dirk drive through his ribs.

When Malcolm arrived, there was little left of Macbeth but a pile of mince. Macduff was panting. "That will teach him," he said, and stopped, exsufflicate.

They laid Macbeth beside Gruach in God's quiet acre in the little churchyard of Dunsinane. Malcolm erected a stately tomb there, for the credit of the institution of kingship; and the epitaph, all things considered, was not unhandsome. There was no reproach in it, no vain bitterness. It said that Macbeth had "succeeded Duncan."

The birds are still singing on Dunsinane. The wood pigeon still coos about the coos; and Malcolm takes them frankly and generously. It is not for us to judge him, or to judge Macbeth. Macbeth was born before his time. Men call him a villain; but had the press existed in his day, a very trifling pecuniary sacrifice on his part would have made a hero of him. And, to do him justice, he was never stingy.

Well! Well!

THE END

There! that is what is called novel writing. I raise no idle question as to whether it is easy or not. Fine art of any sort is either easy or impossible. But that sort of thing I can write by the hundred thousand words on my head. I believe that if I turned my attention to mechanics for a month or two, I could make a typewriter attachment that would do it, like the calculating attachment that has lately come into use. The odd thing is that people seem to like it. They swallow it in doses of three hundred pages at a time; and they are not at all keen on Shakespear. Decidedly, when my faculties decay a little further, I shall go back to novel writing. And Arnold Bennett can fall back on writing plays.

SAMUEL BUTLER: THE NEW LIFE REVIEWED

SAMUEL BUTLER, AUTHOR OF EREWHON (1835-1902): A
MEMOIR. By Henry Festing Jones. (London: Macmillan and
Co. Two vols.)

From the Manchester Guardian, 1 November 1919

IN the great tradition of British criticism a book to review is an occasion to improve. Even if it were not so, the life of Samuel Butler would be an irresistible temptation to any writer with an ounce of homily in him. It is a staggering object-lesson in the villainy (no milder expression is adequate) of our conventional clergyman schoolmaster education, and of the family and class life to which it belongs.

Mr Festing Jones's memoir, though one of the most complete ever written, is nevertheless not quite complete. Butler told the story of his childhood so frightfully well in his novel, The Way of All Flesh, that Mr Festing Jones has recognized the hopelessness of attempting to do that work again and do it better. It cannot be done better: The Way of All Flesh is one of the summits of human achievement in that kind; and there is nothing for it but to require from the reader of the memoir as a preliminary qualification that he shall read the autobiography in the novel. Indeed a good deal of Mr Jones's memoir will be only half intelligible to anyone who has not already come to know Butler's parents as the detestable Theobald and his Christina, whose very names proclaim that they had made their gods as hateful to their son as themselves. Butler is the only man known to history who has immortalized and actually endeared himself by parricide and matricide long drawn out. He slew the good name (and it was such a very good name!) of his father and mother so reasonably, so wittily, so humorously, and even in a ghastly way so charitably, that he convinced us that he was engaged in an execution and not in a murder.

But the moral of this memoir is that not even genius can come through such an education as Butler's with its mind unwounded and unlamed. It was his genius, always breaking through to the truth, that revealed to him, whilst he was still a boy, that this devoted father to whom he could never be too grateful, and this pious angel mother in whose watchful care he was so fortunate, were at best a pair of pitiably perverted and intimidated nobodies, and that he hated them, feared them, and despised them with all his soul. Unfortunately the matter could not stop there. Butler was naturally affectionate to the point of being gulled by heartless people with ridiculous ease. As a child he had sought for affection at home, only to have his feelings practised on by his mother to wheedle confidences from him and have him beaten by his father, who trained him exactly as if he were a performing animal, except that he did not teach him anything amusing. But the child went on assuming that he loved his dear parents, and that they were all happy together in their domestic affection, spotless respectability, and unchallenged social precedence. When he realized how he had been duped and how he had duped himself, he reacted to the opposite extreme with such violence that he set up as a rule in the art of life that the stupidest and most mischievous of mistakes is to force yourself or humbug yourself into liking things that are really repugnant or uninteresting to you. Accordingly, all through this memoir we find Butler "hating," on principle, everything that was not immediately congenial and easy to him at the very first taste. He "hated" Plato, Euripides, Dante, Raphael, Bach, Mozart, Beethoven, Blake, Rossetti, Tennyson, Browning, Wagner, Ibsen, and in fact everyone who did not appeal to his palate instantly as a lollypop appeals to the palate of a child. The exception was Handel, because he had learned to like Handel's music in the days of his childish illusion; but I suspect that if he had never heard Handel's music until after he had set up his rule he would have denounced him as a sanctimonious drum major, and classed him as one of The Seven Humbugs of Christendom.

It is true that these repeated denunciations of great men as impostors and humbugs are made with a tart humor which betrays a subconscious sense of their folly, and saves Butler from being classed as a vulgar nil-admirerist; but the trick is none the less tiresome and even sinister, because it is plain that Butler did seriously narrow his mind and paralyse his critical powers by refusing to take any trouble to find out what our greatest teachers were driving at, or to face the drudgery of learning their peculiar idiom. For a man with his love of music to begin with gavottes and minuets and never get any further (for that is what it came to) was monstrous. I risk his rising from the grave to smite me when I add, as I must, that he never said a word about Handel worth reading; he liked the hailstones running along the ground and the sheep going astray, every one to his own way; but Handel could hardly have said more to him on that than "Thank you for nothing." It is flatly impossible to believe that a man who could see no greatness in Bach was really admiring what is great in Handel, however sincerely he may have relished Handel's more popular vein.

Then, again, Butler's public manners were atrocious. Privately, he was most courteous, most considerate, if anything too delicate in his conscientiousness. But if he did not like a man's public opinion and work, or the man did not like his: in a word, if he did not feel perfectly happy with him, he treated him as a moral delinquent, derided him, insulted him, and even cut him in the street. In other words, he behaved exactly as his father would have behaved if his father had had courage and wit as well as thoroughly bad civic manners. In the war of cliques which never ceases in London, he heaped scorn on the Darwin clique, and not only resented the shallow snobbery which led it to underrate him, and to persuade Darwin himself that it was beneath his dignity to clear up a very simple misunderstanding which had led Butler quite naturally to accuse him of controversial foul play, but retaliated in kind. For there was inevitably a Butler clique as well as a Darwin clique. Butler's bite was so powerful that he may be said to have been a clique in himself in so far as he acted in the clique spirit; but with Miss Savage, Festing Jones, Gogin, Pauli, not to mention Emery Walker, Sydney Cockerell, and the steadily growing outer ring of Butlerites of whom I was one, he was by no means alone *contra mundum*. As the best brains were always with Butler, Darwin, a simple-souled naturalist with no comprehension of the abyss of moral horror that separated his little speciality of Natural Selection from Butler's comprehensive philosophic conception of Evolution, may be pardoned for his foolish estimate of Butler as "a clever unscrupulous man," and for countenancing the belittling of him by Huxley and Romanes that now seems so ridiculous. They really did not know any better. But in the selfsame spirit, without the selfsame excuse, Butler and his clique belittled poor Grant Allen, one of the most amiably helpful men that ever lived, and one, moreover, who recognized Butler as a man of genius, and declared that he "bore its signet on his brow." Butler, with unconscious but colossal arrogance, simply damned his impudence, denying that there was any such thing as genius, and heaping scorn on Allen because he was not at once ready to declare that Butler was right about evolution, and Darwin a disingenuous sciolist. Miss Savage, pretending to forget Allen's name, wrote of him as Allen Grant; and Mr Festing Jones leaves the readers of his memoir to infer that he was an unamiable and rather contemptible man. All the more annoying this because Grant Allen had the same grievance as Butler: he could not live by his serious scientific work, and had to write novels and stories to keep himself and his family alive.

The truth is, we all did that sort of thing in those days; and we are doing it still. Nine-tenths of English criticism today is either log-rolling or bad manners; and at the root of the evil are pure snobbery, bigotry, and intolerance. I will not say that Butler was as bad as his father, because, with his greater powers and opportunities, he was very much worse. Ardent Butlerite as I am, I cannot deny that Butler brought a great deal of his unpopularity on himself by his country parsonage unsociability and evangelical bigotry. One does not get rid of that bigotry by merely discarding the Resurrection and making pious people laugh against their wills with such sallies as "Resist God and He will flee from you," or "Jesus: with all Thy faults I love Thee still." Bigotry in a parson is at least not unexpected, and not unnatural if he is in earnest about the 39 articles; but in a rampant anticlerical like Butler it tempts us to say that as he brought so much of the worst of the Church with him when he came out of it he might as well have stayed in it to please his father.

Still, when all is said that can be said against Butler, the fact remains that when he was important he was so vitally important, and when he was witty he was so pregnantly witty, that we are forced to extend an unlimited indulgence to his weaknesses, and finally to embrace them as attractions. His excessive and touchy self-consciousness; his childish belief that everything that happened to him, no matter how common and trivial, was interesting enough to be not only recorded for the sake of an authentic human document but sold to the public as *belles lettres*; his country parsonage conviction that foreigners with their quaint languages, and working-class people with their ungentlemanlike and unladylike dialects, were funny creatures whose sayings were to be quoted like those of clever children; his patronizing and petting of his favorites and his snubbing and cutting of his aversions: all these, with his petulant and perverse self-limitation and old-bachelorism, would have damned fifty ordinary men; yet they were so effectually redeemed by belonging to Butler, and in fact being Butler, that it never occurs to Mr Festing Jones to conceal, extenuate, or apologize for them.

Those to whom Butler was a stranger did not forgive him so easily. Take, for example, his Alps and Sanctuaries. We have to read it today not only for the promise and beauty of its title, but for the sake of the titbits it contains: in short, because it is by Butler. But barring those titbits it is surely the silliest book ever written by a clever man. Its placid descriptions of itineraries compared to which the voyages of a motor-bus from Charing Cross to Hyde Park Corner are chapters of romance, and its promiscuous quotations from Handel, in which elegiac passages which might conceivably have been recalled by the beauty of an Italian valley are not distinguished from toccata stuff that reeks of the keyboard and of nothing else, explain only too fully why the book was refused by the publisher who had rashly commissioned it, and why its first sale did not reach 500 copies. No Butlerite was surprised or offended when, buying a later book with a title which suggested a pious pilgrimage, he had suddenly sprung on him a most irreverent onslaught on Sir Benjamin Layard, whose only offence was that he was a bigwig, and that to Butler a bigwig meant merely a silk-stockinged calf to fix his teeth in; but Butlerites were few and strangers many; and strangers could not be expected to know that when you bought a book by Butler you never got what you paid for. True, you got something better; but then you did not want something better. A bookseller who responded to an order for La Vie Parisienne by sending The Methodist Times might establish a reputation as a humorist, but he would hardly make a fortune in his business.

There were other ways in which Butler did not live up to his professions. In Erewhon he would have been tried for the serious offence of gullibility, and very severely punished. The Pauli case would have put him quite beyond the pale of Erewhonian sympathy. And Pauli would have been knighted for gulling Butler so successfully. It is all very well to call Butler's forbearance to Pauli delicacy; but in any other man we should call it moral cowardice. I am not sure that it was not something worse. The rectory-born lust for patronage and charity was in Butler's blood: he had absolutely no conscience as to how he demoralized other people provided he could make them his pensioners. If Pauli, infamously pocketing his pension of £200 a year under pretence of penury when he was making £900 as a barrister and a mendicant whilst Butler was on the verge of bankruptcy, had avowed and asserted his independence, I verily believe Butler would have quarrelled with him at once. As it was, when death revealed the fraud, Butler's only regret was that Pauli was not alive to be forgiven. In that Butler was his father all over. Well might he make his prototype Ernest, in The Way of All Flesh, put his children out to nurse with a bargee on the ground that, if he kept them with him, an inexorable heredity would force him to treat them as badly as his father had treated him.

If these things are not firmly said about Butler, his example will corrupt the world. From idiotic underestimate and neglect of him we are already turning to deify him, in spite of his own warnings, as one who could do no wrong. The reviews of Mr Jones's memoirs are as shameless in this matter as the memoir itself. Mr Jones has, on principle, concealed nothing. He even gives the name of the witty and amiable French mistress whom Butler patronized incognito very faithfully but very cautiously for sixteen years, at the end of which he ventured to tell her who he was and where he lived, and admitted her to his circle (one gathers) for the four more years which elapsed before her death. Twenty years ago such a revelation might have pilloried Butler. Today we steadily refuse to overhear Mr Jones's communication.

It is, by the way, a great pity that Butler did not carry out his intention of dealing with the question of marriage as he had dealt with evolution. His reiteration of the not very respectable old proverb that it is cheaper to buy the milk than to keep the cow did not, in spite of the French lady, do Butler justice, being obviously a relic of that shallow Hedonism which seemed to the mid-century Victorians to follow logically when they discovered that the book of Genesis is not a scientific account of the origin of species, and that the accounts given by the evangelists of the Resurrection do not tally so exactly as the depositions of police witnesses in Sinn Fein prosecutions. Instead of concluding that these things were not of the real substance of religion, and that it did not matter one straw to that real substance whether they believed or disbelieved this or that tradition or parable that had become connected with it, they still went on assuming that it mattered so tremendously that they could not get rid of the crudest and most utterly irrelevant miracle story without bringing down the whole ethical structure of religion with a crash. Those were the days when an army officer of my acquaintance said to me gravely, "I know for a fact that the rector's son behaved disgracefully with the housemaid; and you may tell me after that that the Bible is true if you like, but I shall not believe it." The alternative to believing silly things about God seemed to be blank materialist Hedonist atheism. Yet Rousseau had said a hundred years before, "Get rid of your miracles, and the whole world will fall at the feet of Christ." And there you have it. As Butler's education consisted in concealing Rousseau's religious discoveries from him, he imagined that he had lost his faith when he had only lost his superstitions, and that in getting rid of the miracles he had got rid of Christ, of God, of The Church, and of any obligations to pursue anything but his own pleasure. It was in this phase that he nicknamed his father Theobald and his mother Christina, and perhaps decided to buy his milk instead of keeping a cow. His mind was too powerful to be imposed on in that way for long: but it need not have been imposed on for five seconds if his University had treated Voltaire and Rousseau as classics and seers, instead of as "infidels." It was at Shrewsbury School and Cambridge that Canon Butler had been taught to pretend to his son that his mother was killed by Erewhon. That is, his public school and university education had inculcated an ignorance more dense and dangerous than the ignorance of an illiterate ploughman. How silly it all seems now, except perhaps to the hundreds of Canon Butlers still corrupting their sons in our parsonages, and probably beating them if they catch them reading Butler—Butler! who stood for the very roots of religion when Darwin was "banishing mind from the universe"!

I cannot judge whether Mr Festing Jones's exhaustive and very cleverly documented memoir is going to be one of the great British biographies or not. It interests me throughout; but then I knew Butler and many of the other persons with whom the two volumes deal. For strangers, possibly, the death of Miss Savage at the end of the first volume will make it hard for the second to be equally amusing. She was a most entertaining woman who had caught Butler's comedy style so well, and even assimilated his art of life so congenially, that but for her alert feminine touch Butler might be suspected of inventing her letters. Her stories and jokes are all first-rate. Butler is not at his brightest in his remorse for having been occupied with his own affairs instead of with hers: his affectionate feeling that he had treated her badly was, as he would probably have admitted if some robust person had taxed him with it, priggish and childish.

Besides, Butler's bolt is shot in the first volume. In the second he is no longer the great moralist of Erewhon and the forerunner of the present blessed reaction towards Creative Evolution, but a dryasdust dilettante fussing about Tabachetti and Gaudenzio di Ferrara, Shakespear's Sonnets, and the authoress of the Odyssey. His shot about the Odyssey got home. All the pedants thought the attribution of the Odyssey to a woman monstrously improbable and paradoxical only because the Odyssey had always been thoughtlessly attributed to a man; but the moment the question was raised it became, to those who were really familiar with the two epics, not only probable but almost obvious that Butler had hit on the true secret of the radical and irreconcilable difference between the Odyssey and the Iliad. It was equally clear that he was right in his opinion that the first batch of Shakespear's Sonnets was the work of a very young man. But who cared, outside the literary fancy? To the mass of people whose very souls' salvation depended on whether Erewhon and Life and Habit were sound or unsound it mattered not a dump who wrote the Odyssey, or whether Shakespear was 17 or 70 when he wrote the sonnets to Mr W. H. And though Raphael's stocks were down heavily and Michael Angelo's not what they had been, yet the stocks of Tabachetti and Gaudenzio di Ferrara, whose works are not visible to us in England, were not sufficiently up to induce anyone to exchange. His other heroes, Giovanni Bellini and Handel, were very far from being overlooked or needing his assistance in any way, unless, indeed, he had struck a blow at the horrible festivals at which the scattered wheezings and roarings and screamings of four thousand Crystal Palace holiday-makers were making Handel's oratorios ridiculous. He missed that chance of a hook hit at the white chokers. He had nothing new to say about his two pets: he was only a Don Quixote with two Dulcineas. Meanwhile the intellectual and artistic world to which he was appealing was intensely interested in two new giants: Richard Wagner and Henrik Ibsen, the latter carrying on young Butler's battle against old Butler's ideals most mightily. And what had Butler to say about them? "Ibsen may be, and I dare say is, a very wonderful man, but what little I know of him repels me, and, what is worse, bores me." After not only saying this, but actually writing it, could Butler pretend that the worst we can conceive of his father the Canon or his grandfather the headmaster-Bishop in the way of dull arrogance, insolence, snobbery, pomposity, Podsnappery, ignorance half genuine, half wilful and malicious, were not squared and cubed in their gifted son and grandson? And again, "Carlyle is for me too much like Wagner, of whom Rossini said

that he has *des beaux moments mais des mauvais quarts d'heure*—
my French is not to be trusted." Were we to be expected to listen
to a man who had nothing better than that to say about the
composer of The Ring twenty years after that super-Homeric
music epic had been given to the world? Surely we were entitled
to reply that if Butler was too gross a Philistine or too insular an
ignoramus to be civil to Wagner, he might at least have been just
to Rossini, who, with unexpected and touching greatness of
character, earnestly repudiated the silly anti-Wagner gibes attributed to him, and said to Wagner himself—Wagner being then
the worst-reviled musician in Europe, and Rossini classed as the
greatest—that if it had been possible for serious music to exist in
the Italian opera houses, he might have done something; for
"*j'avais du talent*." How disgraceful Butler's sneer appears in the
light of such sublime self-judgment! No doubt Butler did not
know of it; but he could have found it out in less time than
it cost him to learn Shakespear's Sonnets by heart. He could
at least have held his tongue and concealed his ignorance and
spite, which, please observe, was not provoked spite, but
sheer gratuitous insular spite for spite's sake. His own experience should have warned him. Why did nobody say this to
him, and produce that conviction of sin to which he was certainly
accessible? Mr Festing Jones, a serious and remarkable musician,
must have known that when Butler went on like this he was
talking and writing vulgar and uppish nonsense. Perhaps he
did venture occasionally; but he is too loyal a biographer to tell
us about it.

Nothing more is needed to explain why Butler made no head-
way with his books about art and literature, and his records of
his globe trottings. He accounted for it himself by saying that
failure, like success, is cumulative, and that therefore it was inevitable that the longer he lived the less successful he should be. But
the truth is that he spent the first half of his life saying all that he
had to say that was important, and the second half dabbling in
painting and music, and recording the thrills of "a week in lovely
Lucerne" (much as the sisters he derided might have done), with-

out getting beyond mediocrity in painting and slavish imitation in music, or gaining knowledge and sense of proportion in criticism. It is really appalling to learn that this man of genius, having received the very best education our most expensive and select institutions could give him, and having withal a strong natural taste for music and literature, turned from Bayreuth in mere ignorant contempt, and yet made every Christmas a pious pilgrimage to the Surrey pantomime, and wrote an anxiously careful account of its crude buffooneries to his musician friend. Is it to be wondered at that when an investment in house property obliged him to engage a man of the people as his clerk, this recruit, Mr Alfred Emery Cathie, had to constitute himself his valet, his nurse, his keeper, and his Prime Minister and Executive all in one, and to treat him as the grown-up child his education had left him? Alfred is the real hero of the second volume, simply as a good-natured sensible Englishman who had been fortunate enough to escape the public schools and the university. To Butler he was a phenomenon, to be quoted with patronizing amazement and admiration whenever he exploded a piece of common sense in the Clifford's Inn lunatic asylum. What Butler was to Alfred (except a great man) will never be known. Probably a rare good old sort, quite cracked, and utterly incapable of taking care of himself. Butler was at least not ungrateful.

Throughout this later period we see Butler cramped and worried when he was poor, spoilt when he was rich, and all the time uneasy because he knew that there was something wrong, and yet could not quite find himself out, though his genius was always flashing through the fog and illuminating those wonderful notebooks, with their queer strings of over-rated trivialities, profound reflections, witty comments, humorous parables, and family jokes and gibes to please Gogin and Jones or annoy the Butlers.

THE FAULT OF EDUCATION

Now why, it may be asked, do I, who said, and said truly, that Butler was "in his own department the greatest English writer of the latter half of the nineteenth century," now attack him in his grave by thus ruthlessly insisting on his failings? Well, I do so precisely because I want to carry on his work of demonstrating the falsehood and imposture of our "secondary education" and the mischief of treating children as wild beasts to be tamed and broken instead of as human beings to be let develop. Butler held up his father to ridicule and infamy, and exclaimed, "This is what your public school, your university, your Church, made of him." But the world replied, "Oh, yes: that is all very well; but your father was a rotter and a weakling: all public school and university men are not like him." Now if, as is at last possible with this ruthlessly faithful memoir of him in our hands, we can say, "This is what your public school and your university and your country parsonage made, not of a rotter and a weakling, but of a man of genius who was all his life fiercely on his guard against their influence," then we can go one better than Butler, and make his ghost cry "Splendid! Dont spare me. Rub it in; and more power to your elbow!"

For we must not deceive ourselves. England is still governed from Langar Rectory, from Shrewsbury School, from Cambridge, with their annexes of the Stock Exchange and the solicitors' offices; and even if the human products of these institutions were all geniuses, they would finally wreck any modern civilized country after maintaining themselves according to their own notions at the cost of the squalor and slavery of four-fifths of its inhabitants. Unless we plough up the moral foundations of these places and sow them with salt, we are lost. That is the moral of the great Butler biography.

MR GILBERT CANNAN ON SAMUEL BUTLER

SAMUEL BUTLER: A CRITICAL STUDY. By Gilbert Cannan. (Martin Secker.)

From The New Statesman 8 *May* 1915

IN choosing Mr Gilbert Cannan to write on Butler for his critical series, Mr Martin Secker has shewn either luck or cunning; for the book has style and wit, and does its work in a highly readable manner up to the point at which Butler must be left to speak for himself. Its presentation of Butler as a Character with an engaging literary talent and a racy vein of eccentric humor is complete and elegant. It does not present Butler as a man of genius, because Mr Cannan does not consider Butler a man of genius. I do. And I may as well explain the difference.

A man of genius is not a man who can do more things, or who knows more things, than ordinary men: there has never been a man of genius yet who has not been surpassed in both respects in his own generation by quite a large number of hopeless fools. He is simply a man who sees the importance of things. Otherwise every schoolmaster would be greater than Christ. Mr Cannan says that the nearest in spirit to Butler of any man of his time was W. S. Gilbert. This is a staggering statement, because on Butler's plane one does not think of Gilbert; and when we are reminded of him there we feel that Butler mattered enormously more than Gilbert, who in such a comparison seems not to have mattered at all. Yet, on reflection, one has to admit that they have something in common. The particular vein of wit which leads some men to take familiar and unquestioned propositions and turn them inside out so neatly as to convince you that they are just as presentable one way as the other, or even that the sides so unexpectedly and quaintly turned out are the right sides, is one in which Butler and Gilbert were natural adepts. But Gilbert never saw anything in the operation but a funny trick. He deliberately separated its exercise from his serious work, and took it off as a man takes off his hat in church when he attempted serious drama. Whenever Butler performed it he presently realized that the seeming trick was an inspired revelation. His very hoaxes were truths which Providence tempted him to entertain for fun until they made themselves indispensable. "Every jest is an earnest in the womb of time." That womb was incarnated in Butler's head, not in Gilbert's. Butler saw the importance of what he had hit on, and developed it into a message for his age. Gilbert saw it as a quip and left it at that: he could hardly develop a string of quips as far as a second act without petering out. Gilbert was a belittler: he jeered at old women like a street boy with a bad mother. Butler tore off the mask and tripped up the cothurnus of many a pretentious pigmy, thereby postponing public recognition of him until the PPs of his generation had died or doddered out; but he was a man of heroic admirations, whereas the people whom Gilbert admired have yet to be discovered. Mr Cannan himself points out appreciatively that Butler made a Sybil of Mrs Jupp, which may in the books of the recording angel balance his making a booby of Sir Benjamin Layard. There is stuff enough in Trial by Jury and The Pirates of Penzance to set up an Ibsen in his business; but Gilbert, though he could penetrate to the facts, and saw the fun of their incongruity with the glamor through which most of us see them, could not see their importance. Thus Butler forged his jests into a weapon which smashed the nineteenth century, whilst Gilbert only made it laugh. No two men could have been more widely disparate in the scope of their spirit, though their specific humor reacted to the stimulus of human folly in the same manner. Gilbert with the word Chesterton added can turn things inside out and write amusing phrases as well as Gilbert; but he does it to high purpose. Oscar Wilde at his best knew that his gift was divine in its nature. In this they both stood far nearer to Butler than Gilbert did. Gilbert, in short, is an excellent illustration of how useless Butler's specific turn of humor would have been to him had he not been a man of genius; and in this capacity only has he the right to appear in a book about Butler.

Butler's great achievement was his perception, after six weeks of hasty triumph in Darwin's deathblow to the old Paleyan assumption that any organ perfectly adapted to its function must be the work of a designer, of the unspeakable horror of the mindless purposeless world presented to us by Natural Selection. Even with Butler's guidance those of us who are not geniuses hardly see that yet; and we babble about Nietzsche and Treitschke with Darwin's name written all over the Prussian struggle for the survival of the fittest. Mr Cannan, exquisitely appreciative of Butler as a British Worthy, and enamored of Mrs Jupp (who is, by the way, a reincarnation of Mrs Quickly), does not see it in the least, and thereby wholly misses Butler's greatness, being indeed rather ignominiously driven at the end, in spite of the evidence of the earlier chapters to which Butler has stimulated him, to deliver a half-hearted verdict of Spoiled Artist, and Failure, and to dismiss Butler's great vision as the effect of the terror inspired in the ex-evangelical by Darwin, "the greatest figure of the time." Here the word Figure seems well chosen to avoid calling Darwin the greatest man of his time (he *was* the greatest naturalist of his time, and a very amiable person to boot); but the phrase may be a mere *cliché*; for Mr Cannan does not follow up the distinction it implies. "It became a passion with Butler," he continues, "to tell others not to be afraid; and this passion, as fear died down, was congealed into an obsession which is responsible for the tire-some reiteration of the evolution books." This is a settler. Mr Cannan has grasped neither the point at issue nor its importance. That is why he fails to see how Butler was a great man, and in-vents a silly-clever explanation of his quarrel with Darwin. Nothing that I have read in Butler, or gathered from his con-versation, conveys the very faintest suggestion of terror or of the "who's afraid" attitude. On the contrary, he was distinguished by his derisive insensibility to the awe which conventional and pious reputations inspire; and as to Darwin, though it was con-sidered very wicked in Butler's time to countenance Darwin in any way, Butler's attitude towards him was one of strenuous championship until he foresaw how the Darwinians, in their re-volt against crude Bible worship, would empty the baby out with the bath and degrade the whole conception of Evolution by level-ling it down to Natural Selection, which, though a potent method of adaptation, is not true Evolution at all. As a young man, Butler said, in Life and Habit, that Darwin had "banished mind from the Universe." As an old man, he said the same thing to me in private conversation with an intensity that flatly violated his advice to all of us to hold convictions lightly and cultivate Lao-diceanism. Until Mr Cannan grasps the importance of that simple statement through an intuition that the difference between Butler's view of the universe and the Darwinian view of it as a product of Natural Selection is the difference between heaven and hell, he will not begin to imagine what Butler's life was about, though he may write very pleasantly and wittily about Butler's talents and accomplishments and foibles. Nor will he appreciate the grimly humorous satisfaction with which Butler on that occasion added, "My grandfather quarrelled with Darwin's grandfather; my father quarrelled with Darwin's father; I quarrelled with Darwin; and my only regret in not having a son is that he cannot quarrel with Darwin's son."

But Mr Cannan's book is the better in some respects for leaving Butler's message to be taken from Butler himself, especially as it will send people to Butler instead of scaring them off, as mere paraphrases of great writers do. To write a book about a man who has written books about himself is an impertinence which only an irresistible charm of manner can carry off. The unpardonable way of doing it, and the commonest, is to undertake to tell the public what a writer has already told them himself, and to tell it worse or tell it all wrong. Mr Cannan has not committed this outrage. Indeed he interferes too little: for instance, he says not a word of Butler's epoch-making suggestion that poverty and ugliness should be attacked as crimes instead of petted and coddled like diseases. He just allows his mind to play round Butler, and thus makes him the attractive occasion of a book rather than its subject. Here are some samples of his play. "Butler could never respect Darwin when he found humor lacking in The Origin of Species. That was really the beginning and the end of Darwin's offence; and because of it Butler at last could not take anything Charles Darwin said or did seriously." Now this, though quite wrong—for Butler was the only contemporary of Darwin who took him really seriously—is much better than saying that Butler was terrified by Darwin; and it is amusing, anyhow. Again, "In Butler's world there is no freedom except freedom from humbug. He knows nothing of the proud insistence that volition shall proceed contaminated by desire. His view was that volition was in all probability contaminated by the interests of ancestors and posterity, and that there was no help for it." This is better still. And such literary frivolities as "I cannot believe in Butler's God, simply because he does not write about his God with style," have the merits of frivolity; for frivolity has merits: for instance, it is often pleasant. Besides, the laugh here is with Butler, who had the supreme sort of style that never smells of the lamp, and therefore seems to the kerosene stylist to be no style at all. I do not offer these quotations as at bottom more relevant to Butler than to Boccaccio; but a writer who can go on so is readable on his own account, Butler or no Butler; and if the samples encourage my readers to try the whole book, they can judge for themselves its stupendous demerits as a criticism of Butler the Great as distinguished from Butler the Character.

I am disposed to reproach Mr Cannan a little for saying in effect that Butler was no use except as a literary artist, and then giving him away to the so-called scientific people because he was an artist. If Mr Cannan chooses to allow himself to be humbugged by these ridiculous distinctions, he might at least give his own side the benefit of them. But he would do still better if he would revise his book in the light of a serious consultation with himself as to whether he really believes that a naturalist is always, and a thinker never, a man of science; and if so, why? Butler told us a great deal about life and habit, luck and cunning, that nobody had ever told us before, having an extraordinary talent for observing and interpreting both. Darwin told us a great deal about pigeons and worms that nobody had ever told us before, having a remarkable turn for watching pigeons and worms. Why is Darwin classed as a man of science and Butler as an artist of no science? Leonardo da Vinci remarked that the sun did not go round the earth. Galileo made the same remark. Why did nobody believe Leonardo or regard him as a man of science; and why does everybody applaud Galileo as the great scientific discoverer of the fact that it is the earth that goes round the sun? Does anyone seriously suggest that these Galileos and Harveys and Darwins had greater minds than Leonardo or Goethe or Kant or

Butler or any of the great artists and philosophers who have grasped the importance of science and applied their wits to its problems? Even Weismann, who was so much more speculative than Darwin that he developed Darwinism into an extravagant lunacy, and made some brilliant hits in the process, describes how the "discovery" of the cellular structure of living organisms was anticipated fully by a pure mystic whose very name nobody can recollect without referring to Weismann's History of Evolution. Why should Mr Cannan do less justice to the scientific importance of poets and prophets than a naturalist like Weismann?

The real distinction between the two classes is clear enough. The so-called discoverers have been the collectors of evidence and the demonstrators (by put-up jobs called experiments) of facts and forces already divined by men with brains enough not to be wholly dependent on material demonstration. St Thomas, with Christ staring him in the face, refused to believe that he was there until he had put his fingers into his wounds, thereby establishing himself as the prototype and patron saint of all the "discoverers" who, as the Irish say, "would guess eggs if they saw the shells." Darwin's was an exceptionally exasperating case, because he not only got the credit of having discovered Evolution, which had been promulgated and thoroughly established in the period of Goethe and Darwin's grandfather (1790–1830), but had actually substituted for this great general conception an elaborate study of that pseudo-evolution which is produced by external accident (as if a tree could be properly said to have been "evolved" into firewood by the storm which blew it down). This was not Darwin's fault: he did not call the process he demonstrated Evolution, but Natural Selection; still, Darwinism was none the less irritating and disastrous because Darwin was not a Darwinist. The intelligent people jumped wildly at Natural Selection because it knocked Paley and the Book of Genesis clean out. The stupid people took it up because, like St Thomas, they could understand a soulless mechanical process, but could not conceive a vital process like Evolution. The result was half a century of bedevilment, folly, pessimism, despair, and cowardice, of which we are now reaping the fruits in Flanders; and against this Butler stood for years alone; for one cannot count the belated pietists who wanted to go back to the Garden of Eden. In a word, Butler stood alone for science against the purblind naturalists and biologists, with their following of miracle mongers, experiment jobbers, and witch doctors, all absurdly claiming to be *the* men of science. And I contend that Mr Cannan, belonging as he does to Butler's camp, should stand to his guns and defend the apprehensive mind and the intuitive imagination against the peering eyes and the groping fingers. Besides, Butler has won. Why does Mr Cannan, like Frederick at Molwitz, throw up the sponge for him?

THE CHESTERBELLOC: A LAMPOON

From The New Age, 15 *February* 1908

OUR friend Wells is mistaken. His desire to embrace Chesterton as a vessel of the Goodwill which is making for Socialism is a hopeless one for other reasons than the obvious impossibility of his arms reaching round that colossal figure which dominates Battersea Park. Wells is an Englishman, and cannot understand these foreigners. The pages of Who's Who explain the whole misunderstanding. Turn to Wells, Herbert Geo., and you learn at once that he is every inch an Englishman, a man of Kent, not in the least because he was born in Bromley (a negro might be born in Bromley) but because he does not consider himself the son of his mother, but of his father only; and all his pride of birth is that his father was a famous cricketer. It is nothing to Wells that he is one of the foremost authors of his time: he takes at once the stronger English ground that he is by blood a Kentish cricketer.

Turn we now to Chesterton, Gilbert Keith. He is the son of his mother, and his mother's name is Marie Louise Grosjean. Who his father was will never matter to anyone who has once seen G. K. Chesterton, or at least seen as much of him as the limited range of human vision can take in at once. If ever a Grosjean lived and wrote his name on the sky by towering before it, that man is G. K. C. France did not break the mould in which she formed Rabelais. It got to Campden Hill in the year 1874; and it never turned out a more complete Frenchman than it did then.

Let us look up Belloc. The place of his birth is suppressed, probably because it was in some very English place; for Belloc is desperately determined not to be an Englishman, and actually went through a period of military service in the French artillery to repudiate these islands, and establish his right to call himself a Frenchman. There is no nonsense of that kind about Chesterton. No artillery service for him, thank you: he is French enough without that: besides, there is not cover enough for him on a French battlefield: the worst marksman in the Prussian artillery could hit him at six miles with absolute certainty. Belloc's sister is a lady distinguished in letters: she is also in Who's Who, which thus betrays the fact that one of their ancestors was Dr Priestley. Also that Belloc is the son of a French barrister and of Bessie Rayner Parkes. You cannot say that Belloc is wholly French except by personal choice; but still he is not English. Beside his friend Grosjean he seems Irish. I suspect him of being Irish. Anyhow, not English, and therefore for ever incomprehensible to Wells.

Before shutting up Who's Who turn for a moment to Shaw, George Bernard. He, you will observe, is the child of his own works. Not being a Frenchman like Chesterton, for whom the cult of *ma mère* is *de rigueur*, and not being able to boast of his father's fame as a cricketer, like Wells, he has modestly suppressed his parents—unconsciously; for he never noticed this piece of self-sufficiency before—and states simply that he was born in Dublin. Therefore, also eternally incomprehensible to Wells, but, on the other hand, proof against the wiles of Chesterton and Belloc. I cannot see through Chesterton: there is too much of him for anybody to see through; but he cannot impose on me as he imposes on Wells. Neither can Belloc.

Wells has written in this journal about Chesterton and Belloc without stopping to consider what Chesterton and Belloc is. This sounds like bad grammar; but I know what I am about. Chesterton and Belloc is a conspiracy, and a most dangerous one at that. Not a viciously intended one: quite the contrary. It is a game of make-believe of the sort which all imaginative grown-up children love to play; and, as in all such games, the first point in it is that they shall pretend to be somebody else. Chesterton is to be a roaring jovial Englishman, not taking his pleasures sadly, but piling Falstaff on Magog, and Boythorn on John Bull. Belloc's fancy is much stranger. He is to be a Frenchman, but not a Walkley Frenchman, not any of the varieties of the stage Frenchman, but a French peasant, greedy, narrow, individualistic, ready to fight like a rat in a corner for his scrap of land, and, above all, intensely and superstitiously Roman Catholic. And the two together are to impose on the simple bourgeoisie of England as the Main Forces of European Civilization.

Now at first sight it would seem that it does not lie with me to rebuke this sort of make-believe. The celebrated G. B. S. is about as real as a pantomime ostrich. But it is less alluring than the Chesterton-Belloc chimera, because as they have four legs to move the thing with, whereas I have only two, they can produce the quadrupedal illusion, which is the popular feature of your pantomime beast. Besides, I have played my game with a conscience. I have never pretended that G. B. S. was real: I have over and over again taken him to pieces before the audience to shew the trick of him. And even those who in spite of that cannot escape from the illusion, regard G. B. S. as a freak. The whole point of the creature is that he is unique, fantastic, unrepresentative, inimitable, impossible, undesirable on any large scale, utterly unlike anybody that ever existed before, hopelessly unnatural, and void of real passion. Clearly such a monster could do no harm, even were his example evil (which it never is).

But the Chesterbelloc is put forward in quite a different way: the Yellow Press way. The Chesterbelloc denounces the Yellow Press, but only because it dislikes yellow and prefers flaming red. The characteristic vice of the Yellow Journalist is that he never says he wants a thing (usually bigger dividends) or that his employer wants it. He always says that the Empire needs it, or that Englishmen are determined to have it, and that those who object to it are public enemies, Jews, Germans, rebels, traitors, Pro-Boers, and what not. Further, he draws an imaginative picture of a person whose honor and national character consist in getting what the Yellow Journalist is after, and says to the poor foolish reader: "That is yourself, my brave fellow-countryman." Now this is precisely what the Chesterbelloc does in its bigger, more imaginative, less sordid way. Chesterton never says, "I, a hybrid Superman, and Grand Transmogrificator of Ideas, desire this, believe that, deny the other." He always says that the English people desires it; that the dumb democracy which has never yet spoken (save through the mouth of the Chesterbelloc) believes it; or that the principles of Liberalism and of the French Revolution repudiate it. Read his poem in the Neolith on the dumb democracy of England: it would be a great poem if it were not such fearful nonsense. Belloc is still more audacious. According to him, the Chesterbelloc is European democracy, is the Catholic Church, is the Life Force, is the very voice of the clay of which Adam was made, and which the Catholic peasant labors. To set yourself against the Chesterbelloc is not merely to be unpatriotic, like setting yourself against the Daily Mail or Express: it is to set yourself against all the forces, active and latent (especially latent) of humanity. Wells and I, contemplating the Chesterbelloc, recognize at once a very amusing pantomime elephant, the front legs being that very exceptional and unEnglish individual Hilaire Belloc, and the hind legs that extravagant freak of French nature, G. K. Chesterton. To which they both reply "Not at all: what you see is the Zeitgeist." To which we reply bluntly but conclusively, "Gammon!"

But a pantomime animal with two men in it is a mistake when the two are not very carefully paired. It has never been so successful as the Blondin Donkey, which is worked by one Brother Griffith only, not by the two. Chesterton and Belloc are so unlike that they get frightfully into one another's way. Their vocation as philosophers requires the most complete detachment:

their business as the legs of the Chesterbelloc demands the most complete synchronism. They are unlike in everything except the specific literary genius and delight in play-acting that is common to them, and that threw them into one another's arms. Belloc, like most anti-Socialists, is intensely gregarious. He cannot bear isolation or final ethical responsibility: he clings to the Roman Catholic Church: he clung to his French nationality because one nation was not enough for him: he went into the French Army because it gave him a regiment, a company, even a gun to cling to: he was not happy until he got into Parliament; and now his one dread is that he will not get into heaven. He likes to keep his property in his own hand, and his soul in a safe bank. Chesterton has nothing of this in him at all: neither society nor authority nor property nor status are necessary to his happiness: he has never belonged to anything but that anarchic refuge of the art-struck, the Slade School. Belloc, like all men who feel the need of authority, is a bit of a rowdy. He has passed through the Oxford rowdyism of Balliol and the military rowdyism of the gunner; and he now has the super-rowdyism of the literary genius who has lived adventurously in the world and not in the Savile Club. A proletariat of Bellocs would fight: possibly on the wrong side, like the peasants of La Vendee; but the Government they set up would have to respect them, though it would also have to govern them by martial law. Now Chesterton might be trusted anywhere without a policeman. He might knock at a door and run away— perhaps even lie down across the threshold to trip up the emergent householder; but his crimes would be hyperbolic crimes of imagination and humor, not of malice. He is friendly, easy-going, unaffected, gentle, magnanimous, and genuinely democratic. He can make sacrifices easily: Belloc cannot. The consequence is that in order to co-ordinate the movements of the Chester-belloc, Chesterton has to make all the intellectual sacrifices that are demanded by Belloc in his dread of going to hell or of having to face, like Peer Gynt, the horrible possibility of becoming extinct. For Belloc's sake Chesterton says he believes literally in the Bible story of the Resurrection. For Belloc's sake he says he is not a Socialist. On a recent occasion I tried to drive him to swallow the Miracle of St Januarius for Belloc's sake; but at that he struck. He pleaded his belief in the Resurrection story. He pointed out very justly that I believe in lots of things just as miraculous as the Miracle of St Januarius; but when I remorselessly pressed the fact that he did not believe that the blood of St Januarius reliquefies miraculously every year, the Credo stuck in his throat like Amen in Macbeth's. He had got down at last to his irreducible minimum of dogmatic incredulity, and could not, even with the mouth of the bottomless pit yawning before Belloc, utter the saving lie. But it is an old saying that when one turns to Rome one does not begin with the miracle of St Januarius. That comes afterwards. For my part I think that a man who is not a sufficiently good Catholic to be proof against the follies and romancings of Roman Churches, Greek Churches, English Churches, and all such local prayer-wheel-installations, is no Catholic at all. I think a man who is not Christian enough to feel that conjuror's miracles are, on the part of a god, just what cheating at cards is on the part of a man, and that the whole value of the Incarnation nowadays to men of Chesterton's calibre depends on whether, when the Word became Flesh, it played the game instead of cheating, is not a Christian at all. To me no man believes in the Resurrection until he can say: "*I* am the Resurrection and the Life," and rejoice in and act on that very simple and obvious fact. Without that, belief in the gospel story is like belief in the story of Jack the Giantkiller, which, by the way, has the advantage of not being three different and incompatible stories. I should say, too, that a man who is not Individualist and Liberal enough to be a staunch Protestant, is not an Individualist nor a Liberal at all. That is, in the Chestertonian sense of the words. There is a sense in which you can be a Catholic and burn Jews and Atheists. There is a sense in which you can be a Christian and flog your fellow-creatures or imprison them for twenty years. There is a sense in which you can be a Protestant and have a confessor. But not on the Chestertonian plane. Chestertonesse *oblige*.

76

Chesterton and Belloc are not the same sort of Christian, not the same sort of Pagan, not the same sort of Liberal, not the same sort of anything intellectual. And that is why the Chesterbelloc is an unnatural beast which must be torn asunder to release the two men who are trying to keep step inside its basket-work. Wells's challenge to Chesterton is finally irresistible: he must plank down his Utopia against ours. And it must be an intellectually honest and intellectually possible one, and not a great game played by a herd of Chesterbellocs. Nor must it be an orgy of uproarious drunkards—a perpetual carouse of Shakespears and Ben Jonsons at The Mermaid. This may seem rather an uncivil condition to lay down; but it is necessary, for reasons which I will now proceed to state.

It is the greatest mistake in the world to suppose that people disapprove of Socialism because they are not convinced by its economic or political arguments. The anti-Socialists all have a secret dread that Socialism will interfere with their darling vices. The lazy man fears that it will make him work. The industrious man fears that it will impose compulsory football or cricket on him. The libertine fears that it will make women less purchaseable; the drunkard, that it will close the public-houses; the miser, that it will abolish money; the sensation lover, that there will be no more crimes, no more executions, no more famines, perhaps even no more fires. Beneath all the clamor against Socialism as likely to lower the standard of conduct lies the dread that it will really screw it up.

Now, Chesterton and Belloc have their failings like other men. They share one failing—almost the only specific trait they have in common except their literary talent. That failing is, I grieve to say, addiction to the pleasures of the table. Vegetarianism and teetotalism are abhorrent to them, as they are to most Frenchmen. The only thing in Wells's earnest and weighty appeal to Chesterton that moved him was an incidental disparagement of the custom of standing drinks and of the theory that the battle of Waterloo was won at the public-house counter.

Now it will be admitted, I think, by all candid Socialists, that

77

the Socialist ideal, as usually presented in Socialist Utopias, is deficient in turkey and sausages. Morris insists on wine and tobacco in "News from Nowhere"; but nobody in that story has what a vestryman would call a good blowout. Morris rather insists on slenderness of figure, perhaps for the sake of Burne-Jones (who was *his* Belloc). As to Wells, his Utopia is dismally starved. There is not even a round of buttered toast in it. The impression produced is that everybody is dieted, and that not a soul in the place can hope for a short life and a merry one. What this must mean to Chesterton no words of mine can express. Belloc would rather die than face it.

I once met a lady who had a beautiful ideal. Even as Tintoretto chalked up on the wall of his studio "The color of Titian, and the design of Michael Angelo," this lady wrote on the fly-leaf of her private diary, "The intellect of Chesterton, and the figure of Bernard Shaw." I think her bias was rather towards Chesterton, because she concluded, rather superficially, that it is easier to change a man's body than his mind; so instead of sending to me a file of the Daily News and a complete set of Chesterton's books to Chestertonize me, she sent to Chesterton—anonymously, and with elaborate precautions against identification—a little book entitled, if I recollect aright, Checkley's Exercises. Checkley's idea was that if you went through his exercises, your maximum circumference would occur round your chest, and taper down from that to your toes in a Grecian slenderness of flank. I glanced through Checkley and saw that the enterprise was hopeless. His exercises were to be performed without apparatus; and they mostly consisted in getting into attitudes which only a hydraulic press could get Chesterton into, and which no power on earth or in heaven could ever get him out of again. But I, the vegetarian, can do them on my head.

And now I will tear the veil from Chesterton's inmost secret. Chesterton knows about me. I am the living demonstration of the fact that Chesterton's work can be done on a teetotal and vegetarian diet. To Chesterton Socialism means his being dragged before a committee of public health and put on rations from which flesh and alcohol are strictly eliminated. It means compulsory Checkley until his waist will pass easily through a hoop for which his chest has served as a mandril. He sees that all his pleas and entreaties will be shattered on Me. When he says, "Look at Charles James Fox: he was the English exponent of the principles of the French Revolution; and he ate and drank more than I do—quite disgracefully, in fact," they will say, "Yes; but look at Bernard Shaw." When he pleads that a man cannot be brilliant, cannot be paradoxical, cannot shed imagination and humor prodigally over the pages of democratic papers on ginger beer and macaroni, he will get the same inexorable reply "Look at Bernard Shaw: he does not drink even tea or coffee: his austerity shames the very saints themselves; and yet who more brilliant? who more paradoxical? who more delightful as a journalist? And has not he himself assured us that the enormous superiority shewn by him in doing everything that you do and writing epoch-making plays to boot, is due solely to the superiority of his diet. So cease your feeble evasions; and proceed to go through Checkley's first exercise at once."

Whoever has studied Chesterton's articles attentively for a few years past will have noticed that though they profess to deal with religion, politics, and literature, they all really come at last to a plea for excess and outrageousness, especially in eating and drinking, and a heartfelt protest against Shavianism, tempered by a terrified admiration of it. Therefore I will now save Chesterton's soul by a confession.

True excess does not make a man fat: it wastes him. Falstaff was not an overworked man: he was an underworked one. If ever there was a man wasted by excess, I am that man. The Chesterbelloc, ministered to by waiters and drinking wretched narcotics out of bottles, does not know what a real stimulant is. What does it know of *my* temptations, *my* backslidings, *my* orgies? How can it, timidly munching beefsteaks and apple tart, conceive the spirit-struggles of a young man who knew that Bach is good for his soul, and yet turned to Beethoven, and from him fell to Berlioz and Liszt from mere love of excitement, luxury, savagery, and drunkenness? Has Chesterton ever spent his last half-crown on an opera by Meyerbeer or Verdi, and sat down at a crazy pianet to roar it and thrash it through with an execution of a dray-horse and a scanty octave and a half of mongrel baritone voice? Has he ever lodged underneath a debauchee who was diabolically possessed with the finale of the Seventh Symphony or the Wal-kürenritt whilst decent citizens were quietly drinking themselves to sleep with whiskey—and diluted whiskey at that?

Far from being an abstinent man, I am the worst drunkard of a rather exceptionally drunken family; for they were content with alcohol, whereas I want something so much stronger that I would as soon drink paraffin oil as brandy. Cowards drink alcohol to quiet their craving for real stimulants: I avoid it to keep my palate keen for them. And I am a pitiable example of something much worse than the drink craze: to wit, the work craze. Do not forget Herbert Spencer's autobiography, with its cry of warning against work. I get miserably unhappy if my work is cut off. I get hideous headaches after each month's bout: I make resolutions to break myself of it, never to work after lunch, to do only two hours a day; but in vain: every day brings its opportunity and its tempta-tion: the craving masters me every time; and I dread a holiday as I dread nothing else on earth. Let Chesterton take heart, then: it is he who is the ascetic and I the voluptuary. Socialism is far more likely to force me to eat meat and drink alcohol than to force him to take overdoses of Wagner and Strauss and write plays in his spare time. Let him, I say, throw off this craven obsession with my fancied austerity, and instead of declaring that he is not a Socialist when he clearly does not yet know what he is, accept Wells's challenge, and make up his mind as to how he really wants the world to be arranged under the existing conditions of human nature and physical geography.

Wells, like Sidney Webb and myself, is a bit of that totally imaginary Old Victorian England which Chesterton invented in his essay on G. F. Watts. He is intellectually honest. He does not pretend to be the English people, or Democracy, or the indigenous peasant European, or "the folk," or Catholicism, or the Press, or the French Revolution, or any of the other quick changes of the Chesterbelloc. His song is

> My names' *not* John Wellington Wells;
> And I *dont* deal in magic and spells.

He keeps the facts as to WELLS, Herbert Geo. and his difficulties and limitations, and the worse limitations of his much less clever neighbors, honestly and resolutely before you. With wit enough, imagination enough, and humor enough to play with the questions raised by the condition of England quite as amusingly as the Chesterbelloc, he works at it instead, and does what he can to hew out and hammer together some planks of a platform on which a common unliterary man may stand. I also, with a stupendous endowment for folly, have put my cards on the table—even some that are unfit for publication. Webb is far too full of solid administrative proposals to have any time or patience for literary games: when he gets taken that way he puts his witticisms into my printers' proofs, and leaves me to bear the discredit of them and to be told that I should be more serious, like Webb. But, on the whole, we have all three dealt faithfully with the common man.

And now, what has the Chesterbelloc (or either of its two pairs of legs) to say in its defence? But it is from the hind legs that I particularly want to hear; because South Salford will very soon cure Hilaire Forelegs of his fancy for the ideals of the Catholic peasant proprietor. He is up against his problems in Parliament: it is in Battersea Park that a great force is in danger of being wasted.

CHESTERTON ON SHAW

GEORGE BERNARD SHAW. By Gilbert K. Chesterton. (Lane.)

From the Nation, 25 August 1909

THIS book is what everybody expected it to be: the best work of literary art I have yet provoked. It is a fascinating portrait study; and I am proud to have been the painter's model. It is in the great tradition of literary portraiture: it gives not only the figure, but the epoch. It makes the figure interesting and memorable by giving it the greatness and spaciousness of an epoch, and it makes it attractive by giving it the handsomest and friendliest personal qualities of the painter himself.

I have been asked whether the portrait resembles me. The question interests me no more than whether Velasquez's Philip was like Philip or Titian's Charles like Charles. No doubt some mean person will presently write a disparaging volume called The Real Shaw, which will be as true in its way as Mr Chesterton's book. Perhaps some total stranger to the Irish-British environment may produce a study as unexpected, and as unflattering, as the very interesting picture of Nelson by a Turkish miniaturist which hangs in the National Portrait Gallery. Like all men, I play many parts; and none of them is more or less real than another. To one audience I am the occupier of a house in Adelphi Terrace; to another I am "one of those damned Socialists." A discussion in a club of very young ladies as to whether I could be more appropriately described as an old josser or an old geezer ended in the carrying of an amendment in favor of an old bromide. I am also a soul of infinite worth. I am, in short, not only what I can make of myself, which varies greatly from hour to hour and emergency to no-emergency, but what you can see in me. And the whole difference between an observer of genius and a common man is not a difference in the number of objects they perceive, but in their estimate of the importance of the objects. Put one man into Fleet Street and ask him what he sees there; and he may give you an accurate description of the color of the buses, the sex of the horses, the numbers of the motor-cars, the signs of the public-houses, and the complexions and probable ages of the people. Another man, who could not answer a single question on these points, may tell you that what he sees is a Jacob's ladder with angels moving up and down between heaven and earth. Both descriptions are true. The first man, demurring to the other's description, would say that a cabman is not an angel. But the second man, the Jacob's ladder man, would never dream of saying that an angel is not a cabman. Call the taxi a chariot of fire (which it literally is) and the verbal difficulty is half smoothed. But the real difficulty is that the Jacob's ladder man is a man of genius and the other is not; and that difficulty is not to be got over. Mr Chesterton is the Jacob's ladder man. He perceives that I am an angel; and he is quite right. But he will never convince those who cannot see my wings; and for them his portrait will never be a good likeness. Fortunately lots of other people will take his word for it, and some will rub their eyes and look a little more carefully; so his book will be of signal service to me.

All the same, it is in some respects quite a misleading book, not so much because it is here and there incautious, as because its only distinctively English quality is its fundamental madness. First, as to the incaution. Everything about me which Mr Chesterton had to divine, he has divined miraculously. But everything that he could have ascertained easily by reading my own plain directions on the bottle, as it were, remains for him a muddled and painful problem solved by a comically wrong guess. Let me give a screaming example. Here is Mr Chesterton on Major Barbara:

"Sometimes, especially in his later plays, he [Shaw] allows his clear conviction to spoil even his admirable dialogue, making one side entirely weak, as in an Evangelical tract. I do not know whether in Major Barbara the young Greek professor was supposed to be a fool. As popular tradition (which I trust more than anything else) declared that he is drawn from a real professor of my acquaintance, who is anything but a fool, I should imagine not. But in that case I am all the more mystified by the incredibly weak fight which he makes in the play in answer to the elephantine sophistries of Undershaft. It is really a disgraceful case, and almost the only case in Shaw, of there being no fair fight between the two sides. For instance, the Professor mentions pity. Mr Undershaft says with melodramatic scorn, 'Pity! the scavenger of the Universe!' Now if any gentleman had said this to me, I should have replied, 'If I permit you to escape from the point by means of metaphors, will you tell me whether you disapprove of scavengers?' Instead of this obvious retort, the miserable Greek professor only says, 'Well then, love,' to which Undershaft replies with unnecessary violence that he wont have the Greek professor's love, to which the obvious answer of course would be, 'How the deuce can you prevent my loving you if I choose to do so?' Instead of this, as far as I remember, that abject Hellenist says nothing at all. I only mention this unfair dialogue, because it marks, I think, the recent hardening, for good or evil, of Shaw out of a dramatist into a mere philosopher, and whoever hardens into a philosopher may be hardening into a fanatic."

If the reader will now take down the play and refer to the passages in question, he will discover, with a chuckle, first, that the professor of Greek actually does make the precise retort that Mr Chesterton says he ought to make, and, second, that "Pity! the scavenger of the Universe!" is a howling misquotation. I do not disapprove of scavengers any more than I disapprove of dentists. But scavenging is only a remedy for dirt, just as dentistry is only a remedy for decaying teeth. He who aims at a clean world and sound jaws aims at the extinction of the scavenger and the dentist. What Undershaft says is, of course, "Pity! the scavenger of misery!" And my retort to Mr Chesterton is, "If I refuse to permit you to escape from the point by means of mis-quotation, will you tell me whether you approve of misery?" As to the professor making no fight, he stands up to Undershaft all through so subtly and effectually that Undershaft takes him into partnership at the end of the play. That professor, though I say it that should not, is one of the most delightful characters in modern fiction; and that Mr Chesterton, who knows the original (evidently not so well as I do), has failed to appreciate him, is nothing less than a public calamity.

Generally speaking, Mr Chesterton's portrait of me has the limitations of a portrait, which is, perhaps, fortunate in some respects for the original. As a picture, in the least personal and most phenomenal sense, it is very fine indeed. As an account of my doctrine, it is either frankly deficient and uproariously careless or else recalcitrantly and (I repeat) madly wrong. Madly, because it misses the one fact that a sane man should postulate about me: namely, that I am a man, like any other man. And the really amazing thing about this oversight is that Mr Chesterton is aware of it, and, in a magnificent Bacchic rhapsody, finally excogitates, as proof of my superhumanity or sub-humanity, exactly the reason that would have been given by one of Wellington's private soldiers. This reason is, that I, having enough money in my pocket to purchase unlimited beer, do actually pass by public-house after public-house without going in and drinking my fill. I know no extravagance in literature comparable to this. Teetotalism is, to Mr Chesterton, a strange and unnatural asceticism forced on men by an inhuman perversion of religion. Beer drinking is to him, when his imagination runs away with him on paper, nothing short of the communion. He sees in every public-house a temple of the true catholic faith; and he tells us that when he comes to one, he enters ostentatiously, throws down all the shields and partitions that make the private bar furtive, and makes libations to the true god and to my confusion. And he will see nothing but "cold extravagance" in my sure prevision of the strict regimen of Contrexeville water and saccharine in which his Bacchic priesthood will presently end. I dont drink beer for two reasons: number one, I dont like it, and therefore have no interest to blind me to the plain facts about it; and, number two, my profession is one that obliges me to keep in critical training, and beer is fatal both to training and criticism. It makes men cheaply happy by destroying their consciences. If I did not know how unsafe it is to conclude that men practise what they preach (Mr Chesterton doth protest too much, and may be little better than a hypocritical abstainer), I should challenge him to forswear sack and dispute my laurels as a playwright, instead of lazily writing books about me. Is a man to live on my work, and then tell me I was not drunk enough to do it properly? Have I survived the cry of Art for Art's Sake, and War for War's Sake, for which Mr Chesterton rebukes Whistler and Mr Rudyard Kipling, to fall a victim to this maddest of all cries: the cry of Beer for Beer's Sake?

Another insanity of Mr Chesterton's is his craze for fairy tales. I read every fairy tale I could get hold of when I was a child, and in the normal course took to stodgier literature later on. Mr Chesterton, I suspect, began with Huxley or George Eliot, and was caught in later life by that phase of the Oscar Wilde movement which Du Maurier satirized in his picture of the æsthetes raving about the beauty of Little Bo-Peep. He must have read Jack the Giantkiller for the first time in the budding vigor of his manhood, and read it as a work of art; for no child ever loses its head over a fairy tale as he lost his over this one. He does not seem to have ever read another, or to remember whether that one was really Jack the Giantkiller or Jack and the Beanstalk. Jack was enough for him; and, ever since, he has preached an insane cult of that particular fairy tale. The result is that he falls foul of me for pointing out that the true hero is not an average Englishman miserably mortifying his natural badness, but a superior human being strenuously gratifying his natural virtue. I illustrated this by our myths, which shew the hero triumphing irresistibly because he has a magic sword, an enchanted helmet, a purse of Fortunatus, and a horse beyond all motor-cars. This infuriates Mr Chesterton. He declares that I shall never be nearer to hell than when I wrote this; and I hope he is right, as I was not in the least scorched. Thinking of Jack and forgetting Siegfried, he declares that all the fairy tales shew a little man vanquishing a big one. Now, seriously, nothing can be more horrible than the defeat of the greater by the lesser. Even to see the greater driven to vanquish the lesser by cunning and treachery is not pleasant: it is more endurable to pity Telramund in his helplessness against Lohengrin than to exult in David killing Goliath by what was, by all the rules of the ring, a foul blow. All the stories which represent Jack as killing the giant are mean flatteries of our Jacks and gross and obvious calumnies of our giants. In the great world-significant stories the giants are slain with pitiable certainty by the gods, and not by tailors and hop-o-my-thumbs.

There are no consolation prizes for the devil in the book of life. Mr Chesterton has read only one fairy tale, and that a mean one. I have read them all, and I like the ones in which the hero conquers, not because he is a well-plucked little un, but "in this sign."

Mr Chesterton is, at present, a man of vehement reactions; and, like all reactionists, he usually empties the baby out with the bath. And when he sees me nursing the collection of babies I have saved from all the baths, he cannot believe that I have really emptied out their baths thoroughly. He concludes that I am a Calvinist because I perceive the value and truth of Calvin's conviction that once the man is born it is too late to save him or damn him: you may "educate" him and "form his character" until you are black in the face; he is predestinate, and his soul cannot be changed any more than a silk purse can be changed into a sow's ear. Next moment Mr Chesterton is himself Calvinistically scorning me for advocating Herbert Spencer's notion of teaching by experience, and asks, with one of his great Thor-hammer strokes, whether a precipice can be taught by experience, to which I reply, in view of the new railway up the Jungfrau, that I should rather think it can. On another page he is protesting that I exaggerate the force of environment, because I proclaimed the staring fact that Christmas is a gluttonous, spendthrift orgy, foisted on us by unfortunate tradesmen who can just make both ends meet by the profits of the Christmas trade. He concludes that, in my joyless Puritan home (oh, my father! oh, my mother!) I never melted lead on "Holi-eve," never hid rings in pancakes, never did all those dreary, silly Christmas things, until human nature rebelled against them and they were swept out of our domestic existence, like the exchanging of birthday presents and the rest of the inculcated tribal superstitions of the kitchen; and he would have me believe that every Christmas he turns his happy home into an imitation of the toy department at Gamage's, and burns a Yule log ordered, regardless of expense, from the Vauxhall ship-knackers. Chesterton, Chesterton, these are not the spontaneous delights of childhood: they are the laborious acquirements of bookish maturity. Christmas means: "Thank God Christ was born only once a year; so let us get drunk and have done with it for another twelve months." I would not give twopence for a Christian who does not commemorate Christ's birth every day and keep sober over it.

But I must stop arbitrarily or my review will be longer than the book! For there is endless matter in G. K. C. My last word must be that, gifted as he is, he needs a sane Irishman to look after him. For this portrait essay beginning with the insanity of beer for beer's sake does not stop short of the final far madder lunacy of absurdity for absurdity's sake. I have tried to teach Mr Chesterton that the will that moves us is dogmatic; that our brain is only the very imperfect instrument by which we devise practical means for fulfilling that will; that logic is our attempt to understand it and to reconcile its apparent contradictions with some intelligible theory of its purpose; and that the man who gives to reason and logic the attributes and authority of the will—the Rationalist—is the most hopeless of fools; and all that I have got into his otherwise very wonderful brain, is that whatever is reasonable and logical is false, and whatever is nonsensical is true. I therefore ask the Editor of The Nation to open a subscription to send him to Ireland for two years. As I write, with the Kerry coast under my eyes, I can see, breathe, and feel that climate, that weather (changing every twenty minutes more than the stiff, fierce, brain-besotting weather of England can change in a month), which he calls "material and mechanical," mere "mud and mist." His English will, his English hope, he says, are stronger than these mere physical things. Are they? What about the Scotch will, the Yorkshire hope of the Shaws? have they prevailed against that most mystical of all mystical things: the atmosphere of the Island of the Saints? Let Mr Chesterton try that atmosphere for a while. In ten minutes—no more—he will feel a curious letting down, ending with an Englishman's first taste of common sense. In ten months there will not be an atom of English will or hope anywhere in his ventripotent person. He will eat salmon and Irish stew and drink whiskey prosaically, because he will hunger and thirst for food and drink instead of drinking beer poetically because he thirsts for righteousness. And the facts will be firm under his feet, whilst the heavens are open over his head; and his soul will become a torment to him, like the soul of the Wandering Jew, until he has achieved his appointed work, which is not that of speculating as to what I am here for, but of discovering and doing what he himself is here for.

SOMETHING LIKE A HISTORY OF ENGLAND

A SHORT HISTORY OF ENGLAND. By G. K. Chesterton. (Chatto & Windus.)

From The Observer, 4 November 1917

THIS book, and Mr Maurice Hewlett's Hodgiad, raise hopes that the next generation may learn something of what it needs to know about the history of its own country. Hitherto historians have laid hands on the schoolboy, and assumed that their business was to qualify him as a professional historian, just as the classical pedants assumed that their business was to make him a professional grammarian. In my time they always began their histories by saying that true history is not a record of reigns and battles, but of peoples. They then proceeded to give ten times as much information about the reigns and the battles as the older historians, like Robertson, who, in his history of Mary Queen of Scots, introduced an unavoidable allusion to Rizzio with an elaborate apology for mentioning a thing so abysmally beneath "the dignity of history" as an Italian who was only a professional man. Every page of Mr Hewlett's Queen's Quair would have made Robertson blush all over. But I think Robertson had more sense than Macaulay, because he recognized that history, as he understood it, was not a common man's business. Macaulay knew that modern democracy was making history a very important part of a common man's business; but he does not seem to have considered that our common democrats must, if they are to vote with any intelligence and exercise any real power, know not only the history of their own country, but that of all the other countries as well. Otherwise he would have bethought him that it is utterly impossible for common men to learn all these histories in such detail as he gives of his little parliamentary corner of the reigns of Charles II, James II, and William III, whose alliance with the Pope shot forward a gleam of humor (which Macaulay rather missed) over so much subsequent chalked-up polemic in Ulster. Even if you find Macaulay so very readable that you waste on his history the time you should spend on more pregnant documents, the one thing that you do not learn from him is English history.

Mac (if I may thus familiarly abbreviate him) did not improve matters by pointing out how unimportant were kings and queens compared with Hodge and Tom, Dick, and Harry. It was not that when he came to the point he had nothing particular to say about Hodge and the rest, and became obsessed with the insignificant proceedings of a parliamentary dodger entitled Halifax, who, though too intelligent to be a good party man, was much less interesting than his merry monarch. It was rather that Hodge and the rest are not really a bit more important than their masters. The notion that the village champion metabolist, who for a wager consumes a leg of mutton, a gallon of beer, and a hundred oysters at one sitting, is any more important than the king who ate too many lampreys and was never seen to smile again, is much stupider than the contrary notion, that what the king does matters a great deal and what the peasant does matters not at all. England's kings and cardinals were the most important people in England until they were supplanted by England's capitalists: the only wonder about the peasants is that they so helplessly let the kings and cardinals and capitalists do what they liked with them.

No. What the common man wants is not a history of the kings or the priests, or the nobs, or the snobs, or any other set, smart or slovenly, but a vigorously comprehended and concisely presented history of epochs. Nearly fifteen years ago, in a play called John Bull's Other Island, I shewed an inspired (and consequently silenced) Irish priest saying to a couple of predatory commercial adventurers that "for four wicked centuries the world has dreamed this foolish dream of efficiency; and the end is not yet. But the end will come." If anyone had asked me then why I fixed that date (to do the British public and the critics justice, nobody ever did), I should not have been able to refer them to any popular history for an explanation. In future I shall be able to refer them to Mr Chesterton's. For Mr Chesterton knows his epochs, and can tell you when the temple became a den of thieves, though he leaves out half the kings and gives never a date at all. Far from being discursive, as the critics are saying, he is at once the most concise and the fullest historian this distressful country has yet found.

I hope I am not expected to write a brilliant review of Mr Chesterton: I might as well try to write a comic review of Mark Twain. There is nothing worth saying left to be said of his book, because he has said it all himself: he is too good a husbandman to leave much for the gleaners. Let me therefore ask him for another chapter in his next edition. I can even give him subjects for two chapters.

The first is the establishment of the party system in Parliament at the end of the seventeenth century. If Mr Chesterton will discuss this with everyone he meets, from Cabinet Ministers to cobblers, he will discover that nobody has the least idea of what the party system is, and that nobody will take the trouble to find out, because everybody is convinced that he knows already. "You will always have the party system," they will say: "there will always be Conservatives and Progressives: it is human nature." This misunderstanding is the mask under which the system secures toleration. The party system is just two centuries old. Before it was established there were Whigs and Tories, Cavaliers and Roundheads, Papists and Lutherans, Lancastrians and Yorkists, barons and burgesses, Normans and Saxons, Romans and primitive Sinn Feiners; but there was no party system. And to this add that though our municipal councillors include Home Rulers and Unionists, Free Traders and Tariff

Reformers, Churchmen and Dissenters, the party system does not exist in local government, and could not possibly establish itself there, because the constitution and procedure of the local authorities is less adapted to it than a lathe to churning butter. On a local public authority a man can vote on the merits of the measure before him and not on the question whether his party will remain in power or not, because his party is not in power: the public authority is in power. There is no Cabinet, no appeal to the country, no monopoly of administration by any one party. When the Chairman of a Committee brings forward a measure and is defeated, he does not resign: he only sulks; and his Committee goes on as before. The ablest members of the body are always in full activity side by side, no matter how furiously they may differ on politics, religion, or any other controversial subject.

To the wretched members of the House of Commons this seems too good to be true. There the ablest man in the House may be excluded from office and condemned to barren criticism for twenty years if he is in Opposition, and if the elections during that period produce "no change." He never votes on the merits of the measure before the House: he must vote against the very Bill he will himself presently introduce if he comes into office through defeating it; and he must vote for revolutionary measures which he will drop like hot potatoes if a defeat of the Government places him in a position to carry them out himself. He may be noted for the activity of his intellect outside the House, demonstrating it by the alertness with which he keeps up to date in philosophy, science, and art; yet inside the House he must, as a party man, appear a Philistine, an ignoramus, a reactionary, without character enough to rise to the selfish stability of an idiot. And unless he is a party man, he has not the faintest chance of ever taking part in any administration. If he is suspected of having any other price than a place in the Government when his side is in power—if he will once consent to the other side doing the right thing, or hesitate to support his own side when it is bent on doing the wrong thing, he is politically lost. He has, in that case, no more chance of office, or even of a party seat, than

Mr Chesterton, or Mr Sidney Webb, or Mr Maurice Hewlett, or than Ruskin or Carlyle had, or than any other person who is public spirited instead of party spirited, who has less respect for the party game than for golf or skittles, and who, like Hamlet, "lacks ambition," and curses the divine spite that would lay on him the burden of straightening a world out of joint.

The introduction of this amazing system under the pressure of a European conflict prototypical of the present war was, in point of its effect in establishing the parliamentary power of the modern plutocratic oligarchy, epoch making; and as such it demands its place in Mr Chesterton's history. It made Walpole possible; and it made any other sort of man than Walpole impossible except in frightful emergencies: that is, too late. It was by far the most revolutionary act of the glorious, pious, and immortal Dutchman to whom England was nothing but a stick to beat Louis XIV, and who found that without the party system the stick would break in his hand as fast as he could splice it. It was invented and suggested to him by an English nobleman educated abroad; and no English nobleman educated at home has ever been able to understand it. Marlborough, who succeeded to William's throne under cover of Anne's petticoats, understood it so little that he tried to drop it until he was driven back to it, still without understanding it, by the same pressure of the Roi Soleil.

The second chapter which Mr Chesterton's history lacks is a description of the establishment of the modern police by Peel, who thus broke that weapon of the riot which the workers had often used much more effectively than they have since used the vote. Without that new force the nineteenth century, rightly perceived by Mr Chesterton to have been the most villainous and tyrannous period in recorded history, could never have consummated its villainy in the full conviction that it was the proud climax of progress, liberty, and leaping and bounding prosperity. When its attention was drawn by some sensational horror to the cruellest and most bigoted of its own laws, it called them medieval, and believed it. What a theme for Mr Chesterton!

CHESTERTON ON EUGENICS AND SHAW ON CHESTERTON

EUGENICS, AND OTHER EVILS. By G. K. Chesterton. (Cassell.)

From The Nation, 11 *March* 1922

A CRITICISM of Mr Chesterton is in the nature of a bulletin as to the mental condition of a prophet. Mr Chesterton has disciples. I do not blame him: I have some myself. So has Mr Wells. All sorts of people have disciples, from osteopaths to tipsters. But most of them do not get into our way politically. Mr Chesterton's do. Therefore it is important that his pulse should be felt, and his condition reported on; for if he were to go—well, may I say, for the sake of alliteration, off his chump?—the consequences might be serious. He has many magical arts and gifts at his command. He can make anything that can be made with a pen, from a conspectus of human history to a lethal jibe at the Lord Chancellor; and to utilize this practically boundless technical equipment he has enormous humor, imagination, intellect, and common sense.

Now in respect of the humor and imagination, his integrity can be depended on; but when you come to the intellect and common sense, you have to be careful, because his intellect is fantastic and his common sense impatient. That is because his humor and imagination will creep in. It is such fun to take some impossibly obsolete person—say a Crusader—and shew that he was right in his ideas, and that the sooner we get back to them the better for us, that no humorist ingenious enough to do it can resist it unless he has the dogged cerebral honesty of an Einstein. And here again it is so funny to *épater les savants* by arguing that Einstein, being a Jew, invented Relativity to popularize his long-nosed relatives, and that the saints who thought the earth flat were on solid ground, that the cumulative temptation sometimes strains even Chesterton's colossal shoulders. To give way is such an amiable weakness too! When he does it I am always amused; and I am never taken in: at least if I am I do not know it, otherwise, of course, I should not be taken in. But other people may be. Besides, Mr Chesterton may take himself in. He may stray up an intellectual blind alley to amuse himself; for it is the greatest mistake to suppose that there is nothing interesting or useful to be picked up in blind alleys before you run your head into the *cul de sac*. A man like Mr Chesterton finds more diamonds in such an alley than an ordinary man walks over pebbles in the clearest logical fairway. By stopping to pick the diamonds up, like Atalanta, he may not get far enough to discover that the alley is blind. Even if he does, he may find a way out by pretending that he has found one, as the mathematician overcomes an intellectually insuperable difficulty by pretending that there is such a quantity as minus x. Searchlights in blind alleys have illuminated the whole heavens at times; and men have found courage and insight within their limits after finding nothing but terror and bewilderment in the open desert.

Thus Mr Chesterton, who once lived near the Home For Lost Dogs in Battersea, has a whimsical tendency to set up a Home For Lost Causes, in competition with Oxford University, in his half explored blind alleys. Like the Home in Battersea, they are not popular with the lost ones; for the final hospitality offered is that of the lethal chamber. The Lost Causes like their last ditches well camouflaged. Mr Chesterton scorns concealment: he stands on the parapet, effulgent by his own light, roaring defiance at a foe who would only too willingly look the other way and pretend not to notice. Even the Lost Causes which are still mighty prefer their own methods of fighting. The Vatican never seems so shaky as when G. K. C. hoists it on his shoulders like Atlas, and proceeds to play football with the skulls of the sceptics. Pussyfoot's chances of drying the British Isles seldom seem so rosy as they do the morning after Mr Chesterton has cracked the brainpans of a thousand teetotallers with raps from Gargantuan flagons waved by him in an ecstasy in which he seems to have ten pairs of hands, like an Indian god.

Nature compensates the danger of his defence by the benefit of his assault. He went to Jerusalem to destroy Zionism; and immediately the spirit of Nehemiah entered into him, and there arose from his pages such a wonderful vision of Jerusalem that our hearts bled for the captivity, and all the rival claimants, past and present, silly Crusader and squalid Bedouin in one red burial blent, perished from our imaginations, and left the chosen people of God to inherit the holy city. He attacks divorce with an idealization of marriage so superhuman (without extraordinary luck) that all his readers who have not yet committed themselves swear that nothing will induce them to put their heads into the noose of that golden cord. He stated the case for giving votes to women so simply and splendidly that when he proceeded to give his verdict against the evidence it passed as a misprint. Really a wonderful man, this Chesterton; but with something of Balaam in him, and something of that other who went whither he would not.

His latest book is called Eugenics and Other Evils. It is a graver, harder book than its forerunners. Something—perhaps the youthful sense of immortality, commonly called exuberance —has lifted a little and left him scanning the grey horizon with more sense that the wind is biting and the event doubtful; but there is plenty of compensating gain; for this book is practically all to the good. The title suggests the old intellectual carelessness: it seems mere nonsense: he might as well write Obstetrics and Other Evils, or Dietetics or Esthetics or Peripatetics or Optics or Mathematics and Other Evils. But when you read you find that he knows what he is about. The use of the word Eugenics implies that the breeding of the human race is an art founded on an ascertained science. Now when men claim scientific authority for their ignorance, and police support for their aggressive presumption, it is time for Mr Chesterton and all other men of sense to withstand them sturdily. Mr Chesterton takes the word as a convenient symbol for current attempts at legislative bodysnatching—live-bodysnatching—to provide subjects for professors and faddists to experiment on when pursuing all sorts of questionable, ridiculous, and even vicious theories of how to produce perfect babies and rear them into perfect adults. At the very first blow he enlists me on his side by coming to my own position and reaffirming it trenchantly. "Sexual selection, or what Christians call falling in love," he says, "is a part of man which in the large and in the long run can be trusted." Why after reproducing my conclusion so exactly he should almost immediately allege that "Plato was only a Bernard Shaw who unfortunately made his jokes in Greek," I cannot guess; for it is impossible to understand what the word "only" means in this sentence. But the conclusion is none the less sound. He does not follow it up as I do by shewing that its political corollary is the ruthless equalization of all incomes in order that this supremely important part of man shall no longer be baffled by the pecuniary discrepancies which forbid the duchess to marry the coalheaver, and divorce King Cophetua from the beggar maid even before they are married. But that will come in a later book.

Mr Chesterton is implacable in his hostility to the Act for dealing with the feeble-minded. How dangerous these loose make-shift categories are when they get into the statute book he brings out thus. "Even if I were an Eugenist, then I should not personally elect to waste my time locking up the feeble-minded. The people I should lock up would be the strong-minded. I have known hardly any cases of mere mental weakness making the family a failure: I have known eight or nine cases of violent and exaggerated force of character making the family a hell."

This is a capital example of Mr Chesterton's knock-out punch, which is much more deadly than Carpentier's. It is so frightfully true, and illuminates so clearly the whole area of unbearable possibilities opened up by this type of legislation, that it makes the reader an Anarchist for the moment. But it does not dispose of the fact that the country has on its hands a large number of people, including most authors, who are incapable of fending for themselves in a competitive capitalistic world. Many of them do quite well in the army; but when they are demobilized they are in the dock in no time. As domestic servants they are often treasures to kindly employers. Provide for them; organize for them; tell them what they must do to pay their way, and they are useful citizens, and happy ones if the tutelage is nicely done, as between gentlemen. But freedom and responsibility mean misery and ruin for them. What is to be done with them? Mr Chesterton says "Send them home." But that solution is already adopted in most of the cases in which it is possible. How about those who have no home? the old birds whose nest was scattered long ago? You cannot get rid of a difficulty by shewing that the accepted method of dealing with it is wrong. Mr Chesterton's demonstration of its danger actually increases the difficulty; for it is quite true that many of the most hopeless cases are cases not of Defectives but of Excessives. If the Prime Minister were to say to Mr Chesterton tomorrow, "You are quite right, God forgive us: the Act is a silly one: will you draft us another to deal with these people properly?" Mr Chesterton could not fall back on the eighteenth century and cry *Laissez faire*. All the king's horses and all the king's men cannot set that lazy evasion up again. If Mr Chesterton were not equal to the occasion, Mr Sidney Webb and his wife would have to be called in; for the facts will not budge; and it is cruel to abandon the helpless to a mockery of freedom that will slay them.

Mr Chesterton joins the campaign against the quackeries of preventive medicine with zest. "Prevention is not better than cure. Cutting off a man's head is not better than curing his headache: it is not even better than failing to cure it." He shews that the dread of religious superstition is itself a superstition, possible only to a Press that is a century out of date because its journalists are so hurried and huddled up in their stuffy offices that they have no time to observe or study anything, and can supply copy to the machines only by paying out any sort of old junk that has been current for a century past. He says, with a sledge hammer directness that reminds me of Handel, "The thing that is really trying to tyrannize through Government is Science. The thing that really does use the secular arm is Science. And the creed that really is levying tithes and capturing schools, the creed that really is enforced by fine and imprisonment, the creed that really is proclaimed not in sermons but in statutes, and spread not by pilgrims but by policemen—that creed is the great but disputed system of thought which began with Evolution and has ended in Eugenics. Materialism is really our established Church; for the Government will really help to persecute its heretics. Vaccination, in its hundred years of experiment, has been disputed almost as much as baptism in its approximate two thousand. But it seems quite natural to our politicians to enforce vaccination; and it would seem to them madness to enforce baptism."

This, except for the slip by which the essentially religious doctrine of Evolution is confused with the essentially devilish doctrine of Natural Selection, is undeniable, whether you believe in vaccination or not; and it is well that we should be made sharply aware of it, and also of the fact that as much hypocrisy, venality, cruelty, mendacity, bigotry, and folly are using Science (a very sacred thing) as a cloak for their greed and ambition as ever made the same use of Religion. Indeed this is an understatement as far as the mendacity is concerned; for what priest ever lied about the efficacy of baptism as doctors have lied, and are still lying, about such shallow and disastrous blunders as Lister's antiseptic surgery, or have laid hands on children and gouged out the insides of their noses and throats in the spirit of the Spanish grandee who admired the works of God, but thought that if he had been consulted a considerable improvement might have been effected?

But we must not let our indignation run away with us. Let us contemplate a typical actual case. Scene: a school clinic. Present: a doctor, a snuffling child, and its mother. A dramatic situation has just been created by the verdict of the doctor: "This kid has adenoids." The mother is not in the least in a Chestertonian attitude. Far from objecting to State surgery, she holds that her child has a right to it in virtue of the doctor being paid to be there; and she is determined to insist on that right in spite of what she considers the natural disposition of all men, including doctors, to shirk their duties to the poor if they can. Far from crying "Hands off my darling: who but his mother should succor him and know what is good for him?" she demands "Aint nothing to be done for him, poor child?" The doctor says "Yes:

the adenoids had better be cut out."

Now this may not be the proper remedy. It is on the face of it a violent, desperate, dangerous, and injurious remedy, characteristic of the African stage of civilization in which British surgery and therapy still languish. A better remedy may be one of the formulas of Christian Science, or the prayer and anointing of St James and the Peculiar People, or that the child should say every morning between sleeping and waking, "My nose is getting clearer and clearer" twenty-five times over. A million to one the real remedy is half a dozen serviceable handkerchiefs, a little instruction in how to use the nose in speaking and singing, with, above all, better food, lodging, and clothing. The mother does not "hold with" the mystical remedies. Of the two which are not mystical, the last mentioned means spending more money on the child; and she has none to spend, as the doctor very well knows: else, perhaps, he would honestly press it on her. Thus there is nothing for it but the knife. The hospital will cost the mother nothing; and it will be rather a treat for the child. She does not consider the hospital a disgrace like the workhouse: on the contrary, all her human instincts and social traditions make her feel that she is entitled to help in case of sickness, for which her very scanty household money does not provide. Accordingly, the interior of the unfortunate infant's nose is gouged out; and possibly his tonsils are extirpated at the same time, lest he should be overburdened with tissues which surgeons consider superfluous because they have not yet discovered what they are there for.

Now observe that here the mother does not protest: she insists. The doctor operates because there is no money to pay for sane natural treatment. The alternatives are to do nothing, or to throw the mother back on some quack who would promise to cure the child for a few shillings. All the responsible parties, the mother, the doctor, the schoolmaster, and presumably Mr Chesterton, are against doing nothing. What, then, is Mr Chesterton protesting against? He is protesting against adapting the treatment of the child to the low wages of its parents instead of adapting the wages of the parents to the proper treatment for the child.

And he is quite right. From the point of view of the welfare of the community the decision of the doctor can be compared only to that of Grock, the French clown, who, when he finds that the piano stool is not close enough to the piano, moves the piano to the stool instead of the stool to the piano. We have managed to bedevil our social arrangements so absurdly that it is actually easier for our Parliamentary Grocks to move the piano to the stool. But nobody laughs at them. Only exceptionally deep men like Mr Chesterton even swear at them.

Mr Chesterton is, however, too able a man to suppose that swearing at the Government is any use. All Governments are open to Shakespear's description of them as playing such fantastic tricks before high heaven as make the angels weep, just as all men who undertake the direction of other men are open to William Morris's objection that no man is good enough to be another man's master. But when a job has to be done, it is no use saying that no man is good enough to do it. Somebody must try, and do the best he can. If war were declared against us we could not surrender at discretion merely because the best general we could lay hands on might as likely as not be rather a doubtful bargain as a sergeant. Or let us take a problem which arises every day. We are confronted with the children of three mothers: the first a model of maternal wisdom and kindness, the second helpless by herself but quite effective if she is told what to do occasionally, and the third an impossible creature who will bring up her sons to be thieves and her daughters to be prostitutes. How are we to deal with them? It is no use to pretend that the first sort of mother is the only sort of mother, and abandon the children of the others to their fate: the only sane thing to do is to take the third woman's children from her and pay the other two to bring them up, giving the second one the counsel and direction she needs for the purpose. Of course you can put the children into an institution; only, if you do, you had better be aware that the most perfectly equipped institution of the kind in the world (it is in Berlin) acts as a lethal chamber, whilst in the mud-floored cabins of Connaught bare-legged children with a single garment, and not too much of that, are immortal. You have to do something; and since the job is too big for private charity (which is abominable, tyrannical, and humiliating: in fact everything that raises Mr Chesterton's gorge in public maternity centres and school clinics and the like is a tradition from the evil days of private charity) it must be organized publicly; and its organizers must be taught manners by Mr Chesterton and the few others who know that insolence to the poor, though compulsory in our public services, acts like sand in an engine bearing.

But it remains true that as most people do not become "problems" until they become either poor or rich, most of the bad mothers and fathers and sons and daughters could be made passably good by simply giving them as much money as their neighbors, and no more. I am not so much concerned about their freedom as Mr Chesterton; for it is plain to me that our civilization is being destroyed by the monstrously excessive freedom we allow to individuals. They may idle: they may waste; when they have to work they may make fortunes as sweaters by the degradation, starvation, demoralization, criminalization, and tuberculization of their fellow-citizens, or as financial rogues and vagabonds by swindling widows out of their portions, orphans out of their inheritances, and unsuspecting honest men out of their savings. They may play the silliest tricks with the community's wealth even after their deaths by ridiculous wills. They may contaminate one another with hideous diseases; they may kill us with poisons advertized as elixirs; they may corrupt children by teaching them bloodthirsty idolatries; they may goad nations to war by false witness; they may do a hundred things a thousand times worse than the prisoners in our gaols have done; and yet Mr Chesterton blames me because I do not want more liberty for them. I am by nature as unruly a man as ever lived; but if Mr Chesterton could guess only half the inhibitions I would add to the statute book, and enforce by ruthless extermination of all recalcitrants, he would plunge a carving knife into my ribs, and rush through the streets waving its dripping blade and shouting *Sic semper tyrannis*. I see in the papers that a lady in America has been told that if she does not stop smoking cigarets her child will be taken from her. This must make Mr Chesterton's blood boil; for he tells us with horror that when he was in America, people were admitting that tobacco needs defending. "In other words," he adds, "they were quietly going mad." But the truth, I rejoice to say, seems to be that they have given up the defence. What right has a woman to smoke when she is mothering? She would not be allowed to smoke if she were conducting a bus or selling apples or handkerchiefs. A man should be able to turn away in disgust from a railway smoking carriage without being reminded of his mother.

But unless I tear myself away from this book I shall never stop. If, as Mr Chesterton seems to insist, I am to regard it as another round in the exhibition spar with Mr Sidney Webb which he continues through all his books, I must give the verdict to Mr Webb, because the positive man always beats the negative man when things will not stay put. As long as Mr Webb produces solutions and Mr Chesterton provides only criticisms of the solutions, Mr Webb will win hands down, because Nature abhors a vacuum. Mr Chesterton never seems to ask himself what are the alternatives to Mr Webb's remedies. He is content with a declaration that the destruction of the poor is their poverty, and that if you would only give each of them the security and independence conferred by a small property on its owner (when he is capable of administering it) your problems would vanish or be privately settled. Nobody is likely to deny this: least of all Mr Sidney Webb. But Mr Chesterton's Distributive State, which is to bring about this result by simply making us all dukes on a small scale, would not produce that result even if its method were practicable. To many men, possibly to the majority of men, property is ruinous: what they need and desire is honorable service. They need also a homestead; and though for some of them the ideal homestead is a flat in Piccadilly, others want a house in the country, with a garden and a bit of pleasure ground. That is what Mr Chesterton enjoys; but if you were to offer him these things as industrial property, and ask him to turn his garden into a dirty little allotment and make money out of it, he would promptly sell himself as a slave to anyone who would employ him honorably in writing. So would I: so would Mr Belloc: so would Mr Webb. In short, this distribution of property of which Mr Chesterton tries to dream, but to which he has never been able to give his mind seriously for a moment, so loathsome is it, would be an abominable slavery for the flower of the human race. Every Man his Own Capitalist is the least inspiring political cry I know; and when Mr Chesterton raises it my consolation is that it cannot be realized. I urge Mr Chesterton to go on thundering against the tyranny of Socialistic regulation without Socialistic distribution (the Servile State) to his heart's content; but I warn him that if he persists in threatening us with the double curse of peasantry and property as an alternative, he will give the most fantastic extremes of doctrinaire Eugenics an air of millennial freedom and happiness by mere force of contrast.

SIR GEORGE GROVE

BEETHOVEN AND HIS NINE SYMPHONIES. By George Grove, C.B. (London and New York: Novello, Ewer & Co. 1896.)

From The Saturday Review, 14 November 1896

ON cold Saturday afternoons in winter, as I sit in the theatrical desert, making my bread with great bitterness by chronicling insignificant plays and criticizing incompetent players, it sometimes comes upon me that I have forgotten something—omitted something—missed some all-important appointment. This is a legacy from my old occupation of musical critic. All my old occupations leave me such legacies. When I was in my teens I had certain official duties to perform, which involved every day the very strict and punctual discharge of certain annual payments, which were set down in a perpetual diary. I sometimes dream now that I am back at those duties again, but with an amazed consciousness of having allowed them to fall into ruinous arrear for a long time past. My Saturday afternoon misgivings are just like that.

They mean that for several years I passed those afternoons in that section of the gallery of the Crystal Palace concert-room which is sacred to Sir George Grove and to the Press. There were two people there who never grew older—Beethoven and Sir George. August Manns's hair changed from raven black to swan white as the years passed; young critics grew middle-aged and middle-aged critics grew old; Rossini lost caste and was shouldered into the promenade; the fire-new overture to Tannhäuser began to wear as threadbare as William Tell: Arabella Goddard went and Sophie Menter came; Joachim, Hallé, Norman Neruda, and Santley no longer struck the rising generations with the old sense of belonging to tomorrow, like Isaÿe, Paderewski, and Bispham; the men whom I had shocked as an iconoclastic upstart Wagnerian, braying derisively when they observed that "the second subject, appearing in the key of the dominant, contrasts effectively with its predecessor, not only in tonality, but by its suave, melodious character," lived to see me shocked and wounded in my turn by the audacities of J. F. Runciman; new evening papers launched into musical criticism, and were read publicly by Mr Smith, the eminent drummer, whenever he had fifty bars rest; a hundred trifles marked the flight of time; but Sir George Grove fed on Beethoven's symphonies as the gods in Das Rheingold fed on the apples of Freia, and grew no older. Sometimes, when Mendelssohn's Scotch symphony, or Schubert's Ninth in C, were in the program, he got positively younger, clearing ten years backward in as many minutes when Manns and the band were at their best. I remonstrated with him more than once on this unnatural conduct; and he was always extremely apologetic, assuring me that he was getting on as fast as he could. He even succeeded in producing a wrinkle or two under stress of Berlioz and Raff, Liszt and Wagner; but presently some pianist would come along with the concerto in E flat; and then, if I sat next him, strangers would say to me "Your son, sir, appears to be a very enthusiastic musician." And I could not very well explain that the real bond between us was the fact that Beethoven never ceased to grow on us. In my personality, my views, and my style of criticism there was so much to forgive that many highly amiable persons never quite succeeded in doing it. To Sir George I must have been a positively obnoxious person, not in the least because I was on the extreme left in politics and other matters, but because I openly declared that the finale of Schubert's symphony in C could have been done at half the length and with twice the effect by Rossini. But I knew Beethoven's symphonies from the opening bar of the first to the final chord of the ninth, and yet made new discoveries about them at every fresh performance. And I am convinced that "G" regarded this as evidence of a fundamental rectitude in me which would bear any quantity of superficial aberrations. Which is quite my own opinion too.

It may be asked why I have just permitted myself to write of so eminent a man as Sir George Grove by his initial. That question would not have been asked thirty years ago, when "G," the rhapsodist who wrote the Crystal Palace programs, was one of the best ridiculed men in London. At that time the average programmist would unblushingly write, "Here the composer, by one of those licenses which are, perhaps, permissible under exceptional circumstances to men of genius, but which cannot be too carefully avoided by students desirous of forming a legitimate style, has abruptly introduced the dominant seventh of the key of C major into the key of A flat, in order to recover, by a forced modulation, the key relationship proper to the second subject of a movement in F: an awkward device which he might have spared himself by simply introducing his second subject in its true key of C." "G," who was "no musician," cultivated this style in vain. His most conscientious attempts at it never brought him any nearer than "The lovely melody then passes, by a transition of remarkable beauty, into the key of C major, in which it seems to go straight up to heaven." Naturally the average Englishman was profoundly impressed by the inscrutable learning of the first style (which I could teach to a poodle in two hours), and thought "G's" obvious sentimentality idiotic. It did not occur to the average Englishman that perhaps Beethoven's symphonies were an affair of sentiment and nothing else. This, of course, was the whole secret of them. Beethoven was the first man who used music with absolute integrity as the expression of his own emotional life. Others had shewn how it could be done—had done it themselves as a curiosity of their art in rare, self-indulgent, *unprofessional* moments—but Beethoven made this, and nothing else, his business. Stupendous as the resultant difference was between his music and any other ever heard in the world before his time, the distinction is not clearly apprehended to this day, because there was nothing new in the musical expression of emotion: every progression in Bach is sanctified by emotion; and Mozart's subtlety, delicacy, and exquisite tender touch and noble feeling were the despair of all the musical world. But Bach's theme was not himself, but his religion; and Mozart was always the dramatist and story-teller, making the men and women of his imagination speak, and dramatizing even the instruments in his orchestra, so that you know their very sex the moment their voices reach you. Haydn really came nearer to Beethoven, for he is neither the praiser of God nor the dramatist, but, always within the limits of good manners and of his primary function as a purveyor of formal decorative music, a man of moods. This is how he created the symphony and put it ready-made into Beethoven's hand. The revolutionary giant at once seized it, and throwing supernatural religion, conventional good manners, dramatic fiction, and all external standards and objects into the lumber room, took his own humanity as the material of his music, and expressed it all without compromise, from his roughest jocularity to his holiest aspiration after that purely human reign of intense life —of Freude—when

> Alle Menschen werden Brüder
> Wo dein sanfter Flügel weilt.

In thus fearlessly expressing himself, he has, by his common humanity, expressed us as well, and shewn us how beautifully, how strongly, how trustworthily we can build with our own real selves. This is what is proved by the immense superiority of the

Beethoven symphony to any oratorio or opera.

In this light all Beethoven's work becomes clear and simple; and the old nonsense about his obscurity and eccentricity and stage sublimity and so on explains itself as pure misunderstanding. His criticisms, too, become quite consistent and inevitable: for instance, one is no longer tempted to resent his declaration that Mozart wrote nothing worth considering but parts of Die Zauberflöte (those parts, perhaps, in which the beat of dein sanfter Flügel is heard), and to retort upon him by silly comparisons of his tunes with Non piu andrai and Deh vieni alla finestra. The man who wrote the Eighth symphony has a right to rebuke the man who put his raptures of elation, tenderness, and nobility into the mouths of a drunken libertine, a silly peasant girl, and a conventional fine lady, instead of confessing them to himself, glorying in them, and uttering them without motley as the universal inheritance.

I must not make "G" responsible for my own opinions; but I leave it to his old readers whether his huge success as a program writer was not due to the perfect simplicity with which he seized and followed up this clue to the intention of Beethoven's symphonies. He seeks always for the mood, and is not only delighted at every step by the result of his search, but escapes quite easily and unconsciously from the boggling and blundering of the men who are always wondering why Beethoven did not do what any professor would have done. He is always joyous, always successful, always busy and interesting, never tedious even when he is superfluous (not that the adepts ever found him so), and always as pleased as Punch when he is not too deeply touched. Sometimes, of course, I do not agree with him. Where he detects anger in the Eighth symphony, I find nothing but boundless, thundering elation. In his right insistence on the jocular element in the symphonies, I think he is occasionally led by his personal sense that octave skips on the bassoon and drum are funny to conclude too hastily that Beethoven was always joking when he used them. And I will fight with him to the death on the trio of the Eighth symphony, maintaining passionately against him and against all creation that those 'cello arpeggios which steal on tiptoe round the theme so as not to disturb its beauty are only "fidgety" when they are played "à la Mendelssohn," and that they are perfectly tender and inevitable when they are played "à la Wagner." The passage on this point in Wagner's essay on Conducting is really not half strong enough; and when "G" puts it down to "personal bias" and Wagner's "poor opinion of Mendelssohn," it is almost as if someone had accounted in the same way for Beethoven's opinion of Mozart. Wagner was almost as fond of Mendelssohn's music as "G" is; but he had suffered unbearably, as we all have, from the tradition established by Mendelssohn's conducting of Beethoven's symphonies. Mendelssohn's music is all *nervous music*: his allegros, expressing only excitement and impetuosity without any ground, have fire and motion without substance. Therefore the conductor must, above all things, *keep them going*; if he breaks their lambent flight to dwell on any moment of them, he is lost. With Beethoven the longer you dwell on any moment the more you will find in it. Provided only you do not sacrifice his splendid energetic rhythm and masterly self-possessed emphasis to a maudlin preoccupation with his feeling, you cannot possibly play him too sentimentally; for Beethoven is no re-served gentleman, but a man proclaiming the realities of life. Consequently, when for generations they played Beethoven's allegros exactly as it is necessary to play the overture to Ruy Blas, or Stone him to death—a practice which went on until Wagner's righteous ragings stopped it—our performances of the symphonies simply spoiled the tempers of those who really under-stood them. For the sake of redeeming that lovely trio from "fidgetiness," "G" must let us face this fact even at the cost of admitting that Wagner was right where Mendelssohn was wrong.

But though it is possible thus to differ here and there from "G," he is never on the wrong lines. He is always the true musician: that is, the man the professors call "no musician"—just what they called Beethoven himself. It is delightful to have all the old programs bound into a volume, with the quotations from the score all complete, and the information brought up to date, and largely supplemented. It is altogether the right sort of book about the symphonies, made for practical use in the concert room under the stimulus of a heartfelt need for bringing the public to Beethoven. I hope it will be followed by another volume or two dealing with the pianoforte concertos—or say with the G, the E flat, the choral fantasia, and the three classical violin concertos: Beethoven, Mendelssohn, and Brahms. And then a Schubert-Mendelssohn-Schumann volume. Why, dear "G," should these things be hidden away in old concert programs which never circulate beyond Sydenham?

KEIR HARDIE

From The Labor Leader, 14 October 1915

THERE is, I feel sure, a very general feeling of relief in the House of Commons and in the Labor Party now that Keir Hardie's body lies mouldering in the grave. I wish I could revive their dread of him by adding that his soul goes marching on; but I do not feel so sure about that: he seems for the moment to have taken it with him. However, the House of Commons is a less scandalous place now that he is not there. When Keir Hardie rose to ask questions, there was only one thing for the front bench to do, and that was to lie—lie impudently, snobbishly, spitefully, Pecksniffianly, Tartuffily, in the face of records that littered the earth and facts that blotted out the sky, until at last we asked whether, if the Government could not produce a gentleman to stand up to a real man it could not at least produce a respectable liar, a brazen, thundering liar, a liar with convictions and a purpose, a creature with some strength of evil in him to test the strength of good in his challenger. Now that Hardie is gone, the lying will be of the natural House of Commons type: placid, confident, dignified, the liar breathing an atmosphere of general approval, and feeling nothing but an agreeable sensation of good taste.

I really do not see what Hardie could do but die. Could we have expected him to hang on and sit there among the poor slaves who imagined themselves Socialists until the touchstone of war found them out and exposed them for what they are? What was there in common between him and the men who are so heroically determined to resist Conscription that they declare that nothing short of Lord Kitchener's telling them that it is necessary will induce them to embrace it? Of what use to him were the Republicans who will not obey the King unless he orders them to? To Hardie it seemed natural that when a minister had been a lazy, ignorant failure in every department he had been tried in, he should be discarded as incapable. To most of our Labor members, as to the front bench, it seems natural that the Prime Minister's first duty is to find the gentleman another job, and that when the very first measure he brings forward in his new place contains provisions so ridiculous that they are laughed out of existence before they have been debated, he should be not only taken seriously, but applauded in terms that would be rather overdone if applied to Turgot or Adam Smith. Hardie actually thought it quite a serious matter that the Government should imprison Labor leaders under ancient Mutiny Acts; suppress Labor papers; refuse to fix minimum wages on pretexts fifty years out of date; commit the country to war behind the back of the House of Commons; sell the Liberal Party to the Opposition by a secret treaty; deprive the country of its constitutional safeguard against corruption and conspiracy by arbitrarily abolishing the obligation on its accomplices to submit themselves for re-election on accepting office; and, in the face of the protests against the secret incubation of the war, again go behind the back of the Commons to make a treaty depriving us of the power to make peace without the unanimous consent of Russia and France. Hardie, aghast, said: "Are you Democrats? Will you stand this?" They replied, "Oh, for God's sake, shut up. Dont you know that we are at war? Is this a time for Democracy, and truth telling, and Liberty, and Socialism, and all that platform tosh? Cant you wait until the war's over? Then you can twaddle again as much as you like to catch votes for us." And Mr Asquith smiled imperturbably and said, "My friend, they will stand any-thing; and the more I give them to stand, the more loudly they will cheer me."

And as Mr Asquith was quite right, and (not being a Keir Hardie) sees no alternative to governing fools according to their folly, what could Keir Hardie do but turn heavenward and admit that his kingdom was not of this world? He could hardly be expected to live for the sake of MacDonald and Bruce Glasier and a few other brainy Scots, or for Mr Ponsonby's tiny band of sound old Victorian Liberals, or for an Irishman or two here and there, or for the French brains of Mr Morel or the German culture of Mr Norman Angell, or even for his beloved Welsh constituents. What were they against the massive multitude of the English workers, with their superstitious dread of clear thinking, and their ingrained hatred of Democracy, rooted deep in the knowledge that they are not fit for it, and need kind masters to save them from cunning rogues? It was nothing to Hardie that our Junkers and exploiters, with their retinue of professional politicians, should snatch at the war as a pretext for destroying all the liberties won by three hundred years of struggle. He expected that. But that the workers themselves—the Labor Party he had so painfully dragged into existence—should snatch still more eagerly at the war to surrender those liberties and escape back into servility, crying: "You may trust your masters: they will treat you well," loud enough to deafen those to whom Sir Frederick Milner was protesting that some of our heroes were being shamefully left in the lurch: this was what broke the will to live in Keir Hardie.

He was too old to wait for a new generation. Better let them kill him, and be a sort of Banquo's ghost on the Labor benches until his spiritual posterity comes to its own.

Hardie could never, like MacDonald, have mastered the art of manipulating the House of Commons. He often got half a dozen votes when he could easily have got a formidable minority or even a majority, because he worded his amendments in such a way that, if they had been carried, the Cabinet would have had to walk out of the House of Commons, and even out of political life. Hardie's function in the House came at last to be like the function of the crucifix in a French Court of Justice. If the figure in the French Court could talk, it would make the court as uncomfortable as Hardie made the House; and all the smartest barristers would say it ought to be shot. And, like the honorable members who so freely said that about Hardie, they would be quite right—from their own point of view.

Personally, I owe Hardie a debt which I shall now never be able to pay. When my Common Sense About the War appeared, he wrote to me in terms that, in their generosity, cordiality, and intimacy, went so far beyond anything that had occurred in our previous relations (always quite friendly) that I put off answering his letter until I could find time to do so adequately. He died before I carried out my intention. I mention the circumstance because it disposes of the cackle about Hardie being a pro-German. No pro-German could have stood my Common Sense. Everything that honest and humane men wish to defeat, discredit, and destroy in Germany, Hardie wished to defeat, discredit, and destroy there; and he proved his sincerity by spending his life in trying to defeat, discredit, and destroy them here also. He was not the man to shout oaths and abuse at foreign enemies of the people whilst diligently polishing the boots of domestic ones. When history puts all the boots on the right legs, the stupendous impudence of the cry of "unpatriotic" levelled at a man who had devoted his whole life to the service of his country, by people to whom patriotism was such a novelty that they could do nothing but get into everybody's way with their idiotic fussings, and provide a golden harvest for swindlers with their mania for subscribing to something, will be apparent.

Hardie took the war seriously in the face of a House of Commons that had lost all power of taking anything seriously except keeping its parties in power and sharing the official spoils. He had not in him a trace of that easy-going cynical humor which enables the clever man of the governing class to say with a laugh, "My dear fellow, of course the House of Commons cant take care of the war; and a good job, too. The House of Commons has never been able to take care of any war. Wars take care of themselves:

the combatants have to see to that; and, after all, I dont suppose the muddling and jobbing and delaying of the House increase the mortality more than 5 or 6 per cent all round. Leave it to the General Staff: they will work it out because they must." Such an attitude was impossible to Hardie, who knew very well that the General Staff would work it out on reckless assumptions that human life was of no value, and that the treasury was inexhaustible. The war now presents a definite arithmetical problem. To keep up the tornadoes of bombardment, by which alone any advance can be made, must require an ascertainable number of munition workers for each artillerist, because no single munition worker can possibly make shells as fast as a single artillerist can fire them. Other factors are the distance to be covered, the length of front that must advance across it, the time required per mile of advance, the vital expenditure in casualties, and so on. To hear Germans and Englishmen talking of crushing each other's country, and Premiers romancing about fighting to the last drop of blood, and Generals venturing obvious guesses about the duration of the war, without a pretence of having faced this calculation; and to see the Government on whose shoulders the responsibility for it rested having so little intellectual capacity or industry that it could not produce even a Budget that was not silly and inconsiderate, was appalling to a man like Hardie, just because he was thinking of the fate of his country and of Europe, and not indulging the passions of a schoolboy, nor manœuvring for a party opening, nor qualifying for birthday honors. Let us hear no more about Hardie's lack of patriotism: he had more patriotism in his little finger than the Government and its flatterers in all their bodies.

And he had one splendid consolation to end with. His Welsh miners stood to their guns and beat those worst enemies of England who want Englishmen to be brought up on less than three-and-tenpence per day PER FAMILY, when so many others let themselves be outfaced by fools and knaves into throwing their children's bread into the maw of Mars.

MR FRANK HARRIS'S SHAKESPEAR

SHAKESPEARE AND HIS LOVE. By Frank Harris. (F. T. Palmer.)

From the Nation, 24 December 1910

I MUST not affect an impersonal style when reviewing a book in which I am introduced so very personally as in the preface to this play by Frank Harris. He accuses me flatly of cribbing from him, which I do not deny, as I possess in a marked degree that characteristic of Shakespear, Molière, and Handel, which is described as picking up a good thing where you find it. After all, what did Mr Harris mean me to do? He published certain views about Shakespear, just as Darwin published certain views about the origin of species. But whereas Darwin did not expect biologists to continue writing as if Chambers's Vestiges of Creation were still the latest thing in their science, Mr Harris seems seriously to believe that I ought to have treated the history of Shakespear exactly as the Cowden Clarkes left it, and to have regarded his observations as non-existent. The mischief of such literary ethics is shewn in Mr Harris's own work. It is impoverished by his determination not to crib from me, just as my work is enriched by my determination to crib from him. Nothing that he ever said or wrote about Shakespear was lost on me. Everything that I ever said or wrote about Shakespear seems to have been lost on him. Consequently, my Shakespear has everything that is good in Harris and Shaw. His Shakespear has only what is good in Harris. I respectfully invite my friends and patrons to walk up to *my* booth, as offering, on his own shewing, the superior exhibition.

I doubt, however, if our plays would have differed by as much as three words if we had never heard of or met one another. I should not dwell on Mr Harris's complaint (which has been so valuable an advertisement for both of us) if it were not that I want to crush Mr Harris on certain points on which I have a real quarrel with him. I say nothing of his picture of me as a successful and triumphant plunderer of other men's discoveries and picker of other men's brains. But I have a word to say as to Mr Harris's latest picture of himself during this bay-tree-flourishing of mine. Here it is, in his own words:

"Whoever will be one of 'God's spies,' as Shakespear called them, must spend years in some waste place, some solitude of desert and mountain, resolutely stripping himself of the time-garment of his own paltry *ego*, alone with the stars and night winds, giving himself to thoughts that torture, to a wrestling with the Angel that baffles and exhausts. But at length the travail of his soul is rewarded; suddenly, without warning, the spirit that made the world uses him as a mouthpiece and speaks through him. In an ecstasy of humility and pride—'a reed shaken by the wind'—he takes down the Message. Years later, when he gives the gospel to the world, he finds that men mock and jeer him, and tell him he's crazy, or, worse still, declare they know the fellow, and ascribe to him their own lusts and knaveries. No one believes him or will listen, and when he realizes his loneliness his heart turns to water within him, and he himself begins to doubt his inspiration. That is the lowest hell. Then in his misery and despair comes one man who accepts his message as authentic-true; one man who shews in the very words of his praise that he, too, has seen the Beatific Vision, has listened to the Divine Voice. At once the prophet is saved; the sun irradiates his icy dungeon; the desert blossoms like a rose; his solitude sings with choirs invisible. Such a disciple is spoken of ever afterwards as the belovéd, and set apart above all others." [Mr Harris goes on to say that I am not such a disciple.]

This remarkable portrait has every merit except that of re-semblance to any Frank Harris known to me or to financial and journalistic London. I say not a word against finance and the founding of weekly journals; but if a man chooses to devote to them what was meant for literature, let him not blame me for his neglected opportunities. Mr Harris reviles me for not rolling his log; but I protest there was no log to roll. The book called The Man Shakespeare, and this play flung in my venerable face with a preface accusing me of having trodden a struggling saint into darkness so that I might batten on his achievements, might just as well have been published fifteen years ago. If they have been suppressed, it has been by Mr Harris's own preoccupation with pursuits which, however energetic and honorable, can hardly be described as wrestling with angels in the desert in the capacity of one of "God's spies." I have never disparaged his activities, knowing very little about them except that they seemed to me to be ultra-mundane; but I feel ill-used when a gentleman who has been warming both hands at the fire of life, and enjoying himself so vigorously that he has not had time to publish his plays and essays, suddenly seizes the occasion of a little *jeu d'esprit* of my own on the same subject (for I, too, claim my share in the common Shakespearean heritage) to hurl them, not only into the market, but at my head, If he has been neglected, he has himself to thank. If he really wishes to keep in the middle of the stream of insult which constitutes fame for fine artists today, he must give us plenty of masterpieces to abuse, instead of one volume of criticism fifteen years late, a few short stories of the kind that our Philistine critics and advertisement managers do not understand even the need of reviewing, and a play which has been kept from the stage by obvious unsuitability to the resources and limitations of our commercial theatres.

Coming to the play itself, the first thing one looks for in it is Shakespear; and that is just what one does not find. You get "the melancholy Dane" of Kemble and Mr Wopsle; but the melancholy Dane was not even Hamlet, much less Shakespear. Mr Harris's theory of Shakespear as a man with his heart broken by a love affair will not wash. That Shakespear's soul was damned (I really know no other way of expressing it) by a barren pessimism is undeniable; but even when it drove him to the blasphemous despair of Lear and the Nihilism of Macbeth, it did not break him. He was not crushed by it: he wielded it Titanically, and made it a sublime quality in his plays. He almost delighted in it: it never made him bitter: to the end there was mighty music in him, and outrageous gaiety. To represent him as a snivelling broken-hearted swain, dying because he was jilted, is not only an intolerable and wanton belittlement of a great spirit, but a flat contradiction of Mr Harris's own practice of treating the plays as autobiography. Nobody has carried that practice to wilder extremes than he; and far be it from me to blame him, because nobody has discovered, or divined, more interesting and suggestive references. But why does he throw it over when he attempts to put Shakespear on the stage for us? He says that Hamlet is Shakespear. Well, what is Hamlet's attitude towards women? He is in love with Ophelia. He writes her eloquent love letters; and when he has fascinated her, he bullies her and overwhelms her with bitter taunts, reviles her painted face, bids her to get her to a nunnery, and tells her she was a fool to believe him, speaking with even more savage contempt of his own love than of her susceptibility to it. When he finds that he has unintentionally killed her father with a sword thrust, the one thing that never troubles him is the effect on her and on his relations with her. He thinks no more of her until he accidentally finds himself at her funeral, and learns that she has been driven to madness and suicide by his treatment and his slaying of her father. He exhibits rather less of human concern than any ordinary stranger might, until her brother, a man of conventional character and habits, breaks down in the usual way and bursts into melodramatic exclamations of personal grief and vindictive rage against the man who has killed his father and broken his sister's heart. Hamlet's artistic sense is revolted by such rant. He ridicules it fiercely; tells the brother that his own philosophic humanity is worth the "love" of forty thousand brothers; and expresses himself as surprised and hurt at the young man's evident ill-feeling towards him. And with that he puts poor Ophelia clean out of his mind. Half an hour later he is "sorry he forgot himself" with her brother; but for her he has no word or thought: with the clay from her grave still on his boots, he jumps at the proposal of a fencing match, and thinks he shall win at the odds.

If Hamlet is Shakespear, then Mr Harris's hero is not Shakespear, but, in the words of Dickens, whom Mr Harris despises, "so far from it, on the contrary, quite the reverse." "Men have died from time to time; and worms have eaten them; but not for love," says Shakespear. And again, "I am not so young, sir, to love a woman for her singing"—the only thing, by the way, that could move him. "Her voice was ever soft, gentle, and low" is his tenderest praise.

Add to this the evidence of the sonnets. Shakespear treated the dark lady as Hamlet treated Ophelia, only worse. He could not forgive himself for being in love with her; and he took the greatest care to make it clear that he was not duped: that there was not a bad point in her personal appearance that was lost on him even in his most amorous moments. He gives her a list of her blemishes: wiry hair, bad complexion, and so on (he does not even spare her an allusion to the "reek" of her breath); and his description of his lust, and his revulsion from it, is the most merciless passage in English literature. Why Mr Harris, who insists again and again that in the sonnets and in Hamlet you have the man Shakespear, should deliberately ignore them in his dramatic portrait of Shakespear, and make him an old-fashioned schoolgirl's hero with a secret sorrow and a broken heart and a romantic melancholy—rather like Mr Jingle cutting out Mr Tupman with the maiden aunt—is a question I leave him to answer as best he may.

However, I must not pretend not to know the answer. Mr Harris says that his Shakespear is not Mr Jingle, but Orsino in Twelfth Night, and Antonio, the "tainted wether of the flock."

Now, even if we allow this—if we throw over Hamlet, Berowne, Mercutio, and those sprite-like projections of Shakespear's impish gaiety, Richard III (Act I) and Iago—the fact remains that Orsino throws over his dark lady with a promptitude which convinces us that the only thing he really cares about is music. And Antonio does not care about women at all. Even Posthumus, another of Mr Harris's pet prototypes, is much more disgusted at his own folly, and at the wreck of his own life and the unsatisfactoriness of the world in general, than sentimentally heartbroken about the supposed death of Imogen. Macbeth, when his wife's death is announced, says it is a pity she should die at a moment when he has more important matters to attend to. In every case where the Shakespearean man is untrammelled by the catastrophe of a borrowed story, and is touched by sexual sorrow, he is moved, not, like Laertes, to agonized personal grief, but to self-forgetfulness in a deeper gravity of reflection on human destiny. In short, the authority cited by Mr Harris for the authenticity of his heartbroken Shakespear is flatly against him instead of for him.

One crowning intrusion of commonplace sentiment is the exhibition of Shakespear as sentimentally devoted to his mother. I ask Mr Harris, in some desperation, what evidence he has for this. Even if we assume with him that Shakespear was a perfect monster of conventional sentiment, filial sentimentality is not an English convention, but a French one. Englishmen mostly quarrel with their families, especially with their mothers. Shakespear has drawn for us one beautiful and wonderful mother; but she shews all her maternal tenderness and wisdom for an orphan who is no kin to her, whilst to her son she is shrewd, critical, and without illusions. I mean, of course, the Countess of Rousillon in All's Well that Ends Well; and about her I will make Mr Harris a present of a guess quite in his line. Mr Harris, following Tyler and several of his predecessors, identifies Mr W. H. of the sonnets as the Earl of Pembroke, Now, in the sonnets we find Shakespear suddenly beginning to press Mr W. H. to marry for the purpose of begetting an heir. Nothing could be more unnatural as from one young man to another. And nothing could be more natural if Mr W. H.'s mother asked Shakespear to do it. If Mr W. H. was Pembroke, his mother very likely wanted him to marry. Now, "Sidney's sister, Pembroke's mother," the subject of Jonson's famous epitaph, was by all accounts a perfect model for the noble and touching portrait which Shakespear called the Countess of Rousillon. So there you are, with an original for the only sympathetic mother, except Hermione (a replica), in Shakespear's plays, without resorting to the French convention of "ma mère," and flying in the face of all the other plays! Yet Mr Harris will have it that Shakespear idolized his mother, and that this comes out repeatedly in his plays. In the names of all the mothers that ever were adored by their sons, where? Hamlet, for instance? Are his relations with his mother a case in point? Or Falconbridge's, or Richard the Third's, or Cloten's, or Juliet's? The list is becoming thin, because, out of thirty-eight plays, only ten have mothers in them; and of the ten five may be struck out of the argument as histories. Nobody but Mr Harris would cite the story of Volumnia and Coriolanus as Shakespearean auto-biography; and nobody at all would cite Margaret of Anjou, the Duchess of York, or Constance. There are, for the purposes of Mr Harris's argument, just two sympathetic mothers in the whole range of the plays. One is the Countess of Rousillon and the other is Hermione. Both of them are idealized noblewomen of the same type, which is not likely to have been the type of Mrs John Shakespear. Both of them are tenderer as daughter's mothers than as son's mothers. The great Shakespearean heroes are all motherless, except Hamlet, whose scene with his mother is almost unbearably shameful: we endure it only because it is "Shakespear" to us instead of an effective illusion of reality. Never do we get from Shakespear, as between son and mother, that unmistakeable tenderness that touches us as between Lear and Cordelia and between Prospero and Miranda. Mr Harris insists on Prospero and Miranda in his book; but in his play, Shakespear's daughter is a Puritan Gorgon who bullies him. This may be good drama; but it is not good history if Mr Harris's own historical tests are worth anything.

The identification of the dark lady, of which Mr Harris has made so much, is of no consequence. Mr Harris's play would be none the worse if the heroine were called Mary Jones or Mary Muggins. But since he insists on it, it may as well be said that in spite of the brave fight made for the Fitton theory by Thomas Tyler, the weight of evidence is against it. I have myself called the Dark Lady Mary Fitton because one name is as good as another; and for stage purposes I wanted a name that would remind Elizabeth of Mary Queen of Scots. But what does the Fitton case come to? If it were certain that Mr W. H. were the Earl of Pembroke, and if the portraits of Mary Fitton were those of a wonderful and fascinating dark woman like Mrs Patrick Campbell or Miss Mona Limerick, then, no doubt, the case would be a fairly probable one. But Pembroke is not even the favorite among the many guesses at the identity of Mr W. H.; and the portraits are not the portraits of a dark woman. This latter fact would smash the Fitton hypothesis, even though Pembroke were Mr W. H., as, in my opinion, he may have been; for the only weighty argument against him—that a bookseller would not have dared to call an earl plain Mister for fear of the Star Chamber —altogether leaves out of account the likelihood that Pembroke himself, though not averse to being known to an inner circle as "the onlie begetter" of so famous a collection of sonnets, could hardly have allowed himself to be published to all the world as the wicked earl in the little drama of the faithful poet, the wanton lady, and the false friend.

And now, what does all this matter? What has it to do with the merits of Mr Harris's play? Really very little; for though it would be highly interesting and relevant if it explained why Mr Harris has substituted for Shakespear quite another sort of hero, it explains nothing of the sort. Mr. Harris's changeling is not Shakespear: he is Guy de Maupassant. And this is not surprising; for it happens that when De Maupassant's short stories were almost the foremost phenomenon in European fiction, Frank Harris was the only writer of short stories in England for whom we could claim anything of the like quality. So that by depicting himself on his best behavior, Mr Harris has achieved a very good De Maupassant, and called him Shakespear.

What has kept the play from the stage is, no doubt, partly the fact that the pioneer enterprises can neither afford spectacular costume plays nor act them very well (modern realism is their strongest ground), and partly because there is not material enough in the Fitton episode for a big production at, say, His Majesty's. Nor does the melancholy, low-toned, sentimental Maupassant-Shakespear come out with the brilliancy, humor, and majesty that both the public and the actor look for in a part with so famous a name. Yet it is a noble and tender part; and the real difficulty is the slenderness of the material, and the brute fact that the dark lady episode came to no more than an *amourette*. Everything we know about Shakespear can be got into a half-hour sketch. He was a very civil gentleman who got round men of all classes; he was extremely susceptible to word-music and to graces of speech; he picked up all sorts of odds and ends from books and from the street talk of his day and welded them into his work; he was so full of witty sallies of all kinds, decorous and indecorous, that he had to be checked even at the Mermaid suppers; he was idolized by his admirers to an extent which nauseated his most enthusiastic and affectionate friends; and he got into trouble by treating women in the way already described. Add to this that he was, like all highly intelligent and con-scientious people, business-like about money and appreciative of the value of respectability and the discomfort and discredit of Bohemianism; also that he stood on his social position and de-sired to have it affirmed by the grant of a coat of arms, and you have all we know of Shakespear beyond what we gather from his plays. And it does not carry us to a tragedy.

Now Mr Harris's play begins by suggesting that it is going to be a Shakespearean tragedy. It leads up to the brink of a tragedy, and then perforce suddenly stops and skips to the year 1616, when the poet is depressingly ill and presently dies a depressing death as a beaten man. Jonson and Drayton are duly introduced; but instead of having the traditional roaring time with them and killing himself with a final debauch of wit and wine, he allows them to be driven ignominiously from the house by his pious daughter whilst he is in the depths of his next-morning repent-ance. De Maupassant dies of exhaustion, in fact; and that is not the Shakespearean way of dying. All Shakespear's heroes died game. The spectacle of Shakespear dying craven, with rare Ben and Drayton slinking off before the sour and stern piety of Puritan Mistress Hall, is bitterly masterly, but masterly in the modern iconoclastic vein, not in the heroic Shakespearean one.

Nevertheless, the play must be performed; for like everything that Mr Harris writes carefully, it is a work of high and peculiar literary quality. It is also truly Shakespearean in its character drawing: everybody on the stage, brief as his or her part may be, gives some hint, however trifling, of a marked temperament of some recognizable kind. Mary Fitton is quite modern, an *amoureuse* and a *révoltée*. She would be quite in place in a play by Sudermann, and is therefore not credible as the daughter of an Elizabethan squire; but she is vivid in her courage and generosity, and not unworthy of Shakespear's regard. Pembroke, the handsome, daring young gallant, whose number is nevertheless very distinctly number one, is excellent. The attempt to reproduce Falstaff as Chettle is a literary *tour de force*; and though Mr Harris, with his sombre, sardonic, almost macabre touch, takes the fun out of the poor old Bohemian drunkard, and makes him a saddening rather than an amusing spectacle, this very modern and serious turn to an old joke is unquestionably the right turn. The idea of making the prudent Shakespear lend Chettle money from a feeling that he ought to pay him for his unconscious services as a model, is a shrewd one.

Scene after scene in the Fitton episode is interesting and full of literary distinction and tenderness and fancy. The treatment is neither modern nor Elizabethan; or rather it is both by turns. Shakespear sometimes quotes himself and sometimes says such things as "What wine of life you pour!" which comes right dramatically but is impossible historically (Shakespear only once makes a metaphor of wine, when Macbeth, pretending to be horrified at the discovery of Duncan's bleeding corpse, says "The wine of life is drawn; and the mere lees is left this vault to brag of"). Generally speaking, Mr Harris's style, short, mordant, rather grim when it is not almost timidly delicate, excludes Shakespear's. At first we miss the extravagance, the swing, the impetuous periods, the gay rhetoric of the immortal William. But as an attempt to reproduce them could be at best only secondhand Shakespear, we soon admit that original Harris is not only fresher, but better. The curious mixture of eighteenth-century sentiment and modern culture and freethinking (in the literal sense) recalls Oscar Wilde, and perhaps explains an absurd tradition current ten years ago, that Mr Harris was Oscar's "ghost": a tradition that shewed the most desolating lack of literary perception and sense of character. The thumbnail sketch of Elizabeth is brutal; but it bites effectively.

And now, by how many of us could as much success as this be achieved if we attempted to handle such a subject? I could say a good deal more; but I have already gone beyond all reasonable limits of space—Mr Harris's own fault for wasting so much on an idle controversy. I heartily recommend the play to our theatrical reformers. As a full-sized tragedy, it might bewilder, disappoint, and fail, because there was no tragedy in the historic facts. But, as an exquisite episode, it will delight all genuine connoisseurs, if any such exist in England—which I am sometimes tempted to doubt.

HYNDMAN

The Record of an Adventurous Life. By Henry Mayers Hyndman. (Macmillan.)

From The Nation, 21 October 1911

Not many men living have impressed themselves on the consciousness of the political world in such a fashion that, in a political and literary review of picked circulation, one can drop the Mister in heading an article about them. We say Hyndman as who should say Bismarck, or Cagliostro, or Garibaldi, or Savonarola, or Aristotle, or Columbus. A mysterious quality this, when it exists in anyone but a poet. Poets are entitled to it in all the arts: there is nothing in calling Raphael Raphael instead of Messer Sanzio, or Beethoven Beethoven, or Shakespear Shakespear. But why should Hyndman be Hyndman and not Mr Hyndman; or, still worse, *a* Mr Hyndman? Though he is a remarkable person—one would say brilliant if that adjective were not for some reason appropriated by comparatively young men—he has done nothing that has not been done equally well by men who cannot be identified without at least a Christian name, not to mention those who carry their Misters with them to the grave. It is clearly a matter of faith and conviction, not of works, this indefinable quality of personal style that has maintained Hyndman as the figure-head of a great revolutionary movement, even when there was really no movement behind the figure-head. It is not a triumph of tact: no man has done more unpardonable things, or done them so often (within the limits of the pardonable, if you will excuse the contradiction). It is not a triumph of sagacious leadership overcoming all defects of manner: on the contrary, Hyndman has charming manners and is the worst leader that ever drove his followers into every other camp—even into the Cabinet—to escape from his leadership. It is not any item from the catalogue of accomplishments and powers Macaulay kept for advertizing his heroes. Hyndman is accomplished; but his accomplishments are not unique. It is really the man himself that imposes, Heaven knows why! Samuel Foote is said to have stopped a man of striking carriage in the street with the inquiry, "May I ask, sir, are you anybody in particular?" Had he met Hyndman, he would have had the same curiosity; but he would not have dared to ask.

Hyndman has now given us an autobiography that does not do him justice; and yet you can say of it, as you can say of so few volumes of reminiscences, that he is his own hero. He tells you much about people he has met; but he does not hide behind them. And yet he has, to an extraordinary degree, the art of telling you nothing, either about himself or anyone else. Here, for instance, is an account of George Augustus Sala's quarrel with George Meredith in Hyndman's presence. He tells it with an air of telling you everything, and yet at the end you know absolutely nothing that you did not know from the index: namely, that Sala and Meredith quarrelled. You do not know what it was about, or what was said, or how they took it. What you do know is that Hyndman was there; and this, somehow, suffices. Do not hastily conclude that the narrative is so egotistical that Hyndman has insisted on playing the two others off the stage. On the contrary, Hyndman is more reticent about himself than about the others. This is no book of confessions. Confession is not a Hyndmanesque attitude. Not only is it true that, save for a hitherto unpublished fact or two, there is nothing in this book about Meredith, Mazzini, Disraeli, Clemenceau, Morris, and Randolph Churchill (all of them have chapters to themselves) that could not have been compiled by a clever writer who had never met them; there is actually nothing about Hyndman himself that could not have been written, and even considerably amplified, by a constant companion. It is not a revelation of the man: it simply lets you know Who's Who. And yet it is frank to recklessness. Never was there a book where there was less need to read between the lines. Except a few harmless little chuckles over successes that were quite genuine, there is no boasting; indeed, Hyndman does not cut anything like so imposing a figure in these pages as he did in the public eye on several occasions. In the expression of his dislikes he is abusive and positively spiteful without the smallest affectation: his collection of *bêtes noires*, headed by Mr John Burns, is reviled without mercy or justice, and, what is much less common, without hypocrisy or any pretence of superiority to hearty ill-will; whilst, on the other hand, his more congenial friends and faithful followers are praised with equally unscrupulous generosity. Consequently, some of his swans are geese, and some of his geese are swans; but no great harm is done: you can always make allowances for the temper of a man who shews his temper fearlessly, whereas your man of good taste, who is afraid to praise and stabs only in the back, would mislead you seriously if he could lead you at all. And yet, in spite of all this openness, and of a vivacity that never flags and a touch on the pen that never bores, the fact remains that at the end of the book you see no deeper into Hyndman or his friends and contemporaries than you did at the beginning, though you have had a long and entertaining conversation about them. That is, if you already know your Marx and have got over the great Marxian change of mind—the great conversion which made a Socialist of Hyndman. If not, the book may be the beginning of a revelation to you. But if you know all that beforehand, the book will be to you a book of adventures and incidents, not a book of characters.

This will not surprise anyone who knows that there is a specific genius for politics, just as there is a specific genius for mathe-matics or dramatics. Hyndman is a born politician in the higher sense: that is, he is not really interested in individuals, but in societies, states, and their destinies. Apparently he did not care a rap for his own father; and it may be doubted whether he would care a rap for his own son if he had one; but he can see no faults in the Social-Democratic Federation, the ugly duckling which has well-nigh ruined him. He vituperates Mr John Burns, from whom he got no new political ideas, quite callously; but there is enthusiasm, almost tenderness, in his account of Marx, though Marx quarrelled with him, and strove far harder to injure and discredit him than Mr Burns did, even under the strongest pro-vocation. The explanation is that Marx widened his political hori-zon as no other man did. Hyndman began with the nationalism of Cavour and Mazzini: he ended with the internationalism of Marx. After Marx there was nothing to discover in the sphere of pure politics except methods; and for methods Hyndman has no patience, no aptitude, and no qualifying official experience. He never went on from the industrial revolution to the next things—to the revolution in morals, and to the formulation and establish-ment of a credible and effective indigenous Western religion. There is not a word in this book to indicate that the contemporary of Cavour and Marx was also the contemporary of Wagner the artist-revolutionary, of Nietzsche the ethical revolutionary, of Sidney Webb the pathfinder in revolutionary methods, or of Samuel Butler the founder of the religion of Evolution. Hyndman played the flute and played duets with Mrs Meredith without troubling himself about Wagner; dismissed popular religion as superstition and fraud, and was too glad to be rid of it to see any need for replacing it; and found the current morality quite good enough to furnish him with invectives against the injustice and cruelty for which he honorably loathed capitalistic society. His book, though nominally brought up to 1889, really stops with the enlargement of his political conception of the world by Marx, and with his founding of the Democratic Federation. He half promises to bring his history up to date in a future volume; but what has he to add, except a record of his own impatience with the Fabian Society, the Independent Labor Party, and the other bodies and movements which took the tactics of Socialism out of his hands, complicating and obscuring his splendid Marxist vision with all sorts of uncongenial details and elbowing out his poor but devoted disciples with—as he considered them—all sorts of uncongenial, lower-middle-class snobs and heretics?

It is not easy to reduce so exuberant a personality as Hyndman's to a type; but, roughly, we may class him with the free-thinking English gentlemen-republicans of the last half of the nineteenth century: with Dilke, Burton, Auberon Herbert, Wilfred Scawen Blunt, Laurence Oliphant: great globe-trotters, writers, *frondeurs*, brilliant and accomplished cosmopolitans as far as their various abilities permitted, all more interested in the world than in themselves, and in themselves than in official decorations; consequently unpurchasable, their price being too high for any modern commercial Government to pay. On their worst side they were petulant rich men, with perhaps a touch of the romantic vanity of the operatic tenor; and, as the combination of petulant rich man with ignorant poor one is perhaps the most desperately unworkable on the political chess-board, none of their attempts to found revolutionary societies for the advancement of their views came to much. One of the things Hyndman has never understood is the enormous advantage the founders of the Fabian Society had in their homogeneity of class and age. There were no illiterate working-men among them; there were no born rich men among them; there were no born poor men; there was not five years' difference between the oldest and the youngest. To Hyndman the acceptance and maintenance of such homogeneity still seems mere snobbery. He took up the democratic burden (as he regarded it) of working with men and women not of his generation, not of his class, not of his speed of mind and educational equipment. When the Fabians refused to involve themselves in that hopeless mess, he despised them. He even says, wildly, that they killed Morris by their refusal, just as the Unionists say Mr Asquith killed Edward VII. The Labor men knew better. They did not join the Fabian Society; but they made good use of it.

Still, the struggle with incongruity and impossibility on which Hyndman entered in 1881, though it has involved a fearful waste of his talent and energy, had something generous and heroic in it. In the Labor movement the experienced men will allow Hyndman no public virtue save this, that he has kept the flag flying— the red flag. And there are so many men who have every public virtue except this, that the exception suffices. Hyndman is still Hyndman, still, head aloft and beard abroad, carrying that flag with such high conviction that the smallest and silliest rabble at his heels becomes "the revolution." And outside that rabble there are still some friends, though he himself cares for nobody and nothing but the last act of the tragedy of Capitalism.

THE OLD REVOLUTIONIST AND THE NEW REVOLUTION

THE EVOLUTION OF REVOLUTION. By H. M. Hyndman. (Grant Richards.)

From The Nation, 19 February 1921

MR H. G. WELLS shocked the Bolsheviks the other day by blaspheming against Marx's beard. That set us laughing; but, let us hope, it set them thinking. William Blake, following a tradition as old as the Olympian Jove, always represented God as a man with an impressive beard. Marx grew a beard so godlike that, as Mr Wells maintains, it could not have been unintentional. But he did not look like God in Blake's Job. Bakunin, a rival revolutionist who loathed Marx, also cultivated a beard, but was still less like the God of Blake and Job. But Mr Hyndman, who would as soon have thought of aiming at a resemblance to Samuel Smiles as to Jehovah, was born with exactly the right beard (at least, no living man has ever seen him without it), and has always resembled Blake's vision so imposingly that it is difficult to believe that he is not the original, and Blake's picture the copy. Nobody

in the British Socialist movement has ever produced this effect
or anything approaching it. Mr Wells is so hopelessly dehirsute
that his avowed longing to shave Marx may be the iconoclasm
of envy. Mr Sidney Webb's beard *à la Badinguet* is not in the
running. My own beard is so like a tuft of blanched grass that pet
animals have nibbled at it. William Morris's Olympian coronet
of clustering hair, and his Dureresque beard, were such as no man
less great could have carried without being denounced as an impostor; but he resembled the Jovian God in Raphael's Vision of
Ezekiel, not the Jehovah of Blake. Mr Hyndman alone, without
effort, without affectation, without intention, turned his platform,
which was often only a borrowed chair at the street corner, into
a heavenly throne by sheer force of beard and feature. Even he
himself could not ignore his beard, though he was the only man
who could not see it. It compelled him to wear a frock coat when
his natural and preferred vesture would have been a red shirt. He
had to preach the class war in the insignia of the class he was
fiercely denouncing. When in desperation he discarded his silk
hat, the broad-brimmed soft hat that replaced it immediately became the hat of Wotan, and made him more godlike than ever.
Mr Wells has succeeded in making Marx's beard as ridiculous as
a nosebag. Let him try his hand, if he dares, on Mr Hyndman's.
He will try in vain. A glance at the excellent portrait which forms
the frontispiece to Mr Hyndman's latest book will carry conviction on this point.

I expatiate on this solitary majesty of Mr Hyndman's because
it is significant of his part in the Socialist movement. As a Socialist
leader—and he was ever a leader—he was never any good for
team work. It was not that he was quarrelsome (though on occasion he could be a veritable Tybalt); for there was not another
leader in the movement who was not quite ready to meet him
half-way at any moment in this respect. Nor can it have been
that the beard carried with it the curse of the first commandment.
It was that he had what is very rare among practical politicians
in England, the cosmopolitan mind, the historical outlook, the
European interest. For mere municipal Socialism, which he called

Gas and Water Socialism, he had no use. Also, as a thorough re-volutionary Socialist, he knew that Trade Unionism is a part of Capitalism, being merely the debit side of the capitalist account, and that Co-operative Societies within the capitalist system are no solution of the social question.

Now it happened that during the most active part of Mr Hynd-man's public life, the Co-operative Wholesale was developing prodigiously, and the huge new machinery of Local Government throughout this country made an unprecedented extension of Gas and Water Socialism possible for the first time. Mr Sidney Webb saw the opening, and jumped at it with the Fabian Society behind him. Mr Hyndman disdained it, and would not admit that the road to Socialism lay through the suburbs and along the tram-lines. Morris, always fundamentally practical, was no fonder of the suburbs than Mr Hyndman; but he saw that Webb's work had to be done, and gave it his blessing from a distance with the apology (for the distance) that it was not an artist's job. Sidney Webb saw, too, that the efforts made by Morris and Hyndman to organize the workers in new Socialist societies had failed as hopelessly as the earlier attempts of Owen and Marx, and that the Socialists must accept the forms of organization founded spon-taneously by the workers themselves, and make them fully con-scious of this achievement of theirs by making its history and scope known to them. Hence the famous Webb History of Trade Unionism and the treatise on Industrial Democracy: a labor of Hercules which nobody but Webb and his extraordinary wife would face or could have accomplished. Mr Hyndman, interested in the evolution of revolution, frankly scorned such spade work. He was eloquent about Chartism, Marxism, and the First Inter-national, but simply bored by the Amalgamated Society of Engineers and its past.

The result was that during the last ten years of the nineteenth and the first ten years of the twentieth century Mr Hyndman was often sidetracked, whilst Municipal Trading and the organization of a Parliamentary Labor Party by the Trade Unions were being hurried up at a great rate. It was not a business that needed a striking figure-head; and Mr Hyndman is nothing if not a striking figure-head. But it occupied all the capable Socialist sub-alterns and staff officers very fully; and thus it happened that Mr Hyndman was left with a retinue devoted enough, but incapable and disastrously maladroit. Look at his portrait, and you can see in his face a sort of sarcastic despair left by his continually disappointed expectation of intellectual adequacy in his colleagues. But for them he would certainly have won the seat in Parliament which he very nearly did win in spite of them. But it is not clear that he could have done anything in that doomed assembly: he has never suffered pompous fools gladly; and the beard does not conceal his contempt for people who cannot think politically in terms of a very comprehensive historical generalization: that is, for ninety-nine hundredths of his fellow-countrymen, and ninety-nine point nine per cent of their chosen representatives. His real work, like that of Marx, was the pressing of that generalization, in season and out of season, on a civilization making straight for the next revolution without the least sense of its destination or its danger.

It is with this generalization that Mr Hyndman challenges us in his latest book. It is a conspectus of history, and an important one, because it propounds a Sphinx riddle that cannot be answered by mere opportunists. Conspectuses of history are in the air just now. Mr Wells has put his masterpiece into the form of an outline of the world's history. Mr Chesterton, having taken the Cross and followed Godfrey of Bouillon to Jerusalem, has come home in a historic ecstasy. Mr Belloc urges the view of history that the Vatican would urge if the Vatican were as enlightened and as free as Mr Belloc. And all this at a moment when the threatened dissolution of European civilization is forcing us to turn in desperation to history and social theory for counsel and guidance.

I am not sure that Mr Hyndman's book is not the most pressing of all these challenging essays. Mr Wells, though ultra-revolutionary, has deliberately, and for his purpose necessarily, excluded theory from his *magnum opus*, simply preparing a colossal explosive shell crammed with all the relevant historical facts, and hurling it, with a magnificent gesture of intellectual power, at the incompetence, ignorance, obsolescence, and naïve brigandage of the State as we know it. Mr Chesterton, though he never has a theory, has a cry and a theme; and his extemporizations and variations on them are imaginative, suggestive, inspiring, resounding to the last human limit of splendor in that sort of literary orchestration; but the cry is "Back to the Middle Ages," and the theme is *"Cherchez le Juif"*: neither of them in the line of evolution or within the modern conception of the Fellowship of the Holy Ghost. Mr. Belloc is leading a forlorn hope; for Ibsen's Third Empire will not be the Holy Roman Empire. All three either ignore evolution or virtually deny it. Mr Chesterton and Mr Belloc even ridicule it, not without plenty of material, thanks to the antics of some of its professors. But Mr Hyndman has a theory, and an evolutionary one. It is not complicated by Medievalism, official Catholicism, and Judophobia. It has proved itself capable of engaging the faith of small bodies of thoughtful Europeans, and the fanaticism of large bodies of thoughtless ones. The march of events has confirmed it, not only before its promulgation by Marx and Engels (all theories fit the past on the day of publication because they are made to fit it), but since. Mr Hyndman's clear, close writing, always readable, always carrying you along, never confusing, or seducing you by the extravagances, the audacities, the extemporary digressions of writers who, having no military objective, stop repeatedly to play with history, obliges us to entertain his book seriously, and either confute it or let his case win by default. It is quite competently put, with no nonsense about it. There is no attempt to conciliate the reader or propitiate public opinion. Mr. Hyndman does not believe, nor pretend to believe, that *tout comprendre, c'est tout pardonner*: on the whole, he rather concludes that the better you understand history the more you condemn its makers. He spares neither invective nor eulogy; and he words them without the smallest concession to any feeling but his own. He uses tact to make his presentation of his case effective, never to make himself agreeable. In the end you may dislike him, especially if he dislikes you; but his case is there to be answered, and is furthermore a case that must be answered. Mr Wells' case is unanswerable; but its acceptance does not commit you to Marxist Communism. Mr Belloc has a very strong case against Parliament, and would have us discard it and face a really responsible monarchial (not royal) Government by a President and Cabinet; but he associates this with a strenuous advocacy of private property on the ground that it will do us no harm if we have little enough of it and are as ignorant as Tennyson's Northern Farmer. It is Mr Hyndman who shews you that if there is anything in history, private property, in its modern reduction to absurdity as Capitalism, is tottering to its fall, and that we must make up our minds to be ready for the new Communist order or for a crash.

But Mr Hyndman has yet another claim to urgent attention over his competitors in the survey of history. His book comes just when the hugest of the European Powers is putting its doctrine to an experimental test on an unprecedented scale. And this situation is made piquant by the unexpected fact that Mr Hyndman repudiates Lenin as completely as he repudiates Cromwell or Robespierre. The English arch-Marxist has been confronted with the fulfilment of all the articles of his religion: the collapse of Capitalism, the expropriation of the expropriators, the accouchement of the old society pregnant with the new by *Sage Femme La Force*, the dictatorship of the proletariat, and the obliteration of the *bourgeoisie* as a social order. And instead of crying *Vive la Révolution!* and packing his traps for Moscow to inaugurate the latest statue of Marx, he out-Churchills Churchill in his denunciation of the Bolsheviks. This is interesting: we want to know how he justifies it. At first sight he seems to cover his position by setting up the mature Marx as a historic materialist against the immature Marx of the Communist Manifesto, apparently forgetting that in a previous chapter he has knocked historic materialism into a cocked hat. Bolshevist Marxism, I may explain, is the Marxism of the Manifesto, taking a hint from Rousseau by calling its administrators Commissars. Mr Hyndman declares that to make Force the midwife of progress is to discard the full Marxist doctrine (insisted on at the end of every chapter in his book) that Force cannot anticipate the historic moment, and that premature revolutions are bound to fail, like the Peasants' War and the insurrection of Baboeuf.

But this, though true, does not prove Bolshevism premature. The undeniable fact that no midwife can deliver the child alive until its gestation is complete by no means shakes the historical likelihood that the birth will be a difficult one, needing a strong hand and a forceps, and possibly killing the mother. Who is to say that the historic moment has not come in Russia? Certainly not Mr Hyndman, who has so convincingly proved from history that the historic moment is as often as not a psychological moment. All that the Marxian historic moment means when analyzed is the moment when the *bourgeoisie* loses its grip on industry and on the armed forces of the Government, and lets them slip into the hands of the leaders of the proletariat when these leaders are what Marx calls class-conscious: that is, fully aware of the relations, actual, historical, and evolutionary, between the *bourgeoisie* and the proletariat, and well instructed as to the need for and nature of the transition from Capitalism to Communism which they have to operate. Surely these conditions are realized in Russia at present as nearly as they are ever likely to be anywhere. Lenin is as doctrinaire as Marx himself; and the *bourgeoisie* is down and out without having struck a blow. The Soviet Government has made none of the mistakes for which Mr Hyndman reproaches the Luddites and the Paris Commune of 1871. Far from destroying machinery, they are straining every nerve to develop production and open up foreign trade. Instead of superstitiously respecting the banks, and humbly borrowing a little money from the Rothschilds to go on with, they have promptly seized all the specie, bullion, and jewellery they can lay their hands on, and made any attempt to hold it back a capital offence, like the Apostles. They have, on the whole, pounced on the right things, and shot the right people (from the Marxian point of view). They are as ruthless in dealing with the counter-revolution, and with attempts to carry on habitual commercialism, as they are tolerant of mere sentimental regrets for the imaginary good old times of the Tsardom. They have shewn themselves able to handle and dominate both the *bourgeoisie* and the Militarists. Koltchak, Denikin, and Wrangel successively have tried to play the part of Gaston de Foix, only to be cracked like fusty nuts by Trotsky, in spite of the gold of Churchill (*ci-devant* Pitt) and the munitions of Foch. Is there any likelihood of the conditions under which Feudalism and Capitalism accomplished their transformation of society being reproduced more exactly for the transformation of Capitalism into Communism? If, as Mr Hyndman contends, Bolshevism is not real Marxism, but a murderous imposture, what does he think the real thing will be like? He owes us an answer to this question.

If one may infer his answer from his indictment of Bolshevism, he relies on the fact that the colossal peasant proprietary which forms the bulk of the Russian nation is unconverted. This is true; but if Socialism is to wait until farmers become class-conscious Marxists, it will wait for ever. The *bourgeoisie* did not wait for the approval of the farmers before they consummated the Capitalist transformation by establishing Free Trade, which all but abolished British agriculture. We should still be in the Stone Age if Hodge had always had his way. I cannot suspect Mr Hyndman of that romantic cockney idolatry of a politically stupid and barely half-civilized occupation which makes Mr Chesterton and Mr Belloc offer us mud pies as castles in Spain. The antagonism between city civilization and rural primitiveness has underlain all the revolutions just as it underlies this one. Mr Hyndman quotes with indignation a general order to the Red troops in the Don district to exterminate the Cossacks; but it needs only a little hypocrisy and the requisite alteration of names to be eligible for Sir Hamar Greenwood's Weekly Summary. The French Revolution did not stop to convert the farmers of La Vendée: the two parties tried to exterminate one another until the peasants were crushed, as they always are by the city men, because if the peasants had their own way there would not be any towns at all; and the peasants, having by this time forgotten how to make their own clothes and ploughs, cannot do without towns. Mr Hyndman does not deny that the Russian farmers are better off than they were before the revolution: what he insists on is that they refuse to feed the towns, and will produce no more than enough for their own consumption. Now it would perhaps be better, as far as we can judge at a distance, to tax the farmers frankly to their capacity and compel them to produce by compelling them to pay the tax, by distraint if necessary, than to pretend, as the Soviet does, to buy their surplus produce with worthless paper money. But the Soviet leaders disclaim reliance on this expedient: they declare that they are surrounding their factories with communal farms, and that they will extend this system until individual proprietary farming is crowded off the earth in Russia. It is absurd to contend that the historic moment for this has not arrived: far more plausibly might it be alleged that it is overdue. The historic moment is the first moment at which it can possibly be done.

Mr Hyndman, steadily intellectual as a historian at long range, is (being human) prejudiced as a current politician. During the war he was what he still is, a vehemently patriotic "Majority Socialist." But he denounces the German Majority Socialists fiercely for voting the German war credits and not coming out as pro-Britons and Pacifists. Yet he has no words scathing enough for Lenin, because Lenin refused to vote the Russian war credits, and recognized the necessity for securing peace at any price that could be paid by a Micawber note of hand. He is equally intolerant of "the unfortunate Bolshevism and Pacifism of some of the French leaders." He can forgive neither the Germans for fighting us, nor the Bolshevists for surrendering at Brest-Litovsk when they were hopelessly beaten, instead of bleeding to death as England's auxiliaries. This is neither Socialism nor philosophy of history: it is naïve John Bullism. Why should John reproach Fritz because he, too, found in the hour of trial that blood is thicker than gas and water?

However, Mr Hyndman's anti-Bolshevism is not always mere

Jingo resentment of the Brest-Litovsk Treaty. There are moments when he seems to be revolted by the institution of compulsory labor by the Soviet Government, and by the imposition of the will of an energetic minority on the Russian people. But in his own vivid and very favorable sketch of Peruvian Communism under the Incas, he recognizes that suppression of idleness and ruthless punishment of sloth and ca' canny was the political secret of the prosperity and happiness of these people who always sang at their work and did not know what poverty was. For my part, I cannot understand how anyone who has the most elementary comprehension of Socialism can doubt that compulsory labor and the treatment of parasitic idleness as the sin against the Holy Ghost must be fundamental in Socialist law and religion. If Lenin has abolished idleness in Russia, whilst we, up to our eyes in debt, are not only tolerating it, but heaping luxury upon luxury upon it in the midst of starvation, then I am much more inclined to cry "Bravo, Lenin!" and "More fools we!" than to share Mr Hyndman's apparent horror. As to the Bolshevists being in the minority, Mr Hyndman cites with approval "the marvellous transition effected by Japan in forty years from Feudalism to Capitalism." Immediately before this he says that "permanent social revolution and Communist reconstruction can only be successfully achieved when the bulk of the population understands and is ready to accept the new forms which have, consciously or unconsciously, developed in the old society." But he cannot believe that the Japanese man-in-the-street understood what was happening when Capitalism was substituted for Feudalism, or accepted it in any other sense than letting it happen to him just as the British laborer let the New Poor Law and the enfranchisement of the *bourgeoisie* happen to him. There never has been any such conversion of the majority of a people: all the changes have been imposed by energetic minorities. We should still be under the rule of the shepherd kings if Mr Hyndman's Liberal generalization were true or even one-fifth true. What is true enough for practical purposes is that until the live wires of the community are charged with a new current, or with a higher potential of the old one, neither the majority nor the minority can change the social system. Even Peter the Great, with all his gibbets and racks and knouts, could not have imposed his ideas on old Russia if his retinue of able blackguards had not been as tired of old Russia as he was. The old Russians were in a stupendous majority all through. What Mr Hyndman stigmatizes as "the tyranny of the minority" is an indispensable condition not only for moving society forward (or backward, as at present), but for keeping it alive where it stands. In England the majority will never be converted to the need for government at all: ninetenths of us are born anarchists.

Finally, Mr Hyndman falls back once more on Historic Determinism, and declares that the Bolshevists must fail because the economic conditions are not ripe. This impales him on the point of his own spear, because one of the best chapters in his book, called The Limits of Historic Determinism, contracts those limits to a tiny space in which there is room for a monument inscribed *Hic jacet* Carolus Marx, but not room for Russia. It is, he says (and proves it), "a demonstrable truth that similar forms of production sometimes have wholly dissimilar Governments imposed upon them." He shews that a single man with a conviction, like Mahomet, can start a movement which will conquer half the civilized world, whilst movements that have the sympathy of four out of every five men in the country wither and are stamped out by a few unpopular rascals. Does not Mr Hyndman then, as a Socialist leader, take an unnecessarily heavy risk in denouncing as untimely an attempt to do for Communism what Mahomet did for Islam, when he himself has shewn that none of the Determinist arguments against the possibility of its success will hold water? His real reason seems to be that he has set his heart on England being the Holy Land of the Communist faith: John Bull again! Also, curiously enough, on the transition being a peaceful parliamentary one. The old Internationalist is a patriot at heart, the old revolutionist a pacifist.

The petulance of the days when Mr Hyndman was a spoilt child of Nature and Fortune still flashes out from time to time in this book. One can see that he can no more work in double harness today than he could when he and Morris kicked over the traces of the Democratic Federation nearly forty years ago; but the general effect is one of mellowness, which encourages us to believe that Mr Hyndman's later years have not been the least happy of his tempestuous life. Certainly his beard never became him better than it does today.

IBSEN'S NEW PLAY

JOHN GABRIEL BORKMAN: A Play in Four Acts. By Henrik Ibsen. Translated from the Norwegian by William Archer. (Heinemann.)

From The Academy, 16 January 1897

IN this new play Ibsen, always terrible in his character of the Plain Dealer, is plainer than ever; but his terrors this time have the fullest measure of his fascination. No doubt they need it, in view of the world's petulant weakness. If his characters were a whit less intensely interesting, we could not bear the frightfully true things they say and do. If the scenery were less ghostly it could not take us so far out of the prosaic atmosphere in which we have the courage of our Philistinism. Even as it is, cries of outrage arise; and every duffer deplores some "questionable" passage which he (being a duffer) would not have written. Borkman's observation, that "if the worst comes to the worst, one woman can always take the place of another," is deemed out of place in a respectable play; and the elopement, which must needs have been a bad example to the young at best, is voted "unnecessarily" shocking because of a third party—a girl—whose presence is accounted for by the lady in these appalling terms: "Men are so unstable! And women too! When Erhart is done with me, and I with him, then it will be well for us both that he, poor fellow, should have some one to fall back upon."

Our inveterate habit of criticizing fiction on the lines of Mrs Raddle will always get us into difficulties with Ibsen. Mrs Raddle, it will be remembered, had a fixed conception of manliness which included an instant readiness on the part of every true husband to fight cabmen underpaid by his wife. "Raddle aint like a man," she said, when Mr Raddle disappointed her in this particular. That is just how we treat Ibsen. We tell each other with great freedom that there is nobody in the world who cannot be done without, and that there are as good fish in the sea as ever came out of it. We even go so far as to say—in French—that in the dark all cats are grey. But we hold that a man should never admit that the world contains more than one possible woman for him: surely a most dismally idiotic doctrine. So when John Gabriel Borkman delivers himself as above, we cry "Shame!" and console ourselves with the faithfulness of Ella Rentheim, the adorable old maid at whose expense John Gabriel has acted on his more catholic view to the extent of jilting her, on pecuniary consideration, for her twin sister. Even this consolation is a stolen one; for Ibsen remorselessly makes Ella say, when she is complimented on her power of love: "Perhaps it is the lack of love that keeps that power alive," meaning that her infatuation has persisted solely because it has never been gratified. That is the root objection to Ibsen's people: they will not keep up appearances. They come out with our guiltiest secrets so coolly that we feel that if there were such a thing as a hospital for ailing doctors, and a layman were put into a bed there by mistake, the illusionless conversation in the wards might make him feel as we feel when the old people in Ibsen, long finished with chivalry and sentiment, tell each other the frozen truth about their symptoms.

The fact is, enjoyment of Ibsen is a question of strength of mind. The quantity of truth the average man can bear is still very small; and every increase of the dose is met by piteous protests and cries of "Pessimist," "Cynic," "Morbid," and the like. Our own dramatists, in the presence of their sovereign tyrant, the public, are, more or less, like the preacher who, having rashly said in the presence of Louis XIV, "We are all mortal," suddenly caught the monarch's eye and added, "At least, *nearly* all." But the preacher's slip was a very venial one; for there are ten thousand men who can look death in the face for every one who can look life in it. Louis, who no doubt laughed at the courtly preacher, would certainly have had Ibsen broken on the wheel, as a good many excellent people would nowadays if they had the power. To endure the pain of living, we all drug ourselves more or less with gin, with literature, with superstitions, with romance, with idealism, political, sentimental, and moral, with every possible preparation of that universal hashish—imagination. Properly speaking, the opposition to the Awakener is nothing but the natural resistance of the average man to having his standard of temperance and fortitude screwed up to that of the man of genius. This is the whole secret of the eternal war between genius and mediocrity. It has never raged so incessantly as in the present century, because never before have such vast masses of untrained readers been let loose on literature by elementary education and cheap books. It is true that the public relishes a little bitterness in literature as well as in beer. Sentimental or satirical pessimism —the tragic or comic contrast of the frailty of man or the cruelty of Nature with the sublimity of the ideal—is by no means unpopular: in fact, pessimistic sublimity is the characteristic key of the whole romantic-commercial school, from the Renascence onward. Though Swift, having omitted the indispensable feminine interest, may be found too savage, Shakespear, La Rochefoucauld, and Thackeray are highly appreciated, whilst the most fashionable book in the Bible is Ecclesiastes. But the genuine realist, the man who exalts, not the ideal at the expense of life, but life at the expense of the ideal, can only hold the public like a bulldog. Look at the portraits of William Blake, the author of Proverbs of Hell, and of Ibsen! What bulldog ever developed such grip and tenacity in the mouth? One understands at a glance the remark made about Ibsen by Charles Charrington: "No man has any right to have such a mouth." But no less a mouth is needed to carry such a forehead through the idealist wilderness of this world.

Here are a few samples from the new play. Borkman, an old Napoleon of commerce, who, by ill-luck in his first battle, missed his millions and landed himself in prison, is talking to Foldal, an old clerk, whom he has ruined. Foldal, imagining himself a poet, clings to Borkman as the only man who admires his unperformed tragedy. In return, he believes that Borkman's dreams of rehabilitation and success will come true. Ibsen makes short work of the pretty picture of humble devotion faithful to fallen greatness. The course of their mutual admiration is disturbed by a dispute about women.

"BORKMAN [*indignantly*] O, these women! They wreck and ruin life for us. Play the devil with our whole destiny—our triumphal progress.

"FOLDAL. Not *all* of them!

"BORKMAN. Indeed? Can you tell me of a single one thats good for anything?

"FOLDAL. No; thats the trouble. The few that I know are good for nothing.

"BORKMAN [*with a snort of scorn*] Well, then, whats the good of it? Whats the good of such women existing if you never know them?

"FOLDAL [*warmly*] Yes, John Gabriel, there *is* good in it, I assure you. It's such a blessed, beneficent thought that here or there in the world—somewhere—far away—the true woman exists after all!"

This, it will be observed, is poor old Foldal's form of hashish: the imaginary true woman, his consoler for the contempt of his wife, who gives no quarter to his poetic hashish and his worthless tragedies. The conversation presently leads Foldal to betray that his belief in Borkman's rehabilitation is only a pretence. Instantly he is smitten with the terrible retort, "You are no poet." Then all the fat is in the fire.

"BORKMAN. Here youve been lying to me all the time.

"FOLDAL. It wasnt a lie so long as you believed in my vocation. So long as you believed in me, I believed in you.

"BORKMAN. Then weve been all the time deceiving each other. And perhaps deceiving ourselves—both of us.

"FOLDAL. But isnt that just the essence of friendship, John Gabriel?"

And so they part for ever: "for ever" meaning, needless to add, an hour or so.

The idealists will, of course, take all this iconoclasm as mere satire: Thersites up to date. It is not so: it is sympathy and honesty. The proof is in the result. Compare poor Foldal with any attempt in fiction to get sympathy for an old clerk by the ordinary idealist method of painting out all the selfish spots in him: Chuffy in Martin Chuzzlewit, for example. You may wince at every step in Ibsen's process, and snivel with tearful satisfaction at every step in Dickens's; but the upshot is that you are left with a serious belief in and regard for Foldal, whereas Chuffy is nothing but a silly and rather tiresome toy. When Dickens himself, later on, became a serious master of his art, his progress was on the road that leads away from Chuffy and towards Foldal: that is, from sentimental, cowardly, sweet-toothed lying to sympathetic, courageous, nutritious truth.

It is impossible within the limits of a single article to combine a description of the literary and dramatic contents of a play of Ibsen's with its constitutional criticism, so to speak. Nor are such descriptions to the point now that Mr William Archer's translation has placed the text in the hands of all for whom a criticism of Ibsen has any interest. It is sufficient to note that besides the two old men, there are two old women—twin sisters—the married one satisfied and pitiless in her affections, the old maid tender and remorseful, indignant only because she has been cheated, not of a mother's joy and happiness, but of a mother's sorrows and tears, the loss of which moves her to cry out to Borkman, "You are a murderer. You have committed the one mortal sin." In bright relief against this regret is the younger Borkman's impulse towards happiness and "living his own life," and his youthful revolt, in full illusion as to the boundlessness of his choice, against the apparent selfishness with which his elders have disposed of his career. The whole play is a wonderful chapter on the illusions of youth and the illusions of age: a wise and power-ful work, which will purify and strengthen dramatic literature, and help to educate dramatic criticism, very much against their own wills no doubt, but all the more effectually on that account.

One of our best dramatic critics, Mr A. B. Walkley, has pointed out the happy chance by which this play exactly fits the Lyceum company. But Sir Henry Irving's insensibility to Ibsen is notorious: there is no chance, unfortunately, of the hint being taken. Yet it is difficult to believe, especially after the success of the long-delayed Little Eyolf, that John Gabriel Borkman will have to wait and beg for two years as Little Eyolf waited and begged. Who speaks first?

OUR GREAT DEAN

OUTSPOKEN ESSAYS. By William Ralph Inge, C.V.O., D.D., Dean of St Paul's. (Longmans.)

From Everyman, 22 November 1919

WILLIAM RALPH INGE is our most extraordinary Churchman, our most extraordinary writer, and in some very vital respects our most extraordinary man. He is a living paradox, a Church-man who does not stone the prophets, a prophet who is a high dignitary of the Church, and so many other contradictory things as well that we have to analyze and explain him before his exist-ence becomes credible.

To begin with, he has had to struggle from his birth, and in-deed for generations before his birth, with disadvantages that would have crushed any common spirit and sterilized any com-mon mind. His heredity and environment are appalling. His father was the head of an Oxford College, and his mother the daughter of an archdeacon. And he met this black-coated destiny by that gamest sort of defiance which consists in embracing it; for he deliberately married the granddaughter of a bishop and the daughter of an archdeacon. I have not the privilege of know-ing his sons; but if ever I meet them I shall regard them with anxious curiosity. If I had a son with such fearfully unfair ante-cedents I should bring him up as an ignoramus and an atheist, so as to give him at least half a chance of acquiring a mind of his own.

I need hardly add that Dr Inge has been every sort of scholar and prizeman a Cambridge Don can be at his worst; that he has been an Eton master as well as an Eton boy; that he is a Doctor of Divinity and a Dean; and that he is allowed to say what he likes on the assumption (safe in ninety-nine per cent of similar cases) that after going through such a mill he cannot possibly have anything new to say. But the miracle is that he has. By all human calculation he ought to be exactly like either Samuel Butler or Samuel Butler's father. He is like neither. Without one of the disreputable advantages enjoyed by Mr H. G. Wells, Mr Gilbert Chesterton, and myself, he is as complete a Freethinker as any of us, and has compelled us to take off our hats to his in-tellect, his character, his courage, and—speaking professionally, as one author to another—his technique. If you do not read these outspoken essays of his, you will be as hopelessly out of the movement as if you had not read my latest preface, or Mr Ches-terton's book on Ireland, or Mr Wells's Joan and Peter, or The Undying Fire. For the truth is, the undying fire is in the Dean; and as it is a fire of such exceeding brightness that it blinds people with weak eyes instead of enlightening them, he is commonly called "The Gloomy Dean" by these poor ophthalmics.

The highest business of a critic is to proclaim the man: his next concern is to indulge the smaller self by nagging at the man's book. These essays, dazzling as they are, have done much to confirm me in a conviction which has been deepening in me for years, that what we call secondary education as practised at our public schools and universities is destructive to any but the strongest minds, and even to them is disastrously confusing. I find in the minds of all able and original men and women who have been so educated, a puzzling want of homogeneity. They are full of chunks of unassimilated foreign bodies which are much more troublesome and dangerous than the vacancies I find in the minds of those who have not been educated at all. I prefer a cavity to a cancer or a calculus: it is capable of being filled with healthy tissue and is not malignant. In the mind of the Dean, which is quite unmistakeably a splendid mind, I find the most ridiculous substances, as if, after the operation of educating him, the surgeon-pedagogue had forgotten to remove his sponges and instruments and sewn them up inside him. When a Dean has a rigid bearing, as Deans are apt to have, it is commonly said of him that he has swallowed a poker. Dean Inge, though not excessively stiff in his deportment, has swallowed a whole set of fire-irons; and it is too late now to extract them. There they are, and there they must remain until he extrudes them naturally, as he has extruded bits of them already.

I know how long such things stick. When I was a child I was told that a gentleman who had paid us a visit was a Unitarian. I asked my father what a Unitarian was; and he, being the victim of a sense of humor and a taste for anticlimax which I have to some extent inherited, thoughtlessly replied that the Unitarians are people who believe that our Lord was not really crucified at all, but was seen "running away down the other side of the Hill of Calvary." Childlike, I accepted this statement *au pied de la lettre*, and believed it devoutly until I was thirty-five or thereabouts, when, having occasion one day to make some reference to Unitarianism in print, and being led thereby to consider it more closely, I perceived that my father's account of the matter would not stand the fire of the Higher Criticism.

Now it is clear that somebody, perhaps the Dean's father, but more likely some benighted university tutor preparing him for an examination, told him (a) that the Rev. Thomas Malthus had satisfied himself that a single human pair could, with unlimited food, cover the habitable earth three deep with people in a thousand years or so; (b) that therefore if there were only one man in the world he could have all the food in it, but that if there were two he could only have half, or a third if there were three; (c) that the eternal law of life is the "law of diminishing return;" (d) that the more people there are in the world the poorer they must be (except the upper class, who are exempt from nature's laws); (*e*) that it follows logically that an Englishman cannot spin cotton or weave carpets unless he eats less than a Hindu or a Parsee; (*f*) that anyone capable of a syllogism must conclude that the skilled laborer is the natural enemy of the professions, and that the commercial brigands who exploit him are their devoted patrons; (*g*) that without Capitalism the workers must perish; (*h*) that the Industrial Revolution impoverished England by producing an excessive population; (*i*)—I spare you the rest of the alphabet.

I hope, now that I have exposed this farrago of nonsense to the Dean in its nakedness, he will recant his economic fatalism as frankly as I have recanted the much more plausible and pardonable error of my father on Unitarianism. Indeed, his own conclusions are a sufficient *reductio ad absurdum.* One of them is that both industrialism and population will disappear if we practise birth control, and will leave us as we were in the early eighteenth century, grouped in our proper stations round the squire and his relations, not forgetting, I hope, the country parsonage. Another—a real breath bereaver this—is that the best thing the Russians can do is to restore the monarchy!!!

If the Dean is unappalled by the hopelessness of the first conclusion and the wickedness of the second (he evidently does not realize how much better the worst we know of Lenin is than the best we know of the Tsardom), I would ask him to contemplate the career of Mr Asquith. Mr Asquith came up from his university with his very lucid mind carefully furnished with the standard set of university excuses for robbing the poor, called by the Dean himself "the old political economy." Firm and calm in its entrenchment, he condescended to impart its synthesis of society to an audience, mainly of Socialists, at The Working Men's College. They listened, and awaited the ignobly easy task of wiping the floor with him. But he baffled them completely by simply refusing to debate or discuss the matter. One does not discuss the inexorable destiny of humanity: one abides it. One does not debate with persons so ignorant as to suppose that there is any room for debate on matters that were settled, and settled for ever, as long ago as the year 1830. He left the room haughtily, and proceeded, as front bench man and finally Prime Minister, to deal with Socialism and the Labor Movement on the assumption that Socialists are ignorant of political economy; that the Collectivism which was growing up under his nose was a tinker's Utopia; that employers are still competing with one another in the public interest instead of combining against it; and that the establishment of a minimum wage is contrary to the laws of nature. The Dean describes the social result in one of his unforgettable phrases as "a condition of septic dissolution."

The truth is that all this sham political economy has not been even academic since Mill, in the process of writing the treatise in which he began by accepting it all, was irresistibly driven to Socialism before he finished it. It is true that up to so late a period as the date of the Dean's birth it was still possible to admit that Capitalism, or the substitution on principle of Mammon for God, had, in spite of all its infamies, broken the shell for a rebirth of society and incidentally done more harm than good. But since that time the evil of its central sin of godless selfishness has been working itself out. God is not mocked after all. Capitalism is now hindering more than it ever helped; and it will be the ruin of our civilization, as it has been the ruin of so many previous ones, if the Dean (among others) does not purge his education out of his system; go to his religion for his politics; and reconcile Christ-Logos to Christ Communist. To put it shortly, the Dean's economics will not wash; and we are all by this time Marxist enough to fear that if we go wrong in our economics, we shall go wrong in everything.

I conclude that the secret of a genuine liberal education is to learn what you want to know for the sake of your own enlightenment, and not let anybody teach you anything whatever for the purpose of pulling you through an examination, especially one conducted by persons who have been taught in the same way. You may think you can discard it all when it has served its turn; but it sticks all the more treacherously because you have a theory that you have cleared it all out. Before you know where you are, you have tripped over a block of it.

Both Democracy and Socialism need continuous and fierce criticism; but unless the critic understands them and knows that their theory is impregnable, and that the shutters are up on the Manchester School, he will produce no more impression on them than Archbishop Ussher's ghost would on the Dean if it reproached him with his ignorance of the fact that the world is only 5923 years old. In the Church Dr Inge is like a refiner's fire: he puts it to its purgation and purification as no atheist could. But when he turns to industrial politics he is worse than ineffectual: he discredits birth control by giving the wrong reasons for it, because he has never drawn a curve of production per head of population through time in the light of modern economic science, and therefore never discovered that the curve begins as a curve of prodigiously increasing return, with diminishing return so far ahead that the prospect of a world crowded right up to its utmost resources in edible carbohydrates and nitrogen (or whatever posterity will call its bread and butter) would appal the most sociable man alive. If Malthus himself were with us now, he would be worrying about the decline of population, not about its increase. For the increase which startled him produced such leaping and bounding prosperity, as Gladstone called it, that the classes benefited by it became too dainty and thoughtful to breed recklessly as they had done before; and now we have the very poor pullulating, and the better sorts sterilizing themselves. The Dean sees the danger, and comes down rightly and boldly on the side of control; but he imagines that we produce less per head as we increase in numbers, whereas the fact is that we produce more, though we are foolish enough to use the increase in supporting more idlers, instead of making the laborers rich enough to revolt against uncontrolled child-bearing.

But it is exasperating to have to cavil at the Dean's economics when there is so much to be said in praise of his divinity. In that sphere he is beyond praise. I suppose I think so because he comes out at last as a great Protestant; and I am so thorough an Irish

Protestant myself that I have all my life scandalized the Irish Protestant clergy, and made the Irish priests chuckle, by declaring that a Protestant Church is a contradiction in terms. The true Protestant is a mystic, not an Institutionalist. Those who do not understand this must read the Dean's superb essay on Institutionalism and Mysticism, which contains an inspired page (232) which ought to be included in the canon. His essay on St Paul convicts me of having taken too static a view of a developing spirit, and almost persuades me that the Supplanter of Christ found his soul at last.

I shall not stand between the Dean and his readers by any attempt to describe or paraphrase his doctrine: I simply agree and admire. Snobs will be scandalized, and some timid souls terrified, by the passages that suggested the epithet "outspoken," such as the curt dismissal of Bible science as "a cosmology which has been definitely disproved," and the declaration that if the bishops refuse to ordain all those postulants who cannot swallow the creeds, the infallibility of the scriptures, the thirty-nine articles, and the virgin birth in the old-fashioned way, the clergy will consist of fools, bigots, and liars. But it is now clear that the Church can be saved, if it is not past salvation, only by men with character and mental force enough to be able to say such things without conscious audacity. Whether the Dean will stay in it when he has saved it is not quite a foregone conclusion. He is so much more a prophet than a priest that one's first impulse on learning that he is Dean of St Paul's is to cry *"Que diable allait-il faire dans cette galère?"* As it is, he helps the lame dog over the stile with a roughness that betrays the imperfection of his sympathy with Institutionalism. His treasure is in a wider region than The Church of England, or any other such local makeshift; and where his treasure is, there must his heart be also.

AGAIN THE DEAN SPEAKS OUT

Outspoken Essays. Second Series. By William Ralph Inge, C.V.O., D.D., Dean of St Paul's. (Longmans.)

From The Nation, 9 December 1922

In reading a book for review it is convenient to mark the passages which call for comment, and note the numbers of the pages. This book contains 275 pages. The number of passages which call for notes of pure admiration is considerably more than 275. The passages which call not merely for comment, but for whole treatises, more or less controversial, are almost as numerous. The task is impossible: the book is review proof. The man with enough faculty and knowledge for it—and he would be a rare bird indeed—would not have the space for it; and so there is an end of the matter as far as reviewing is concerned. One can only say again that here is a mind so splendidly efficient, and a character so gentle and noble, that the otherwise somewhat deplorable aspect of the Church of England is transfigured by the strange accident that their possessor is Dean of St Paul's.

The explanation of this anomaly is that Dr Inge is Dean Inge not by faith but literally by benefit of clergy. Both historically and actually The Church has always had to depend on its scholarship for the reverence of the laity. A great scholar has The Church at his mercy: it must have him at all costs; therefore, if he will only condescend to step into its fold and stay there, he may do what he likes, say what he likes, and be what he likes. To a soul with so fine a conscience as Dr Inge's this freedom means much less than it would to the blunt and arrogant successful examinees who often carry off the trophies of scholarship without a scrap of genuine learning. But it accounts for the facts that Dr Inge, being by open and reiterated confession a Platonist Quaker, is Dean of the Metropolitan steeplehouse (a dome-house as it happens) of the British Empire; that he steadfastly warns his Church that if it insists on its ministers really believing all the articles they have to subscribe on ordination, its pulpits will presently be occupied exclusively by fools, bigots, or liars; and that the only sort of mothers' meetings he treats with marked respect are Birth Control meetings. The ordinary plain parson, when he is not too much impressed by the Dean's dignity to dare look his activities squarely in the face, gasps, and whispers to himself "What will he say next? What will he do next? What will he be next? What would happen to *me* if I went on like that?"

Thus has the Dean's scholarship enabled him to be at once our greatest Churchman and our greatest Freethinker. But for that scholarship he has paid a heavy price: the old price paid by Wotan when he won the spear that governed the world at the cost of one of his eyes. For not even the Dean's wonderful mind has been able to resist that disastrously successful swindle which we call secondary education. I solemnly curse the inauspicious hour in which William Ralph Inge went to Eton, and the dark day on which he passed thence to Cambridge. Of Bell and Porson, Craven and Browne and Hare, whose prizes tempted him to pursue unnatural knowledge, I say "Let the day perish wherein they were born, and the night in which it was said 'There is a pedant child conceived.'" Why was he not inspired in his childhood to cry "Surely I would reason with the Almighty, and I desire to reason with God; but ye are forgers of lies: ye are all physicians of no value: oh that ye would together hold your peace! and it should be your wisdom"? Civilization is being visibly wrecked by educated men; and yet, with a hideous infatuation, we seek to cure ourselves by a hair of the dog that bit us, clamoring for more education instead of razing Eton, Harrow, Winchester, Oxford, Cambridge, and the rest of them to the ground, and sowing their sites with salt rather than with dragons' teeth.

I daresay many men who have learnt things for the corrupt purpose of passing examinations instead of in the natural pursuit of knowledge, have said to themselves, especially when they were being carefully coached in the admittedly false answers they must give to satisfy obsolete examiners, that it would be easy to discard all that stuff when the examination was over, and the prize won. But God is not mocked so easily. I have never yet discussed with an academically educated man without finding his mind obstructed and deflected and let down by the *débris* and the unfilled excavations left by his academic course. Men like Bunyan, Blake, Dickens, differ from university men in the respective ignorances of the university training and the Sam Weller training; but they point the way to the light whilst the educated are stumbling through a dense fog of inculcated falsehood towards the pit. Bunyan fell in head foremost when he became an academic theologian: never in literature has there been such an aberration as that which led from the humanities of The Pilgrim's Progress to the grotesque figments of The Holy War. The true Fall of Man occurred when he lost his intellectual innocence by trying to pluck the apple of knowledge from the upas tree of the teaching profession.

When any subject of knowledge becomes what is called a teaching subject, it is taught, not that the student may know it, but that he may make his living by teaching it to somebody else who has the same object in view. After two generations it loses all touch with life; and the so-called learning and science of the professors becomes spuriously different from the learning and science of the practitioners. Yet we go on—but I have no patience. Readers of the Dean's outspoken essays must not be surprised when, finding themselves in a valley of diamonds glittering with gems of thought and wisdom, they are tripped up now and then by some battered old kettle or wisp of barbed wire lying about. These are part of the impedimenta of the university prizeman.

To drop metaphor, Dean Inge believes in the Wages Fund; accepts existing poverty as proof that the world has entered on the phase of Diminishing Returns and is over-populated; thinks that the Manchesterism which seeks to get as much as possible for as little as possible is a state of grace for the employer and of damnation for the ca' canny Trade Unionist; and believes that all clergymen who have sons are like his own father and not like Samuel Butler's father, and that the actual gentleman produced by our social system is the ideal gentleman.

In Dean Inge's case these inculcated delusions do not matter so directly, because he is not a politician. But consider the case of Mr Asquith. He, too, has a mind which is a remarkable instrument, and a character which is proof against demagogy. Unfortunately, he was educated. At a moment when his whole career depended upon his having Karl Marx at his fingers' ends, and realizing that Malthus and Nassau Senior are as dead as Queen Anne, he entered on his Parliamentary career with a complete 1832 equipment, and an unshakeable conviction that only very ignorant persons are unaware that the last words in political economy were said by Bastiat and popularized by Cobden and Bright. That has made a considerable difference to the history of England during the last thirty years; and to Mr Asquith himself it has resulted in his being unable either to withstand Joseph Chamberlain's abysmal ignorance of Free Trade, or to save himself from being elbowed off the front bench by the up-to-date economic knowledge of Mr Ramsay MacDonald and Mr Sidney Webb.

But there is something else entangling the footsteps of Dean Inge beside the obsolete special pleadings of the Devil's advocates of the Manchester School. There is the materialist pseudoscience of the second half of the nineteenth century, which still constitutes the "modern side" of our university education. And it is the oddest experience to find the real Inge, the Inge In Itself, smashing this heathenish nonsense with one contemptuous punch of his pen, and then suddenly relapsing into the Cambridge class room and assuring us that there is nothing for us to do but to wait as best we can until our extinction is completed by the cooling of the sun. For example:

"Progressism takes the world of common experience as the real world, and then seeks to improve it by building upon this foundation an imaginary superstructure in the future: an unending upward movement, which science itself knows to be impossible. . . . The fate of every globe must be, sooner or later, to become cold and dead, like the moon."

Would anyone believe that only four pages before the latter sample of the science of lunacy occurs the following:

"Even if those physicists are right who hold that the universe is running down like a clock, that belief postulates a moment in past time when the clock was wound up; and whatever power wound it up once, may presumably wind it up again"?

Precisely. Then away with melancholy; and leave we our university scientists to watch the cooling of the sun (which is not known with any genuine scientific certainty to be cooling at all, or even to be on fire) and to live like the hero of Poe's story of The Pit and the Pendulum, counting the seconds between them and extinction.

I will quote only one more of these stumbles over university science:

"The development of life out of the inorganic is a fact, though it has not yet been produced experimentally."

The implication here, that nothing can be accepted as a fact until somebody has faked an imitation of it in a laboratory, is a rudiment, in the Darwinian sense, of the collegian Inge. Why did they not warn him that the last century is white with the dust of exploded theories of natural operations that have all been "produced experimentally"? The Baconian phase in which science was pursued by the method of put-up jobs had and has its uses; but as Dean Inge shews in the first half of the sentence I have quoted that he has found out its limitations, why did he finish with that quaint little gesture of homage to its most ridiculous pretension?

The centre of interest in the new book is, of course, the Dean's Confession of Faith; and here I am on holy ground, and feel a delicacy which does not inhibit me when I am jollying its author into emptying his academic economics and science into the dust-bin. And yet it seems to me that here again there are different planes of thought: a traditional plane and an original plane: a plane which he would never have dreamt of if nobody had told him anything about it, and a plane which he would have reached if he had never read a book or seen a church in his life. There are, indeed, two different men in the case, a philosopher and a Dean; and one cannot but wonder what will happen if the two ever meet face to face. They need not; for experience shews us that though we are each at least half a dozen different persons, nothing is rarer than a meeting between any two of the six, much less a parliament of the lot. But the Platonist philosopher and the Dean sometimes come so close that I hold my breath. Listen:

"THE PHILOSOPHER. True faith is belief in the reality of absolute values.

"THE DEAN. The Incarnation and the Cross are the central doctrines of Christianity.

"THE PHILOSOPHER. Heaven and hell are not two places; they are the two ends of a ladder of values.

"THE DEAN. It is impossible that God should not create, after His own image, any good thing which it is possible for Him to create.

"THE PHILOSOPHER. There is no evidence for the theory that God is a merely moral Being; and what we observe of His laws and operations here indicates strongly that He is not."

The Dean is very hard on persons who, like myself, get over the problem of evil by the very simple assumption that the creative Energy, as yet neither omnipotent nor omniscient, but ever striving to become both, proceeds by the method of trial and error, and has still something to live for. He clings to the vision of an existing and accomplished Perfection; and I cannot laugh at him as I had to laugh at a lady of title who repudiated my fallible God on the ground that nothing but the best of everything was allowed in *her* house. Yet what am I to make of the following passages?

"We are at liberty to cherish the inspiring thought that we are fellow workers with God in realizing His purpose in time. . . . But surely Christ came to earth to reveal to us, not that He was like God, but that God was like Him."

158

For me the Dean does not solve the problem of evil. Indeed he says that it cannot be entirely solved; but his contribution to its solution, which is, that "the eternal world must contain crushed evil, illustrating negatively the triumph of the positive values," seems to me the most desperate venture in official theology on record, quite hopeless as a reply to the multitude of people who are made atheists by the spectre of so much uncrushed evil in the temporal world.

But I think the supreme heresy of Inge the philosopher against the Incarnation which he declares a central doctrine of Christianity is his repeated denunciation of anthropolatry. I myself have never lost an opportunity of warning Man that he is not God's last word, and that if he will not do God's work God will make some more serviceable agent to supplant him. But hear the Dean of St Paul's to the same effect:

"It is an unproved assumption that the domination of the planet by our own species is a desirable thing, which must give satisfaction to its Creator. . . . There are many things in the world more divine than man: anthropolatry is the enemy: true philosophy is theocentric."

This seems to me to be perfectly true; but then when God incarnated Himself as Man, He was an anthropolator; and the Roman Catholic Church, which Dr Inge rightly denounces for its refusal to recognize that non-human creatures have rights as against the abuse and cruelty of Man, could put him in a polemical corner on this point.

But I am drifting into a polemic myself, which is the last thing I desire to do. I break off hastily, and take refuge in a few random quotations as samples to shew that every thoughtful person will find something of importance to him in this book:

"It is only occasionally that I can pray with the spirit and pray with the understanding also: a very different thing from merely saying one's prayers."

"I have never understood why it should be considered derogatory to the Creator to suppose that He has a sense of humor."

"The ironies of history are on a colossal scale, and must, one is tempted to think, cause great amusement to a super-human spectator."

"Ancient civilizations were destroyed by imported barbarians: we breed our own."

"Roman Catholicism everywhere confronts modern civilization as an enemy; and that is precisely why it has so much more political power than Protestantism."

"The Churches have little influence; and if they had more they would not know what to do with it."

HENRY IRVING AND ELLEN TERRY

[*Henry Irving died on the 14th October* 1905. *I was asked by the Neue Freie Presse of Vienna to contribute an obituary notice, as I was then somewhat prominently in practice in London as a critic of plays and players. Unfortunately the translator made a slip or two in his haste, and gave a malicious turn to some of my comments. These were retranslated by the London papers; and the malicious turn lost less than nothing in the process. And when the retranslation was paraphrased by scandalized admirers of Irving, or by enemies of his who did not dare to disparage him at first hand, there arose a nine days fuss, including a heated correspondence in The Times, in which I was pilloried as a heartless slanderer of the dead. All I could do finally was to circulate the original text of my article to all the newspapers in the kingdom and place it freely at their disposal for literal reproduction. Only one of them, and that not a London one, availed themselves of my offer; for there is no getting over the hard journalistic fact that as quarrels and vituperations make thrilling reading whilst vindications are dull and disappointing, it is much easier to get a calumny published than its refutation, unless, as in France, the paper is legally obliged to give equal space to the attack and the defence.*

Those who are curious about the affair will find it more intimately dealt with in my published correspondence with Ellen Terry.

HENRY IRVING AND ELLEN TERRY

The Neue Freie Presse promptly demanded an article on Ellen Terry to supplement the one on Irving. Accordingly I republish the two together here. But they do not by themselves reveal the subjective relations of the three parties to them. For that I must refer readers not only to the correspondence aforesaid, but to the criticisms of Irving's enterprises and Ellen Terry's part in them contained in my volumes entitled Our Theatres in the Nineties.]

SIR HENRY IRVING, who has just died suddenly after an evening spent in the only way he cared to spend an evening: that is, on the stage, was 68 years old, and had been for thirty years the foremost actor in London. His death, like his life and his art, is an event of personal interest only. He was an extraordinarily interesting actor, enthusiastically admired by some, violently disliked by others, but never ignored, never insignificant, always able to force the world to accept him as a public dignitary standing quite alone in his eminence. The crowning event of his life was his admission to the order of knighthood. He was the first English actor whose social status was ever officially confirmed in this way; and, what is still more remarkable, he actually compelled the Court to knight him by publicly and explicitly demanding that he, as the head of the London stage, should be treated as the peer of the President of the Royal Academy of Arts, who is always knighted in England as a matter of course. The demand was made at a lecture which Irving delivered at the Royal Institution on the 1st February 1895, ostensibly on some dramatic subject, but really on the claims of his profession and of himself to official recognition. Any other actor would have been laughed at. Irving was knighted with apologies for the delay, and with gratitude for his condescension in accepting a title which he never afterwards deigned to print on a playbill.

There is nothing more to be said about him. When I was asked, the day after his death, to pay a tribute to his memory, I wrote: "He did nothing for the living drama; and he mutilated the remains of the dying Shakespear; but he won his lifelong fight to have the actor recognized as the peer of all other artists; and

this was enough for one man to accomplish. *Requiescat in pace.*"
The truth is that Irving took no interest in anything except himself; and he was not interested even in himself except as an imaginary figure in an imaginary setting. He lived in a dream which he was so loth to have disturbed that when an actor told him once that he was being scandalously robbed, he thanked him and begged him not to tell him anything of the kind again. His scholarship and his connoisseurship in art and literature were equally imaginary. He was willing to have a retinue of writers, with Lord Tennyson, the Poet Laureate, at the head, and the journalists who helped him to write his lectures and speeches at the tail; but he had no literary sense, and was quite outside the intellectual life of his time. He was ignorant even of the theatre, having seen nothing of it since about thirty years ago, when he became master in his own playhouse, and shut the world out. He murdered Shakespear's Lear so horribly in cutting it down that he made it unintelligible; and he allowed one of his retainers to turn Goethe's Faust into so cheap a spectacular melodrama that it was repeated every night for a year. He played Macaire, the Corsican Brothers, Richelieu, Claude Melnotte, and all the old repertory of Charles Kean without a thought that they could be in the least old-fashioned. In the case of Macaire the new version by Robert Louis Stevenson, a masterpiece of literature, lay ready to his hand; but he used the old traditional version which is still played in booths and barns. Many persons were indignant at his supposed pretensions to be a thinker, a scholar, a connoisseur; but though such pretensions were undoubtedly made for him, he never made them himself. The truth is, his bearing was so dignified that the world made all possible pretences for him. When they saw him as Becket, they could not doubt that he was a great statesman and churchman; when they saw him as the Vicar of Wakefield, they recognized the scholar and the divine in every silver hair in his wig; when they saw him as Charles I, they felt that the patron of Van Dyck could not be ignorant of painting.

And yet this artist, who could produce every illusion about

himself off the stage by the mere force and singularity of his personality, was prevented by just this force and singularity from producing any great range of illusion on it. He had really only one part; and that part was the part of Irving. His Hamlet was not Shakespear's Hamlet, nor his Lear Shakespear's Lear: they were both avatars of the imaginary Irving in whom he was so absorbingly interested. His huge and enduring success as Shylock was due to his absolutely refusing to allow Shylock to be the discomfited villain of the piece. The Merchant of Venice became the Martyrdom of Irving, which was, it must be confessed, far finer than the Tricking of Shylock. His Iachimo, a very fine performance, was better than Shakespear's Iachimo, and not a bit like him. On the other hand, his Lear was an impertinent intrusion of a quite silly conceit of his own into a great play. His Romeo, though a very clever piece of acting, wonderfully stage-managed in the scene where Romeo dragged the body of Paris down a horrible staircase into the tomb of the Capulets, was an absurdity, because it was impossible to accept Irving as Romeo, and he had no power of adapting himself to an author's conception: his creations were all his own; and they were all Irvings.

Technically he became very skilful. He was too much interested in himself not to cultivate himself to the utmost possible degree; and he was both imaginative and industrious in devising and executing stage effects, and what is called on the English stage "business." His Vanderdecken was a stage effect from first to last, and a most weirdly and beautifully effective one. His Mathias in The Bells and his Charles I were elaborated to the most extreme degree. They were such miracles of finished execution that they raised a melodrama of no importance and a surpassingly bad historical play into dramatic masterpieces. Just as Paganini fascinated the world with trumpery music by his own skill and strangeness, so Irving fascinated London with trumpery plays. But he had some serious physical defects and peculiarities; and though he succeeded in making the peculiarities interesting and characteristic, the defects limited him to the last. His voice was so poor that it would have prevented him from attaining any success at all had he not had a large and cavernous nose. By throwing his voice forward into it he gave it an impressive resonance which sometimes produced a strikingly beautiful effect in spite of its nasal tone. But this was only practicable when he could deliver a speech slowly. In rapid, violent, energetic passages, his nasal method produced a hysterical whinnying which was ridiculous; and for many years after he began playing heavy tragic parts he was the butt of every mimic and the object of continual ridicule from vulgar people who could see his obvious physical defects but could not appreciate his artistic qualities. It was not until he abandoned all pretence of robust acting that the laughter stopped. He was thus driven into a very slow method; and the more subtly he elaborated it, the worse became the performances at his theatre; for though he himself was always effective, those who were on the stage with him had to wait so long for his replies, and were so hurried in the vain attempt to make up for the time he was losing (if they had all played as slowly as he the play would never have ended), that they soon gave up all attempt to act, and simply gave him his cues as he wanted them. Under our English actor-manager system they could not remonstrate. They were his employees, completely in his power, and he simply could not get his effects in any other way.

In judging Irving, Austrians must remember that he had to assume a very high position without having had the training and culture that can be given only by a great national theatre with a highly trained audience and an established artistic tradition. There is nothing of the sort in England. Imagine a lad with his head full of nothing but romances, pitchforked into a city office, and leaving it to go on the stage as a member of the stock company in provincial cities where the theatre was abhorred as the gate of hell, and playing a piano on Sunday considered an unpardonable crime, by many of the most respectable citizens! Imagine him, after picking up his profession technically in this way, being enabled, by a private subvention from a charitable lady, to lease a metropolitan theatre and become its absolute and sole director, and you will get some idea of Irving's position in

London. It would carry me too far to go into the whole question of the deplorable intellectual and artistic condition of the English theatre in Irving's time. Suffice it to say that the environment and tradition which an actor can obtain in Vienna cannot be obtained in England, and that Irving had to do his best to supply them out of his own romantic imagination, without much schooling and virtually without any general artistic culture. His success under such disadvantages was extraordinary; but in the end he had to give up his theatre and take to the provinces to live on his reputation. A theatre without a living drama is in the long run impossible; and when Irving had exhausted the old plays in which his personality was effective, he was—to be quite frank—too ignorant and old-fashioned to know how to choose fresh material. His greatest achievement was his social achievement, the redemption of his profession from Bohemianism, the imposing himself on the nation as one of the most eminent men in it, and the official acknowledgment of that estimate by the accolade.

Contributed to the Neue Freie Presse (Vienna) of the 24th December 1905 by request after the death of Henry Irving.

ELLEN TERRY, apart from her professional accomplishments as an actress, is so remarkable a woman that it is very difficult to describe her to the Austrian public without writing her private rather than her public history.

The part she has played in the life of her time will never be known until some day—perhaps fifty years hence—when her correspondence will be collected and published in twenty or thirty volumes. It will then, I believe, be discovered that every famous man of the last quarter of the nineteenth century—provided he were a playgoer—has been in love with Ellen Terry, and that many of them have found in her friendship the utmost consolation one can hope for from a wise, witty, and beautiful woman whose love is already engaged elsewhere, and whose heart has withstood a thousand attempts to capture it. To me— for I am one of the unsuccessful lovers—Ellen Terry's skill as an actress is the least interesting thing about her. Unlike Irving, to whom his art was everything and his life nothing, she found life more interesting than art; and when she became associated with him in his long and famous management of the Lyceum Theatre, she—the most modern of modern women, the most vital of modern personalities—set to work, more in the spirit of a thrifty intelligent housekeeper than of a self-obsessed artist, to fill up the leading feminine rôles in the old-fashioned plays he delighted in. Fortunately these plays included the handful of Shakespearean comedies and tragedies which still keep the stage in England as stalking horses for ambitious actors. We therefore had at the Lyceum Theatre Ellen Terry as Portia, as Beatrice, as Juliet, as Imogen, as Ophelia, though never as Rosalind in As You Like It, which she would certainly have insisted on playing if she had cared as much for her own professional renown as for helping Irving.

Probably there were never two eminent members of the same profession so unlike one another as Ellen Terry and Henry Irving. They both had beautiful and interesting faces; but faces like Irving's have looked at the world for hundreds of years past from portraits of churchmen, statesmen, princes, and saints, whilst Ellen's face had never been seen in the world before. She actually invented her own beauty; for her portraits as a girl have hardly anything in them of the wonderful woman who, after leaving the stage for seven years, reappeared in 1875 and took London by storm. The much abused word "unique" was literally true of Ellen Terry. If Shakespear had met Irving in the street, he would have recognized a distinguished but familiar type. Had he met Ellen Terry, he would have stared as at a new and irresistibly attractive species of womankind. Her portrait as Lady Macbeth, by Sargent, will stand out among all the portraits of famous women as that of a woman who was like nobody else. Again, Irving was simple, reserved, and slow. Ellen Terry is quick, restless, clever, and can get on the most unembarrassed and familiar terms in an instant with even the shyest strangers. Irving did not like writing: his correspondence was carried on by the late L. F. Austin, Bram Stoker, and perhaps others of his retinue: the few letters he really wrote himself owing their charm to their unaffected and unskilled lack of literary pretence and the handwriting not remarkable. Ellen Terry, on the other hand, is one of the greatest letter writers that ever lived. She can flash her thought down on paper in a handwriting that is as characteristic and as unforgettable as her face. When you find a letter from her among your morning's correspondence, you see the woman as vividly as you see the handwriting; and you open that letter first and feel that the day is a fortunate one. Her few published writings give no idea of her real literary power. All her letters are too intimate, too direct, too penetrating to be given to anyone but those to whom they are addressed. And here we come to another difference from Irving. Irving was sentimental and affectionate, and like most sentimental and affectionate people was limited and concentrated in his interests. He never understood others, and indeed never understood himself. Ellen Terry is not sentimental and not affectionate; but she is easily interested in anybody or anything remarkable or attractive: she is intelligent: she understands: she sympathizes because she understands and is naturally benevolent; but she has been interested oftener than deeply touched, and has pitied and helped oftener than loved. With all her ready sacrifice of her stage talent and skill, first to domestic ties, and then, on her return to the stage, to the Lyceum enterprise, she has never really sacrificed her inner self. In sacrificing her art she only sacrificed a part of herself. Irving's art was the whole of himself; and that was why he sacrificed himself—and everybody and everything else—to his art. It is a curious piece of artistic psychology, this, and will be misunderstood by stupid people and Philistines; but one does not write about artists of genius for people who know nothing about genius.

I have never, either in public or private, made any secret of my opinion that the Lyceum enterprise, famous as it became, was on the purely dramatic side of theatrical art a deplorable waste of two of the most remarkable talents of the last quarter of a century. In a former article I described how Irving used the plays of Shakespear as settings for figures which were the creations of his own fancy—how his Shylock was not Shakespear's Shylock, his Iachimo not Shakespear's Iachimo, his Lear not Shakespear's Lear. I may now add that if circumstances had forced Irving into the living drama of his own time—if he had gone forward from his early successes as Digby Grant in Albery's Two Roses to Ibsen's Master Builder and John Gabriel Borkman —if he had played Bishop Nicolas instead of Shakespear's Wolsey and Tennyson's Becket and Sardou's Dante—he would have carried the English theatre forward into line with the Scandinavian and German-speaking theatre instead of being, as he actually was, the most conspicuous obstacle to its development. Now in precisely the same way as he wasted his own talent on obsolete reactionary or Shakespearean drama, so also he wasted Ellen Terry's. He did so, of course, quite unconsciously: if anyone had accused him of it, he would have pointed to The Lady of Lyons, The Amber Heart, Wills's Faust, Olivia (an adaptation of Goldsmith's Vicar of Wakefield), the Shakespearean repertory, and finally, as a daring concession to the ultra-modern spirit made expressly for Ellen Terry's sake, Madame Sans Gêne. He would have asked whether anyone but a madman could say that a talent which had triumphed in all these masterpieces had been wasted. What more could any actress desire? Was not Shakespear the greatest of all dramatic poets, past, present, or future? Was not Goethe, though a foreigner, at least worthy to be "adapted" by Wills? Was not Lord Tennyson the Poet Laureate? Were obscure, eccentric, and immoral Norwegians and Germans—Ibsens, Hauptmanns, Sudermanns, and their English imitators—to be accepted at the Lyceum Theatre merely because literary cliques talked about them, and because Duse, Réjane, and English actresses poor enough to play for such private subscription enterprises as the Independent Theatre and the Stage Society occasionally played a new and objectionable sort of stage heroine like Nora Helmer, Magda, Hedda Gabler, etc., etc.?

All this seemed, and even still seems, sound common sense to the bulk of our English playgoers and their critical bellwethers. In Germany and Austria the position of Ellen Terry at the Lyceum Theatre will be more intelligible. It meant that she was completely cut off from the modern drama and all its intensely interesting heroines. And her opportunities in the older drama were much less satisfying than Irving's, because she understood Shakespear and played Beatrice, Juliet, Portia, Imogen, etc., intelligently and charmingly just as Shakespear planned them, whereas Irving, as Benedick, Romeo, Shylock, or Iachimo, was embodying some fancy of his own, the irrelevance of which only made it more enigmatic and consequently more Irvingesque and fascinating. It was inevitable that she should at last break loose from the Lyceum and practise her art under her own management.

But the question remains, why did she stay so long? The answer to that is that the Lyceum, whilst it starved her dramatically, gave great scope to her wonderful sense of pictorial art. Ellen Terry has always been adored by painters. She was married almost in her childhood to one of the greatest painters of her time.

Now whatever the Lyceum productions may have lacked in intellectual modernity, they never failed as stage pictures. If Ellen could not collaborate with Ibsen to explain the revolt of Nora Helmer, she could collaborate with Burne-Jones and Alma Tadema to make living pictures of Guinevere and Imogen. I quite forget what Tennyson's first play at the Lyceum Theatre was about; but I shall never forget Ellen Terry as Camma. I can recall picture after picture in which she and Irving posed as no other artists of that time could pose. Her incomparable beauty and his incomparable distinction: there lay the Lyceum magic: that was the spell that blinded everyone to the fact that the converts of the grim old gentleman in Norway were biding their time, and that when the enchantment of youth was no longer added to the enchantment of beauty, the Lyceum would come down like the walls of Jericho.

I escaped the illusion solely because I was a dramatist, and wanted Ellen Terry for my own plays. When her son, Mr. Gordon Craig, became a father she said that nobody would write plays for a grandmother. I immediately wrote Captain Brassbound's Conversion to prove the contrary. I had already tried to tempt her by writing into my play called The Man of Destiny a description of the heroine which is simply a description of Ellen Terry: a very faint one, by the way; for who can describe the indescribable? But Irving checkmated me on that occasion by announcing his desire to perform the play; and it was impossible for me to evade the compliment, though, of course, nothing came of it. In the case of Captain Brassbound's Conversion, it was impossible for Irving to persuade himself even momentarily that he could produce it. Yet it was clear that it was in plays of this modern kind, with parts for women which were intellectually interesting and of commanding importance, that Ellen Terry's future business lay. Of this she said nothing; but she could not be restrained from telling the world that she was born in 1848 and that her apparent youthfulness was an illusion: in short, that the day had gone by for the Lady of Lyons, Gretchen, and Juliet. Her withdrawal from Sir Henry Irving's company at last became inevitable, though she postponed it long after it had become urgently advisable in her own interest if not in his.

Even then her first step shewed all her old indifference to her own career. She produced Ibsen's Vikings in Helgeland solely to enable Mr Gordon Craig to make an expensive experiment in his peculiar methods of stage presentation. It was a most unnecessary maternal extravagance; for Mr Gordon Craig's new development of the art of the theatre had already been convincingly demonstrated in London. No doubt his processions of Vikings coming up the cliffs from the sea in the moonlight, with their spears used as cunningly for decorative purposes as the spears in Velasquez's Surrender at Breda, or in the pictures of Paolo di Uccello, were very striking, and very instructive as to the possibility of doing away with the eternal flat wooden floor and footlight illumination which are so destructive of stage illusion; but they could not enable Ellen Terry to contradict her own nature by playing the fierce Hiordis of Ibsen convincingly. The public wanted Ellen Terry in an Ellen Terry part, and was too Philistine to see the beauty or care about the importance of Mr Gordon Craig's art. So Mr Gordon Craig shook the dust of London off his feet, and went to Germany. And Ellen Terry at last did what she should have done many years before—devoted herself to a modern play written for her by a modern playwright. She made a decisive success in creating Sir James Barrie's Alice Sit by the Fire; and she will follow that up next March [1905] by at last appearing as Lady Cicely in Captain Brassbound's Conversion, which has waited seven years for her. And here for the present I must leave her; for her saga is not yet ended.

P.S. 1930. Her saga as an actress ended with her impersonation of Lady Cicely, which she played on her final tour through America as her farewell to the stage. But she lived to be eighty and Dame Grand Cross of The British Empire. To the generation that grew up with the Great War, to which horror she never deigned to hold a candle, she had become a legend. She was born in 1848 and died in 1928.

THE INVECTIVE OF HENRY ARTHUR JONES

MY DEAR WELLS. A Manual for the Haters of England. By Henry Arthur Jones. (Eveleigh Nash & Grayson.)

From The Sunday Chronicle, 20 November 1921

I AM a patient man, being naturally timid; but really my old friend Henry Arthur Jones has been a little inconsiderate this time. He has written a book abusing me and Mr H. G. Wells up hill and down dale. Such vituperation has not been current in English print since the days of Milton and Salmasius.

Now dear Jones knows that he is welcome to abuse me until he is black in the face without estranging me in the least. But in this book he not only vilipends me with the most amazing copiousness merely to exercise his own powers of invective: he actually finishes by appealing to me in the most moving terms to come and keep up the game with him, because Wells will do nothing but call him the most fearful names, and compare his mind to threepenn'orth of cat's meat.

Wells, you see, is under no ancient obligations to Jones; he has never committed himself, as I have, to Jones's eminence among British playwrights; and, as he and Jones are both English through and through, they are natural enemies, and can pitch into one another wholeheartedly.

But if I pretend to think that Jones's mind is no better than threepenn'orth of cat's meat, he will dig up my old Saturday Review articles and confute me from my own pen.

If I take him on as an Optimist Imperialist, as the Hammer of the Bolshevists and the champion of victorious England As She Is, he will remind me of the days when he read revolutionary plays to William Morris, Emery Walker, and myself, and quote triumphantly his latest psalm of faith:

> In some respects our present civilization
> Is the most hideous that the world has ever known;
> There are many things in it that sadly need to be changed,
> And some things that need to be destroyed.
>   I do not seek
> To perpetuate the present social order
>   It must inevitably submit
> To vast and ever-swiftening changes,

to shew that I am a piffling Constitutionalist compared to him. He talks of the inhabitants of Europe as "the blind, helpless, tortured masses"; and if I remonstrate, he will probably call me a bourgeois. I should never know where to have him.

He denounces Wells for *scandalum magnatum* because Wells is not impressed with the wisdom with which Parliament has handled the peace; but Jones's own name for the House of Commons is The Bauble Shop. If I take the other tack and hail him as an ultra-incarnadined Red and try to sing the Internationale with him, he will call the police.

Again, if I apologize for occasionally chaffing his countrymen for being a little thoughtless, he will revile me for being as pitiable a gull as Wells, to whom he says, "If statistics were available we should find that the number of non-thinkers in Europe would enormously exceed your estimate of half the population."

If I disparage human nature, he will call me the enemy of England: if I extol it, he will out-Swift Swift by repeating that "old lace is one of those graceful perquisites of her sex whereby the mate of man has made herself something different from the mate of the gorilla."

If I agree with him that "the late disastrous world-conflict was immediately caused by the failure of a certain number of European politicians to think clearly, honestly, and righteously," he will call me a traitor. If I disagree with him, he will call me a liar.

SOCIALISM AS WE HAVE IT

He pledges himself to become a good Socialist if I can shew him Socialism "in actual operation even upon the smallest scale among the smallest community"; but I know very well that if I point out to him that London, which is not a particularly small community, depends for its very existence and possibility on pure Communism in highways and bridges, scavenging and lighting, police protection, military and naval defence, public health service, the Throne and the Church, the National Gallery and the British Museum library, the parks and open spaces, not to mention the Collectivism to which we owe our municipal electric light services, our public baths, and so forth, he will throw his boots at me, and go on telling Wells on every third page that he owes the quiet enjoyment of "his motor-car and cosy dividends," not to our Communist police force, but to the private capitalists who are standing heroically between Wells's garage and that notorious motor-car snatcher, Lenin.

There is no reasoning with Jones. He goes to America because he finds himself better off there than in England, and then turns round and tells Wells, who sticks patriotically to his native soil, that "the British Empire, however imperfect it may be, and open to improvement in many ways, does yet offer to its hundreds of millions of citizens an average degree of security, comfort, and happiness, immeasurably greater than they would enjoy if it were pulled to pieces"—America, which has tried the experiment, being, if you please, one of the pieces.

He asks: "Have you ever considered what would be the effect of a general repudiation of national debt on the entire civilization of the world? Are you able even to imagine the incalculable misery and ruin it would work for a generation to come?"

This to me, who am one of the creditors, and have already had between 30 and 40 per cent of my loan repudiated by the Commissioners of Inland Revenue! This to a world where the nations are discussing repudiation all round (cancel is the expression they use), because payment means just that misery and ruin that Jones threatens if they dont pay. Why, most of them have not paid a farthing of interest yet.

IDEAL AND FACT

He exhorts Wells to observe "those great unchanging rules of life and conduct, those sovereign laws of communal and national well-being, eternally fixed, and as old as the world itself, whereby through all time past nations have established themselves in peace and prosperity and happiness," as if our whole trouble were not that neither in Wells's Outline of History nor in any other human record can we find a single civilized nation or empire in which more than one-tenth of the population could feel sure of their daily bread from one year to another, or whose history is not that of a rapid rise to a plutocratic pseudo-prosperity followed by a Gibbonian decline and fall, through the buffleheadedness of those citizens who, though leisured and educated enough to be capable of social criticism, remained the same dear old Henry Arthur Jugginses, and let themselves be persuaded that capitalist laws lead straight to an earthly paradise, and that communal ones must land them in "a filthy bog of misery, disease, starvation, and despair."

It is useless for Jones to adjure me to face him and answer him. I cannot do it. I am beaten. I throw up my hands. Kamerad! Kamerad!

Yet I make one condition before surrendering. That is, that Jones, if he must quote Sheridan, will quote him correctly, and not turn his blank verse into octosyllabic couplets. Sheridan did not write—

> The Spanish fleet thou canst not see,
> Because it is not yet in sight.

The line, so delivered, would be utterly spoilt. He wrote—

> The Spanish fleet thou canst not see, because
> It is not yet in sight.

Really, Henry Arthur, you might at least join your flats. You remind me of a chairman I once had, who, in the presence of Morris himself, quoted Goldsmith thus:

> Curst be that wretched land,
> To hastening ills a prey,
> Where wealth accumulates,
> And working men decay.

WELLS'S METHOD

Wells, who is not a Socialist for nothing, has countered Jones with the *coup de Lassalle*. It is a stroke that can be played only by a man in a commanding intellectual position against an opponent manifestly his inferior in knowledge of the subject in hand.

Lassalle used to say: "Sir, I will not argue with you. If I call you a fool, everyone will believe me. If you call me a fool, all Europe will laugh at you." Wells has resorted to this counter ruthlessly, varying it only by substituting for the crude word fool a volley of more amusing epithets.

And Jones, who, by the way, has achieved the extraordinary feat of losing his head without quite losing his sense of humor, finds himself quite helpless, and can only fall back on Shakespear by embracing the epithets merrily, and bringing down the house with "Forget not that I am an ass."

But he does not consider this fair fighting; for he adjures me at the top of his eloquence not to play those tricks on him.

"Take up my challenge which he refuses," he cries. "*You* will not pompously and fatuously announce, as he does, 'I never argue with Henry Arthur Jones.' You will not throw up your hands and scuttle to that miserable shelter. Face me and answer me. Heres much matter for you to jibe at. You, who so long have jibed at England, to the applause of your addled English worshippers, now jibe at me. Your pen! Quick! You scent your job. About it, straight."

Who could resist such an appeal? But what am I to say? I do not want to jibe at Jones. I have to jibe at England because that is the classical English way to make her sit up, as practised by all the great novelists and playwrights from Fielding to Dickens, and from Dickens to Henry Arthur himself.

But what good will jibing at Jones do? On the face of it he has got himself into a mess. If I mount the literary high horse, and stand on the common civility due to Wells as one of the greatest living English writers, I must say with pompous austerity that this book is a shocking book; that it should never have been written; and that no reputable court of honor, literary or general, could pronounce any other judgment on it.

But how can I mount the high horse and deliver a moral lecture (that exercise so dear to Englishmen!) when my rebuke would be provoked by a book which is an example of moral lecturing gone mad?

Besides, this is not a shocking book. It is a crazy book. It calls for a psycho-analyst, not for a Pecksniff. My friend Jones is suffering from a suppressed desire. I will not argue with him. I will not jibe at him. I will explain him.

Thirty years ago there were only two playwrights in London who counted seriously when it came to full-length original work. They were Pinero and Jones. Carton had not fully arrived; Grundy was successful only as a translator and adapter. Never again, probably, will the British stage narrow to the width of two men; but it had done so then; and one of the men was Jones.

Max Beerbohm and I, as critics, praised Jones for all we were worth. Pinero was passing through a temporary Feminist phase, from which we wanted to drive him back to social criticism; but he had a splendid Press behind him, headed by our friend William Archer. Just then a frightful blow was struck at the position of every playwright in Europe by the impact of Ibsen, who for a while made even Shakespear unbearable; but the London play-goers remained faithful to Pinero and Jones.

It seems impossible today, when Pinero has more than half a dozen fully-established colleagues who are no disgrace to him, that he should have had only one serious rival even before he had quite sowed his wild oats; but so it was.

Then a strange thing happened. Jones suddenly shook the dust of the London stage from his feet, and went to America. Our young lions today, roaring about Dunsany and Stravinsky, ask quite sincerely: "Who on earth is Henry Arthur Jones?"

Pinero they know, Barrie they know, me they know, as figures surviving to prove that the remote past was not wholly fabulous; but they are only vacantly curious about Jones because they have never felt the touch of his vanished hand.

Mr Jones much alive

Yet Jones has not lost his vigor: never in his life has he been more obstreperous. Read the eighteen pages (265-283) he has consecrated to me in this book. Read the sentence beginning on page 274 with "Know that this is your appointed lot," and ending on page 277. It contains more than 800 words, and stops then only because the printer, in desperation, has bunged in a full-point.

I read that sentence to my wife, and at the end we found ourselves cheering with excitement. "Whaurs your Jeremiah, your Junius, your Ruskin, your Carlyle the noo?" we exclaimed. What a speech for the stage!

I have not room to quote it at length; but take this other little sentence as a sample:

"Believe and build upon this centrepiece of truth, that whatever changes and convulsions may shake and split asunder the peoples, no world chasm shall ever open that shall not find America and England standing together on the same side of its pit."

Hooray! I repeat, Hooray! I defy Wells not to join in the applause.

The pit may be only the pit of the theatre, or it may be that bottomless pit in which so many Americans and Englishmen have perished together in mortal strife; but can you deny that this is good stage stuff, and that it is a tragedy that the man who at seventy can still write it easily, profusely, 800 words at a mouthful, should be driven from the London stage to waste himself in writing nonsense books against his most distinguished fellow-countryman and his pet Irishman, sooner than sit miserable, like a giant set to peel potatoes, with his rhetorical muscles atrophying from disuse?

And there you have the explanation of the whole matter.

Jones, a more amiable man personally, perhaps, than either Wells or myself, has a genius for paper violence, for stage hatred, for comminatory rhetoric, which would have found scope in Elizabethan England or Periclean Athens.

The London stage offered him no opportunity of exercising it to his heart's content. Finding no anvil there for his hammer, he tried smashing teacups and flattening out butterflies with it.

His plays became more and more splenetic; the vehemence with which he made himself disagreeable to insignificant and uninteresting people jarred on our easy-going public; and the string of great successes, from The Silver King in 1882 to Mrs Dane's

Defence in 1900 (how many playwrights can boast such a career?), was succeeded by the Hegira to New York, and the disappearance of a new play by Henry Arthur Jones from the list of important and inevitable features of our theatrical seasons.

It is a great pity, and it is a reproach to our national culture as well. If we had had a theatre big enough for him to declaim in, and a drama big enough at its summit to bear Jeremiads without making Jeremiah ridiculous, we should still have our Henry Arthur doing his proper work, instead of desperately pretending that Wells is a mischievous and brainless ignoramus, and I "a freakish homunculus germinated outside lawful procreation."

He is just launching at us, *à tort et à travers*, all the baffled stage tirades he has been bursting with in exile for the last twenty years.

By the way, as the statement that I germinated outside lawful procreation has caused some people to conclude that either Henry Arthur is quite mad, or else my mother must have been of the mould of the Mothers of Falconbridge and Dunois, I had better explain that my family traces its descent from one Shaigh, the third son of Macduff, immortalized by Shakespear as having been "from his mother's womb untimely ripped."

I think it must have been some vague recollection of this interesting piece of genealogy that moved Jones to so scandalous an invective.

I protest I am the unquestioned lawful heir of my mother's property and my father's debts; and if Jones will come to tea (or any other meal) with me, not only will he be cordially welcomed, but he can inspect the family photographs, which will convince him that, extraordinary as I am, I am none the less unmistakeably the son of my reputed father.

I flatter myself that his publishers would never have ventured on such a roaring libel if he had not given them his guarantee that my friendship could be depended on. And he was quite right.

KEATS

From a Memorial Volume

IT is very difficult to say anything about Keats except that he was a poet. His merits are a matter of taste. Anyone who can read his best lines without being enchanted by them is verse-deaf. But whether the enchantment works or fails there is nothing more to be said. Other poets have other strings to their bows. Macaulay could have written a very interesting essay on Shelley without liking or even mentioning a line of his verse. He did write a very interesting essay on Byron, which would have been equally readable had Byron been an amateur like Count D'Orsay. Societies have been established to discuss Browning; and they would not have held a meeting the less if Browning had been a revivalist preacher who had never penned a rhyme in his life. But out of Keats Macaulay could not have made two pages; and a Keats Society would be gravelled for lack of matter half-way through its first sitting unless it resolved itself into a Fanny Brawne Society, when it might conceivably make good for a few evenings of gossip. Being at this moment asked to write about Keats, a thing I should never have dreamt of doing on my own initiative, I find myself with nothing to say except that you cannot write about Keats.

Another way of putting this is to say that he was the most literary of all the major poets: literary to the verge of being but the greatest of the minor poets; only, if you go over that verge you achieve a *reductio ad absurdum*; for the strength of a poet is the strength of his strongest lines; and Keats's strongest lines are so lovely, and there are so many of them, that to think of him as a minor poet is impossible. Even his worst lines: for example,

> A bunch of blooming plums
> Ready to melt between an infant's gums,

have nothing minor about them; they are not poor would-be lines: they are brazenly infamous, like Shakespear's

> In a most hideous and dreadful manner,

which I once accused Ellen Terry of having improvised to cover a lapse of memory, so incredible it seemed that Shakespear should have perpetrated it.

What I mean by a literary poet is one who writes poetry for the sake of writing poetry; who lisps in numbers because he prefers that method of utterance; who wants to be a poet as if that were an end in itself. Such a one will force the forms and graces of poetry on the most prosaic subject matter, and turn a page of prose into a thousand lines of epic. Poe, a master of both prose and verse, complained that epics are not really homogeneous poems, but patches of poetry embroidered on long stretches of prosaic fabric disguised as poetry by the arts of versification. Even Milton did this, though no man knew better than he that prose has a music of its own, and that many pensters write verses because their ears are not good enough to enable them to write readable prose, and because, though nobody will give them any credit for calling a window a window, lots of people will take them for poets if they call it a casement.

Now Keats was the sort of youth who calls a window a casement. That was why the reviewers told him to go back to his gallipots. Critics who are only waiting for a chance to make themselves disagreeable trip themselves by jumping at the chance, when it comes, without looking before they leap. If an apothecary's apprentice happens to be born a poet, one of the first symptoms of his destiny will be a tendency to call windows casements (on paper). The fact that if he is born a poetaster the symptoms will be just the same, may mislead a bad critic, but not a good one, unless the good one (as often happens) is such a snob that when he has to review the poems of a shopman the critic in him is killed by the snob. If Keats had ever described a process so remote from Parnassus as the taking down and putting up of the shop shutters, he would have described them in terms of a radiant sunrise and a voluptuous sunset, with the red and green bottles as heavenly bodies and the medicines as Arabian Balsams. What a good critic would have said to him was not "Go back to your gallipots," but "If you can call a window a casement with such magical effect, for heaven's sake leave your gallipots and do nothing but write poetry all your life."

The other sort of poet is the one for whom poetry is only a means to an end, the end being to deliver a message which clamors to be revealed through him. So he secures a hearing for it by clothing it with word-garments of such beauty, authority, and eternal memorableness, that the world must needs listen to it. These are prophets rather than poets; and for the sake of being poets alone would not take the trouble to rhyme love and dove or bliss and kiss.

It often happens that a prophet-poet begins as a literary poet, the prophet instinctively training himself by literary exercises for his future work. Thus you have Morris exercising himself in his youth by re-writing all the old stories in very lovely verses, but conscientiously stating at the beginning that he is only "the idle singer of an empty day." Later on he finds his destiny as propagandist and prophet, the busy singer of a bursting day. Now if Morris had lived no longer than Keats, he would have been an even more exclusively literary poet, because Keats achieved the very curious feat of writing one poem of which it may be said that if Karl Marx can be imagined as writing a poem instead of a treatise on Capital, he would have written Isabella. The immense indictment of the profiteers and exploiters with which Marx has shaken capitalistic civilization to its foundations, even to its overthrow in Russia, is epitomized in

> With her two brothers this fair lady dwelt
>   Enrichéd from ancestral merchandise;
> And for them many a weary hand did swelt
>   In torchéd mines and noisy factories;
> And many once proud-quivered loins did melt
>   In blood from stinging whip: with hollow eyes
> Many all day in dashing river stood
> To take the rich-ored driftings of the flood.
>
> For them the Ceylon diver held his breath,
>   And went all naked to the hungry shark:

For them his ears gushed blood: for them in death
  The seal on the cold ice with piteous bark
Lay full of darts: for them alone did seethe
  A thousand men in troubles wide and dark.
Half ignorant, they turned an easy wheel
That set sharp racks at work to pinch and peel.

Why were they proud? Because their marble founts
  Gush'd with more pride than do a wretch's tears?
Why were they proud? Because fair orange-mounts
  Were of more soft ascent than lazar stairs?
Why were they proud? Because red-lin'd accounts
  Were richer than the songs of Grecian years?
Why were they proud? Again we ask aloud,
Why in the name of Glory were they proud?

Everything that the Bolshevik stigmatizes when he uses the epithet "bourgeois" is expressed forcibly, completely, and beautifully in those three stanzas, written half a century before the huge tide of middle-class commercial optimism and complacency began to ebb in the wake of the planet Marx. Nothing could well be more literary than the wording: it is positively euphuistic. But it contains all the Factory Commission Reports that Marx read, and that Keats did not read because they were not yet written in his time. And so Keats is among the prophets with Shelley, and, had he lived, would no doubt have come down from Hyperions and Endymions to tin tacks as a very full-blooded modern revolutionist. Karl Marx is more euphuistic in calling the profiteers *bourgeoisie* than Keats with his "these same ledger-men." Ledger-men is at least better English than bourgeois: there would be some hope for it yet if it had not been supplanted by profiteer.

Keats also anticipated Erewhon Butler's gospel of Laodicea in the lines beginning (Shakespeareanly) with

How fever'd is the man who cannot look
Upon his mortal days with temperate blood!

triumphantly driving home the nail at the end with (Words-worthily)

> Why then should Man, teasing the world for grace,
> Spoil his salvation for a fierce miscreed?

On the whole, in spite of the two idle epics, voluptuously literary, and the holiday globe-trotting "from silken Samarcand to cedar'd Lebanon," Keats manages to affirm himself as a man as well as a poet, and to win a place among the great poets in virtue of a future he never lived to see, and of poems he never lived to write. And he contributed a needed element to that august Communion of Saints: the element of geniality, rarely associated with lyrical genius of the first order. Dante is not notably genial. Milton can do a stunt of geniality, as in L'Allegro; but one does not see him exuberantly fighting the butcher, as Keats is said to have done. Wordsworth, cheerful at times as a pious duty, is not genial. Cowper's John Gilpin is a turnpike tragedy. Even the thought of Shelley kills geniality. Chesterton's resolute conviviality is about as genial as an *auto da fé* of teetotallers. Byron's joy is derision. When Moore is merry he ceases to be a poet so utterly that we are tempted to ask when did he begin. Landor and Browning are capable of Olympian joviality: their notion of geniality is shying thunderbolts. Mr Pecksniff, saying "Let us be merry" and taking a captain's biscuit, is as successful as most of them. If Swinburne had attempted to be genial he would have become a mere blackguard; and Tennyson would have been like a jeweller trying to make golliwogs. Keats alone remains for us not only a poet, but a merry soul, a jolly fellow, who could not only carry his splendid burthen of genius, but swing it round, toss it up and catch it again, and whistle a tune as he strode along.

But there is no end to talking about poets; and it often prevents people reading them; so enough.

VERNON LEE'S WAR TRILOGY

Satan the Waster: A Philosophic War Trilogy. With Notes
and Introduction. By Vernon Lee. (Lane.)

From The Nation, 18 September 1920

This book is something more than the latest literary product of
a well-known author. It is a trophy of the war for England. It
proves what everyone has lately been driven to doubt, that it is
possible to be born in England and yet have intellect, to train
English minds as well as English muscles, and to impart knowledge to Britons. The problem remains, how is it then possible
for a nation to produce a woman like Vernon Lee, and at the
same time choose Mr Lloyd George and Sir Edward Carson as
its dictators? The contrast is overwhelming. Put the Prime
Minister's most important speech—say that on the Polish crisis
the other day—beside the most trifling of Vernon Lee's notes
to Satan the Waster, and it immediately becomes apparent that
Mr Lloyd George leads the English people only as a nurserymaid
leads her little convoy of children, by knowing her way about
within a radius of half a mile or so, and being quick at guessing
what promise or threat will fill them with childish hopes or
terrors, as the case may be. As for Sir Edward, he becomes the
policeman who misdirects the nurserymaid because he has
rashly undertaken fixed point duty in a strange district much too
big for his powers of comprehension. One sees the nurserymaid
turn in her bewilderment from the policeman who does not know
his job to the soldier who does, raising her little song of "Another
little war, and another little war, and another little war wont do
us any harm." "Certainly not," says the soldier: "it will do you
a lot of good. Besides, it is absolutely necessary to prevent
another big war." And the poor nurserymaid is not clever enough
to ask why wars should be prevented if they are so wholesome.
So she takes on the airs of a nursery-governess, and gives a
history lesson, starting with the announcement that the independence of Poland is indispensable to the peace of Europe, the

children being too young to know that Poland has been dependent and subjugate for a century and a half or so without protest from the nurserymaid, and with a most pacific effect on Central Europe, whatever the effect may have been on the Poles themselves. What the Foreign Office wanted her to say was that Polish independence may be worth a war from the point of view of Balance of Power diplomacy now that there is a possibility of Russia and Germany combining *contra mundum*, the officially correct remedy being the establishment and maintenance of a buffer State between them. What will happen when the buffer State sees the obvious advantage of making a Triplice (as Belgium had to) with the two adjacent bogies is a speculation outside the nurserymaid's half-mile radius. After all, the European reactions of a war are uncertain and remote: the khaki votes and profits at home are certain. Norman Angell said that wars do not pay; but the nurserymaid has never had her mouth so full of chocolates in her life, and therefore thinks she knows better. If it were not for the sudden appearance of certain hooligans (for so the nurserymaid scornfully classes the working man in Council of Action) with bricks in their hands, and a very evident disposition to shy them, the unfortunate children would be up to their necks in blood literally before they knew where they were, as in 1914.

The nurserymaid has, as she thinks, some clever ideas about war. For instance, why declare war on Russia? Just send Poland arms and ammunition and food, and make our gallant fellows in Dantzig work for her behind the lines whilst our splendid navy blockades and if necessary bombards the Russians. The Russians will not be able to retaliate because we shall not be at war with them; so that we shall have all the fun of being at war without any of the unpleasantness of being torpedoed or bombed or reading casualty lists. Do not suppose that the nurserymaid is sagacious enough to be calculating on what would actually happen: namely, that Russia would be forced to declare war on us, and that the moment she killed a British soldier we should rush to arms and accept conscription again. If she were Machiavellian enough for that, she would also have gumption enough to know that a forced choice between conscription or revolution might make Lenin master of the situation. The nurserymaid cannot understand Lenin—finds him "incoherent" when every intellectually competent person in Europe finds him only too terribly logical. Lenin keeps on saying to the British workman, "Why dont you remove these aristocratic Curzons and Churchills and these *bourgeois* Carsons and Georges who are standing in our way and yours? You know you will have to do it some day: why not do it now?" He is too much the gentleman and diplomatist to use a shorter word than remove; but his meaning is clear; only the poor nurserymaid cannot grasp it, because she is not accustomed to be spoken to like that. She takes refuge with Mr Balfour, crying "Speak to this sarcastic man for me, will you, sir?" And he, having wasted the last thirty years of his life helping political nurserymaids over stiles and escorting them past strange cows, does his best for a hopeless client.

Now why do I push this similitude of the nurserymaid so far? Because I cannot get away from it whilst Vernon Lee is standing beside Mr Lloyd George. You cannot read a page of Satan the Waster without feeling like that about the Prime Minister. Vernon Lee has the whole European situation in the hollow of her hand: Mr Lloyd George cannot co-ordinate its most obviously related factors. Vernon Lee knows history philosophically: Mr Lloyd George barely knows geography topographically. Vernon Lee is a political psychologist: Mr Lloyd George is a claptrap expert. Vernon Lee, as her dated notes to this book prove, has never been wrong once since the war began: Mr Lloyd George has never been right, as his speeches will prove if anyone will take the trouble to dig them up. Vernon Lee, by sheer intellectual force, training, knowledge, and character, kept her head when Europe was a mere lunatic asylum; Mr Lloyd George hustled through only because, in matters of wide scope, he had no head to lose. And remember, Vernon Lee is an Englishwoman. Had she been Irish, like me, there would have been nothing in her dispassionateness: the three devastated streets of Louvain would have been balanced (not to say overbalanced) by the three hundred devastated acres of Dublin; and "the broken treaty" would have meant for her the treaty of Limerick. No wonder I had a comparatively mild attack of war fever. But Vernon Lee is English of the English, and yet held her intellectual own all through. I take off my hat to the old guard of Victorian cosmopolitan intellectualism, and salute her as the noblest Briton of them all.

I will now ask the reader to look back a few lines to the string of contrasts which I have drawn between Vernon Lee and Mr Lloyd George, and ask him to read them again, substituting the name of Lenin for that of our Prime Minister. They immediately become ridiculous; and that is a very serious matter for us. Lenin can say to Vernon Lee, "Let the galled jade wince: *our* withers are unwrung." Lenin has made mistakes of practice, and admitted them. Lenin has made, or at least been forced to tolerate, mistakes in industrial organization which the Sidney Webbs would not have made, and has scrapped them frankly and effectively. Like all the other European statesmen, he has had to wade through atrocities; though he alone has neither denied them nor pretended that they were all inevitable. But Lenin has kept his head; has talked no manifest nonsense; has done nothing without knowing what he was doing; has taken the blether of his enemies as he has taken the bullets their assassins shot into him, without flinching intellectually. And he has surrounded himself, as far as the supply would permit, with men of his own calibre. Lord Curzon was able to hang up the Russian question in England for many months because he was too uppish to communicate with Mr Litvinoff, just as Lord Randolph Churchill was too haughty to speak to Mrs Asquith at dinner, when she was "only a Miss"; but Lenin and his extremely able envoy Krassin were not too uppish to communicate with Lord Curzon, even when he was so absurd as to offer his services with a magnanimous air to negotiate between Russia and General Wrangel, as between one European Power and another, on the question of which shall possess that well-known dependency of the British Empire called the Crimea.

What can we expect if we go on pitting British rabbits against Russian serpents, British boodle and bunkum against Russian fanaticism and realism: in short, sixth-rate political intellects against first-rate ones, and the education and outlook of Henry VII, piously preserved by taxidermist pedagogues in scholastic museums, against the ideas and outlook of Buckle, Marx, Nietzsche, Bergson, and the rest of the live wires of our super-charged time? The whole capitalized world is bursting with an impulse towards "the dictatorship of the proletariat," because the proletariat means simply the whole body of people who live by working, as against the handful who, as the Duke of Northumberland put it, live by owning, or, as Ruskin put it, by begging and stealing. Mr Smillie can floor Mr Lloyd George by challenging him to prevent the coal strike, or any strike, by simply making industrial and social service compulsory for all classes (and all incomes) as Lenin has done. Democracy and liberty have no meaning except as affirmations of the vital need for this supremacy of the proletariat; and yet our Prime Minister, ignorant of the meaning of the words, thinks he has only to hold up the phrase as a bogy to the children he is nursemaiding to defeat an antagonist of Lenin's quality. If he can do no better than that with Red Armies ready to spring into existence in every country in Europe and every State in America at a wave of Lenin's hand, the sooner we put Vernon Lee into the position occupied three hundred years ago by Queen Elizabeth the better.

But this is by way of being a review of Vernon Lee's book, and not a phrenologist's chart of Mr George's bumps. The book, of first-rate workmanship from beginning to end, is far too thorough to leave the reviewer anything to say about it that is not better said in the book itself; but to aid the contrast I have suggested between Vernon Lee's braininess and Mr George's bumptiousness, I append a few samples of the good things with which Satan the Waster is stuffed on every page, merely adding that the dramatic power and stage dexterity with which the work has been framed are quite adequate, and that there is no reason in the world why Vernon Lee should not have been a successful playwright except that her subject matter is above the heads of our theatrical caterers, and, doubtless, of the suburban playgoers whose taste in high politics is for hanging the Kaiser.

"The long duration of this war has resulted less from its hitherto undreamed of military machinery, less from the even more unprecedented wholesale fabrication of public opinion, than from the spiritual mechanism of errors and myths which the vastness, the identity of this war's dangers and sacrifices automatically set up in the minds of all the warring peoples." [The word long should now be omitted, as the war is now seen to have been, in fact, an amazingly short one.]—(Page 20.)

"When war suddenly bursts out among people who are thinking of other matters, the first thing they become aware of is that, in the Kaiser's symbolic words, *they did not want it.* And feeling certain that it was not of their willing, they inevitably lay hold of the belief that the other party must have wanted and willed it."—(Page 22.)

"To the modern conscience in time of peace, war is a monstrosity complicated by an absurdity; hence no one can believe himself to have had a hand in bringing it about."—(Page 23.)

"I need not introduce to you our old friend, Clio, Muse of History by profession, but, may I say it? by preference and true vocation, dramatic critic."—(Page 33.)

"Self Interest, a most industrious fellow. It is he who, on week days, plays unremittingly the ground bass of Life."—(Page 34.)

"Sin, whom the all-knowing Gods call *Disease.*"—(Page 35.)

"Hatred, the stupidest of all Passions, yet the most cunning in deceit, brought with him a double-bass of many strings: shrill and plaintive gut, rasping steel, and growling bronze, and more besides; some strange comforting in their tone like a rich cordial, although they heartened men to massacre each other."—(Page 36.)

"Ye are going forth, O Nations, to join Death's Dance even as candid high-hearted virgins who have been decoyed by fair show into the house of prostitution."—(Page 45.)

"Calamities of this kind do not spring from the small and

negligible item which suffering and angry men call *guilt*."—
(Page 94.)

"Not the air and the waters and the earth's upturned soil, nor
the grass and the forests, nor the moon and the stars, are, as
our ancestors thought, full of unseen and malevolent spiritual
dwellers, but a place more mysterious and perilous, namely,
the spirit of man, where they lurk unsuspected, and issue forth
working subtle or terrific havoc. The spells by which they are
let loose are *words*. And the thoughtless magician's apprentice,
the unhallowed hierophant, who plays with them, is the man or
woman whom we pay to teach us, preach to us, and, above all,
to write."—(Page 134.)

"Certain states of the nerves, nay of the muscles, are incompatible with certain thoughts: a clenched fist, for instance, with
the notion that there is something to be said for the other side."—
(Page 161.)

"The importance of the notion of evolution and all it has
brought with it, lies largely in its teaching us to think genetically,
which means thinking in terms not of stability, but of change.
And this has led a small school of thinkers of today, whose
thought will perhaps be dominant tomorrow, to the recognition
that, in order *to understand what a thing is*, we must ask ourselves:
What has it been, and what will it become?"—(Page 178.)

"What was the name of that retired Admiral who went about
the country sowing acorns in order that England might never
lack for oaken timbers, just at the very moment when the first
iron ships were on the stocks? We are like that old gentleman;
only, instead of acorns, we are sowing hatred, injustice, and
folly." [Collingwood. But where is the first iron ship? Nothing
of the kind is visible so far except a coffin ship with League of
Nations painted on it, and a black flag in its locker. Perhaps
something better may come out of the Russian dockyard.]—
(Page 180.)

"Indeed, our optimistic talk about *extracting good out of evil* is,
perhaps, one of Satan's little ironical tricks for, in his way, extracting evil out of good."—(Page 191.)

"Patriotism, as a collective though compound passion, requires for its existence segregation, opposition, antagonism, and I venture to add: hostility. . . . Patriotism can be considered virtuous or vicious only according to circumstances; and hence cannot be called virtuous or vicious taken in itself and, so to speak, in its own right."—(Page 234.)

"Statesmen prudently insisting on Preparedness, imprudently overlook that it calls forth Preparedness on the other side; and that the two Preparednesses collide, till both parties find themselves at war; and, in immeasurable, honest (or well-feigned) surprise, accuse the other party of breaking the peace, thus elaborately and expensively safeguarded."—(Page 245.)

"But what the poor world of reality really requires are heroes who can be heroic, and saints who can be saintly, on their own account, without a crowd to back them."—(Page 285.)

"Indignation (let us admit and try to remember this depressing truth!), Indignation is a passion which enjoys itself."—(Page 287.)

"Our guides and guardians, moralists, philosophers, priests, journalists, as much as persons in office, stand to cut a sorry figure before posterity, singling out, as they do, one of themselves, *e.g.*, the deposed and defeated Kaiser, as most convenient for hanging, but with no thought for some quiet Potter's Field suicide for themselves."—(Page 289.)

"The Nations were not aware of what war might do with their bodies and especially with their souls. But how about their guides and guardians?"—(Page 291.)

"Freedom of the Will, in the least metaphysical, the most empirical sense, is not, as theologians used to teach, a permanent possession of the soul. Its very essence is that it lapses by surrender; and that nine times out of ten, the freedom to do, or to refrain, is lost by the initial choice; and, as regards love or war, can be recovered only when the new circumstances which that decision has brought about, and that new self of yours, have run their course and been exhausted. You are a free agent so long as you have not set that stone, *yourself*, a-rolling. Once the push

given, the brink left behind, the forces outside and inside yourself, the strange unsuspected attraction, weight and velocity,
reduce you to helplessness."—(Page 295.)

H. W. MASSINGHAM

Contributed to a Memoir, 1925

SOMETIME in the eighteen-eighties I became conscious of
H. W. Massingham in the journalistic world. Of our first
meeting I have no recollection. I was certainly not introduced
to him: he arises in my memory as a person known to me quite
intimately, and often called The Boy. The name was not suggested by his bodily build; for at that time the slenderness and
fragility of his later time was covered up by big high shoulders
into which his cheeks sank readily when his unsleeping sense of
humor set him chuckling; and his shirt front seemed at least
twice as broad as anyone else's when he was in evening dress.
But he was always what we call youthful, in virtue of a quality
which is certainly not youth at all, as it is proof against years.
But we call it so; and the term will serve. There are people who
are born forty, and die forty plus some years of decay. There are
people who are born twenty and do not grow up. Massingham
was one of the young ones: he never became venerable or stiff
or solemn; and he never ceased to chuckle. He was physically
thinskinned (I remember his shrieks when a friendly cat once
fleshed its claws on his knee with a fearful facility of laceration),
and mentally fine to a degree most unusual in his profession.

He must have formed the incurable habit of journalism, which
may be defined as the habit of stating public problems without
ever having time to solve them, very early in life; for he was
quite well qualified to write books, and might have been a notable
author, much as a station master at one of the great European
railway centres might be a notable traveller if he were not too
busy despatching trains to all the cities of the earth ever to visit
them himself. As far as I know, he never wrote a book or a play,
nor even tried to. He knew nothing of those dull and dreadful

moments when the writer of books sits down to his desk and wonders what story to spin out of his unfurnished entrails. To Massingham the world daily handed endless stores of material with both hands, material that played vigorously on his alert political sympathies, on his unfailing interest in contemporary life, and on his sense of humor. To him the stuff of fiction was too insipid, too unreal, too hackneyed, to nerve him to pen a line: it was much better fun making Campbell-Bannerman Prime Minister than helping a fictitious long-lost earl to his coronet in the last chapter of a novel which he could not have endured to read if in a moment of aberration he had succeeded in writing it. He was an enthusiastic amateur of literature, and a first-rate critic of it and of the theatre as well as of Parliament; but it must have been apparent to him that his work as a journalist required much more ability, knowledge of the world, and skill with the pen than ordinary fiction, and that the extraordinary authors who were his heroes were really great journalists whose journalism was too good for any newspaper to make its living by. The technical proof that he was not condemned to editorship by inability to succeed as an author is that he proved himself one of the best feuilletonists in London. I was a feuilletonist myself almost exclusively; and he was the only editor who could do my job as well as his own. The feuilletonist is the man who can write a couple of thousand words once a week in such a manner that everyone will read it for its own sake, whether specially interested or not in its subject, which may be politics, literature, music, painting, fashion, sport, or gossip at large. Many able editors can no more do this than the Archbishop of Canterbury can preach Billy Sunday's sermons. But Massingham could. His parliamentary feuilletons, his occasional theatre feuilletons, and finally his Wayfarer gossip feuilletons were as good as any written in his time by men who made feuilleton writing their sole work in journalism.

Of course he paid for all this exciting activity, and the influence and interesting acquaintances it brought him. Editing, especially daily editing, involves a great deal of drudgery, mitigated only by the impossibility of spending enough time on each job, since the clock is racing the editor all the time, and the leading article, well or ill written, must be ready for the newspaper trains. The physical strain is not mitigated at all; and Massingham, like Voltaire, was never quite well for a week together.

Then there was the disability I have already mentioned: the provisional solutions or no solutions at all of the political problems of the day. Political warfare is like military warfare: no journalist can keep up with it. During the war of 1914–18 I tried to keep up with the race of events. It was quite impossible. Long before I could form a considered judgment and write it carefully down the situation had changed, and what I had written was hopelessly out of date.

There is another element of impermanence in journalism. In the party warfare of Parliament as in the field, we have to make the best of the commanders we can get. Kitcheners and Joffres have to be upheld and encouraged in terms that would provoke contradiction if applied to Alexanders and Napoleons. When a Cabinet has to be formed the case is worse; for the Kitcheners and Joffres, having at least gone through the military mill from their lieutenancy upward, know their business technically; but the British politician need neither know his job scientifically nor even be an adept in its procedure. Massingham had more than once to back ambitioners who let him down pretty badly; and on such occasions he did not hesitate to let them know it.

In the end these disappointments of his might have claimed that they beat him out of every paper he edited. They beat him out of The Star, only to find him in a stronger position editing The Daily Chronicle. They beat him out of The Daily Chronicle into weekly journalism as editor of The Nation. And they finally beat him out of The Nation when he was too old to face another editorship. At least that is one way of summarizing his career; and it is an important one as an illustration of the final control of the Press by those whose power has hardly any effective check on it except newspaper criticism. But as it took the politicians a long time to discover that they could not buy Massingham; and as it also took Massingham, politically suckled in an out-wearing creed, a long time to discover that they were hopeless, he was never silenced, though he was always going to be. He ran his full career as a journalist; and the fact that he was driven from Stonecutter Street to Whitefriars Street, and from Whitefriars Street to Adelphi Terrace—less than ten minutes walk both times—really made no difference in his total output or in his effect on public opinion. Thus his defeats were not fatal: they were the evidences of his integrity.

To have a career in politics under our party system a man must have his price; and it must be the standard price of putting party before everything, denouncing fiercely every leader and every measure on the other side even when your side has just lost an election by advocating it with your hearty support. Nobody ever dreamt of pressing the grosser forms of corruption on Massingham; but this established one was pressed on him as the obvious duty of an English gentleman and loyal supporter of his party. It never occurred to him to pay it: his pride, enormous and unconscious, would not tolerate it. When some leader had gained his enthusiastic support by advocating the reforms that all leaders advocate in Opposition, and proved no exception to the rule that no leader advocates them in office, Massingham would fall slaughterously on him, and set the financial backers of the paper demanding why Liberal leaders were being attacked in a Liberal paper, and what party the editor thought he belonged to, anyhow.

On the whole, by sheer talent and character, Massingham had a pretty good run, not only as a journalist but as a martyr who always rose from his ashes with ludicrous promptitude and success. What really handicapped him and yet helped him (all helps are handicaps too) was that in his politics he was a transition journalist, and that the transition was for him a development of Liberalism as the specifically progressive force in politics into Socialism as the next step ahead. This estranged him at once from the spirit of the old essentially anti-Socialist Liberalism and the new essentially Marxian Socialism which regarded the change, not as a development of Liberalism, but as a complete repudiation of it. Massingham would laugh at the bourgeoisie as heartily as Molière or Dickens, and be hotly indignant at its bigotries and snobberies and muddles and mismanagements; but he had not the Marxian abhorrence of the whole bourgeois epoch, and the Marxian conviction that a radically different culture must replace its outlook on life. In his view, to despair of Liberalism politically was to despair of humanity, because he could see no hope in any Marxian leadership known to him. Thus in a certain altercation with Hyndman, the Socialist leader (with whom discussion generally ended in altercation), his final shot was "You are the most entirely negligible man in England," which was true in a parliamentary sense, just as it would have been true of Marx himself, but hardly so in a seriously political one, as the Russian Revolution presently proved.

In the end, when the Labor Party became established in Parliament, and developed a new personnel, Massingham calmly took The Nation over to it, and made the paper the organ of a fierce attack on French Imperialism, coupled with the name of M. Poincaré, and, on occasion, with that of Mr Lloyd George, who, in spite of his exploits in Coalition, still ranked confusedly as a Liberal asset. Now The Nation, though artistically and journalistically entirely a creation of Massingham's, was financed by Liberal money to be a Liberal organ; and he found for the third time that they who pay the piper will finally call the tune, however masterfully the piper may play.

There was another weakness in his position. Party warfare is very newsy. When the parliamentary warfare flags there is always plenty of personal gossip to go on with. But warfare for Socialist principles will not keep a journal going with fresh material when it is so much in the air as it was during most of Massingham's time. Even a parish magazine cannot live on the creeds; and when an editor has stated his position in principle fifty times without echo or controversy in Parliament, the problem of how to keep the paper alive, fresh, and in the movement becomes almost insoluble. Some time before his last displacement Massingham, discussing this difficulty with me, said that he and his devoted staff had said all they had to say, and said it too often. We repeated the usual commonplaces about new departures and new blood; but we knew that this was useless: the paper, already ahead of events, could do nothing but mark time until events caught up. As it happened, they caught up (by the advent of a Labor Government) just too late to save the situation for him. Had he been a younger man this would have been very hard luck. As it was, it happened in the nick of time: he could not have begun life again as a Labor journalist. He had not gone stale: he was youthful to the last; but his number was up: he was dying.

Massingham lived so eagerly in the present, and was so full of all sorts of public and cultural interests, that he never reminisced or talked about himself. Well as I knew him, especially in his later years in the Adelphi, where he so often came upstairs to lunch with us, I knew very little about him except what I saw. I gathered that he was an East Anglian; and I wondered that Norfolk had produced so supple and susceptible a mind and temperament until I discovered that his suppleness did not prevent his being extremely obstinate. He always held on to a position for weeks after it had become obviously untenable. I am aware somehow that he was not his mother's pet son, and that there was a sort of feud between them; but this situation appealed to his sense of humor rather than to any kind of rancor in him. He told me that as a boy he had been engaged in the class wars of juvenile gentry and proletariat, and had at first suffered agonies of terror, but had got over them and acquired an insatiable taste for this sort of street fighting.

We occasionally made Sunday morning excursions of a kind then in vogue among journalists. They had a double object: first, to walk four miles from home and thus become *bona fide* travellers in the legal sense, entitled to obtain drinks as such, and, second, to buy a copy of The Observer. This was pure tradition; for I was a teetotaller; and Massingham, though convivial enough, was no toper. I only once saw him intoxicated (drunk is hardly the word); and then he was in the wildest high spirits, and had to be restrained from dropping over the bannisters in his soaring disdain for the stairs. But this was at one of those dreadful men's dinner parties at which all the guests get drunk to save themselves from going melancholy mad.

As to The Observer, it was very different then from the Garvinian Observer of today. It cost fourpence; and its sale was a superstition from the Franco-Prussian war of 1870–71, when, as it happened, some big battles were fought at the end of the week. The Observer had a good foreign news service, and thus made itself indispensable on Sunday to all journalists, and in all the clubs and country houses and rectories where political news still meant diplomatic and military news. The habit thus established persisted; so that long after the Franco-Prussian war had faded into a reminiscence of our boyhood Massingham would solemnly waste fourpence every Sunday morning on The Observer when any of the penny weeklies would have served him better. The revival of The Observer by Mr Garvin after some rather desperate vicissitudes is one of the great journalistic feats of our time.

During one of these walks Massingham told me the story of his brother's startling end. He regarded this as something that he never spoke of to anybody; and he soon forgot having spoken of it to me. All men have certain sacred subjects which they firmly believe they never mention to a living soul, though as a matter of fact they mention them sooner or later to their more intimate and congenial friends. Some time afterwards I made unscrupulous use of this confidence at a bogus spiritualistic séance to which I treated a friend of ours with whom we were spending a week-end. He had expressed himself so contemptuously about people who believed in such things that I thought it allowable to demonstrate to him that he himself could be taken in with the utmost ease. One of my earliest steps in the demonstration was to call up a spirit who, after admitting that he was a relative of someone present, gradually eliminated, question by question, myself, our host, and every possible relationship except that of brother to Massingham, who was so visibly and unmistakeably upset by this communication that I was rather shocked by the success of my own trick. As to our host, it was impossible for him, after seeing Massingham change color as he did, to doubt his entire good faith; and this was his undoing; for when, as usually happens, he made Massingham hold me hand and foot on one side whilst he did the same on the other, the rappings and other phenomena proceeded as impressively as ever. Of course what happened was what always happens on these occasions. I took Massingham into my confidence without a word by working away with the foot he was supposed to be holding down; and he, much relieved and enormously amused, threw himself ecstatically into the game, and was presently treating our host to manifestations on which I should never have ventured. All professional mediums know that if they can only get hold of one of these stories that the teller regards as never told, and his friends nevertheless know by heart, they need not be afraid of the amateur detectives he will set on them, as none of them ever resist the temptation to become confederates.

Beyond such confidences as the above I knew nothing of the external circumstances of Massingham's life except what I saw. I knew his mind; and, I repeat, his mind was far too active and comprehensive to be occupied with himself or with the past. He changed very little. A country house, two marriages, and a family of children who all grew up graver, more posed, more serious than himself, made no mark whatever on him: he carried them with all his old combination of levity of mood with hectically fierce fits of political conviction, and was easily first juvenile among them to the day of his death.

As I write these lines comes the news of the death of our friend and contemporary William Archer. The two vacant places seem to make a prodigious gap in the surviving front rank of late Victorian journalism. But Archer, like myself, was a journalist only, inasmuch as he wrote for the papers to boil his pot. Massingham was the perfect master journalist: the born editor without whom such potboiling would have been for many of us a much poorer and more sordid business. If he had left behind him a single book it would have spoilt the integrity of his career and of his art. I hope I have made it clear that this was his triumph, not his shortcoming. I could lay my hand more readily on ten contributors for his successor than on one successor for his contributors. A first-rate editor is a very rare bird indeed: two or three to a generation, in contrast to swarms of authors, is as much as we get; and Massingham was in the first of that very select flight.

WILLIAM MORRIS

THE LIFE OF WILLIAM MORRIS. By J. W. Mackail. Two vols. (London: Longmans, Green and Co.)

From The Daily Chronicle, 20 April 1899

WHEN the biography of a great man has to be written, a friend of the family, unless he is cynically reckless of other people's feelings, is hardly the happiest man for the work, although he has often the richest stores of information. In this case there are two families to be considered. William Morris and Burne-Jones were much closer friends than even Mr Mackail, Burne-Jones's son-in-law, conveys. Remarkable as Morris's judgment was on all questions of art, his opinion was not worth having when its value depended, however subtly or indirectly, on an impartial estimate of Burne-Jones's work. He smelt a rival to his friend at forty removes, and was probably jealous of even his own share in the tapestries and windows which they produced together, Burne-Jones as designer, Morris as colorist. When Mr Mackail, at Burne-Jones's request, undertook to write the life of Morris, he probably had to face every difficulty and exercise every discretion that would confront a biographer of his father-in-law as well.

But the family difficulties are trifles compared to those raised by the chapters that deal with such larger and unrulier circles as the Social Democratic Federation, the Socialist League, and the Hammersmith Socialist Society. Fortunately for himself, Mr Mackail knows little more about this part of Morris's life than might be gathered by any stranger from the available documents. Even his literary judgment leads him astray when Socialism is the topic. For example, in the futile Joint Socialist Manifesto drafted by Morris in 1893, and reduced in committee by himself, Mr H. M. Hyndman, and the present writer to the greatest common measure of the Fabian Society and the Social Democratic Federation in that year, Mr Mackail detects the hand of Mr Sidney Webb! He declares that "it fairly represents the moderate and practical views which Morris held in the last years of his life." As a matter of fact, it contains, under cover of certain plausible general sentiments, no views at all; and though this is exactly what "moderate and practical" usually mean in England, it was not in the least what they meant to Morris. The situation was really a piece of comedy. Morris, like the Corsican brother who has to reconcile Orsini and Colonna, had to act as moderator between two politicians who were exceedingly incommoded in their respective tactics by the coalition which was being forced on them in the name of the universal brotherhood of all Socialists. At least I can answer for my own bad faith, of which Morris was perfectly aware. But he finally got us to sign a document which avoided expressing any of our views, though it contains recognizable interpolations from the pens of the other triumvirs. It fell flat, and neither is nor was of the slightest importance. The manifesto of the Hammersmith Socialist Society is a far better exposition of Morris's later attitude towards Socialism.

That Morris's notions of how the social changes he desired would come about altered from a point at which he saw nothing for it but a forcible overthrow of the proprietary classes by the proletariat, to an attitude so Fabian that he practically left Socialism to work itself out in the ordinary course of politics, and returned to his work as an artist-craftsman, may be gathered from his platform lectures in the eighties and nineties, which are extant in his own handwriting. Thus, in the early days, after a description of society class by class, he comes to the professional class, and first says what he can of its advantages:

"Surely we at least are bound to be contented, whoever else

above or below us is discontented.

"Is it so, indeed? Yet here I stand before you, one of the most fortunate of this happy class, so steeped in discontent that I have no words which will express it—no words, nothing but deeds, wherever they may lead me to, even if it be ruin, prison, or a violent death."

He told the Oldham weavers, as he told all his working-class audiences at that time, that there was "no hope save revolution" for them; and by "revolution" he meant armed insurrection as much as his hero John Ball did.

In 1895 all this is changed. "Almost everyone has now ceased to believe in the change coming by catastrophe," he says; and again, "We used to be a sect; now we must be a party, since it is admitted that we must go into Parliament." At this time, in an excellent paper on Communism, he says, "I do declare that any other state of society than Communism is grievous and disgraceful to all belonging to it." But there is no longer a word of revolution; the tone is cheerful and humorous; he is even disposed to chuckle at his favorite butt, the politically fussy Fabian, as having hit on a stupendously prosaic solution of the problem that was once so tragically difficult.

Mr Mackail's conception of the way in which this evolution of Morris's tactics took place is typical of the weak side of his biography. He ascribes it to the soothing effect of translating the Odyssey into English verse. After this, the reader will not be surprised to learn that Mr Mackail thinks that Morris was strikingly like Dr Johnson, and that he slips in some remarks on the elasticity of the epic hexameter between the Norwich riots and "Bloody Sunday." Mr Mackail has forgotten that the change from revolutionary to Fabian Socialism was not peculiar to Morris. It occurred to many of his comrades who never translated the Odyssey, and who were not in the least like Dr Johnson. It is abundantly explained by the immense extension of political organization since the foundation of the Socialist League. At that time the franchise was restricted; the Metropolitan Board of Works and the unreformed vestries governed London. There were no Parish Councils, no County Councils, no District Councils, none of that new machinery which makes Progressivism possible, and enables it to carry out as much Socialism as the people care for. To suppose that this change in the condition of the London laborer, from helplessness to a "moral minimum" of sixpence an hour, accompanied as it was by a change from the starvation and window-breaking of 1886 to the comparative prosperity which set in in 1887, produced no effect in Morris, is to assume that he still lived in the old circle with books and pictures, looms and dye-vats, instead of in the very rough jostle with real life which followed his step down into the streets to preach Socialism. The turning-point with him was a personal experience: the battle of Trafalgar Square. Mr Mackail seems to have been in the square on that occasion; for he describes the scene picturesquely, but remarks that "Morris himself did not see it till all was nearly over." He misses the point of what Morris did see. Morris joined one of the processions in Clerkenwell Green, where he made a speech, urging the processionists to keep steadily together and press on if they were attacked. It was the speech of a man who still saw in a London trades procession a John Ball fellowship. He then placed himself at the head of the column, and presently witnessed the attack on it by a handful of policemen, who must have been outnumbered fifty to one at least. The frantic stampede that followed made a deep impression on Morris. He understood at once how far his imagination had duped him. The translation of ten Odysseys would only have deepened the illusion that was dispelled in that moment. From that time he paid no more serious attention to the prospects of the Socialist bodies as militant organizations. The promptitude with which he took the hint was part of that practical sense which suggests Dr Johnson to Mr Mackail; and the revival of trade and absorption of the unemployed which were just then beginning did the rest.

Of these free speech difficulties with the police Mr Mackail writes sympathetically and intelligently, but not intimately, missing in consequence many opportunities for a sense of humor, which elsewhere does him good service, as well as for some deeper strokes. He describes how Morris spoke in a street off the Edgware Road, and, refusing to stop at the request of a "mighty civil inspector," was fined a shilling. What he does not describe is the contrast between the apologies and compliments of the prosecution, flattering the prisoner and demanding only a nominal fine, with the treatment of his working-class friend John Williams, who repeatedly suffered imprisonment for the same offence. I met Morris on his return from the police-court on the Edgware Road occasion. With Williams in his mind, he described himself as "a funkster" for letting himself get off so easily. He then got one of Dumas' novels (Dumas père, of course), and sat in his garden to air himself morally and physically after the contamination of the police-court, from which he shrank sensitively. On one occasion, when he went there to bail a comrade, his fellow surety was the late Charles Bradlaugh. Morris afterwards described to me his own nervousness among the officials, and his envy of the tremendous *aplomb* of Bradlaugh, who behaved as if the whole place belonged to him, and was deferred to with awe by everybody. The physical worry of this sort of thing to a man of Morris's temperament was much greater than that of open-air speaking, which Mr Mackail thinks must have injured his health, though it probably rather tended to counteract the bad effect of lectures and committee squabbles in crowded, stuffy rooms.

The free speech contests were perhaps the worst worries which Socialism brought on Morris. Mr Mackail underrates the burden to such a character of the feeling, whenever a poor man went to prison, that he should have gone instead. On being remonstrated with for proposing to do so at Edgware Road, he betrayed this feeling by replying, "Noblesse oblige": one of the few occasions on which he let slip his consciousness of his noblesse. Mr Mackail often misses both the fun and the seriousness of these matters. In one of his references to the Dod Street affair (another free speech difficulty) he says that there had been " a distinct breach of faith as regards the order of the speeches."

The truth is much funnier than that. Three victims had been selected for sacrifice to the police on the day in question; to wit, Dr Aveling, Mr George Bateman, and myself as representative of the Fabian Society. But on the night before the morning of the meeting the police called on Dr Aveling, and announced the welcome news that they had orders to surrender. The news spread; and next morning, instead of three condemned speakers, the entire oratorical force of the Socialist movement turned up, resolute to assert their right of Free Speech or die on the place. They all wanted to speak first; but Aveling, who had faced the music before the danger was over, claimed first place, and got it. A quarrel ensued, in which nothing was agreed on but a general denunciation of Aveling, although the Dod Street incident was perhaps the most creditable incident in his morally somewhat chequered career. But it must be remembered that the struggle at Dod Street had been going on for months, during which Morris had been kept in continual anxiety, not only as to its upshot, but as to the extent of his own obligation to take his turn with the arrested and imprisoned speakers. Finally, it was arranged that he and Mr Stewart Headlam should speak and be arrested; and he was looking forward to this very disagreeable ordeal when the Home Office capitulated, and the melodrama became a farcical comedy.

Trivial as these particulars now seem, they form the real history of Morris's plunge into politics as distinguished from the account given by Mr Mackail. In the book we are shewn him as going through a certain curriculum of lectures and propaganda, like a man who takes up a subject and works his way through it much as a university student does, except in a rather eccentric and ungentlemanly way, and in a perhaps rather shady set. But that was not how it happened. Morris brought to the professed Socialists of the Leagues and Federations a conception of life which they never assimilated, and concerning which they could teach him nothing; whilst on the general public, already educated to some extent by Ruskin, it gained to an extent which Morris himself was the last to realize. The Socialists boasted of him as their tame great man; and all the Skimpoles and Autolycuses in the ranks borrowed money from him unmercifully, besides occasionally dragging him from his bed with untimely applications for prompt bail at police stations. It is true that these good-fornothings were very few in number; but in capacity for worrying Morris, and wasting his time, they easily outdid the whole capitalist system against which he was warring. Yet he was infinitely more tolerant of them than he was of the classically minded and respectable members of the movement. If a man was a humorous vagabond who seemed to have come straight out of George Borrow's books: one to whom war with society, including the police, was as natural as a frock-coat and a literary style were to Mr Hyndman, then Morris would bail the Borrowite out, and lend him money to get drunk with, with inexhaustible patience; whilst he would quarrel with Mr Hyndman or with an academically correct Fabian at a moment's notice. Morris's observation of these "comrades" educated him in a new way; and that is why his Socialism cannot be conveyed by a portrait of himself alone, however faithful the likeness and correct the accessories. A great conversation piece is required, in which bald phrases, as "an extremist named ——," and a string of mere names are replaced by full-length studies. This baldness does not matter in the case of Mr Hyndman, Mr Sidney Webb, Mr Philip Webb, Burne-Jones, or any of the personalities which have impressed themselves independently on the public consciousness; but the Socialist League contained many obscure tragic comedians, who were at first taken by Morris with perfect seriousness, and whose subsequent development opened his mind as it had never been opened before. From the Burne-Jones point of view (which I take to be Mr Mackail's also) this is the more likely to be misunderstood, because in stepping from the Pre-Raphaelite circle down into the streets, Morris found himself, with a shock, no longer an eccentric young man nicknamed "Topsy," and patronized by men who had taken permanent root as artists, but an elder and a sage. "These fellows treat me as an elderly buffer," he used to say; but he was mistaken: they thought him not merely elderly, but old;

for, as Mr Hollyer's frontispiece to the second volume shews, Morris, at fifty-three, looked sixty-five. And yet he was still experimenting, still learning, still regarding his life's work as ahead of him instead of behind or abreast of him. At that time Burne-Jones was an ascertained quantity both for himself and the public. His method was fixed; his scope was surveyed and fenced; it was clear that time could add to the number of his pictures, but not to the height of his achievement nor to the variety of his accomplishment. Not so with Morris. Nobody could tell what he would be doing five years in advance. If he were alive now he would probably be making fiddles, as he often said he should like to do; and the Kelmscott Press, having done its work, would be as much a thing of the past as the wall-papers which in his later years he disparaged in favor of whitewash. The result was that Burne-Jones felt towards him as an old, settled, and sensible man feels towards a young and unsettled one. Thus in the old circle he remained more than ever a marvellous boy called Top: in the new one he was a patriarch, and was instinctively looked to for leadership when he was seeking for it himself. He began by humbly describing himself as ready to do what he was told as well as he could; and when at last it dawned on him that the leadership he was looking for did not exist, and that he would have to do it himself and build up an organization from the beginning, he set to at it with all the practicality that distinguished him as an artist, though with much less natural aptitude, and no pleasure whatever in the result, which he finally threw aside like a spoiled Kelmscott page of letterpress. In the meantime, he had only to step back into the old *milieu* to be Top again, the Socialism making no difference there except perhaps a slight intensification of the paternal attitude towards him, and a tacit understanding that Burne-Jones's acceptance of a baronetcy had better not be mentioned between the two friends.

The worst that can be said of Mr Mackail's book is that it describes Morris, especially in his later days, too much from the Burne-Jones point of view. It is the life of a phenomenon rather than of a man; and it has not only the inevitable amiable weakness of sparing the affections which grew up round Morris every serious criticism of his faults, especially his intellectual petulances; but it sometimes treats the street corner exploits on which Morris rightly valued himself with an indulgence which implies that Mr Mackail regards them as slightly vulgar follies. Mr Mackail is entitled to that opinion; but whilst he holds it, he cannot make the Socialist League as interesting and vivid as it was to Morris; and he is consequently at his best only in dealing with Morris as an artist. He evidently does not care for the "comrades," and in his indifference commits apparent errors of tact, as, for instance, when on one page he does not tell us that "a speaker" by whom Morris stood in a Hyde Park disturbance was Mr John Burns, whilst on the next page he plumps out Mr Hyndman's name in connection with an explosion of wrath which might just as well have descended on half a dozen other people. In fact, not being interested himself in this part of his work, he does not make it very interesting to others, and makes Morris's Socialism produce, on the whole, the effect of a mere aberration.

On the art side, he is also so far under the family tradition that he thinks of Pre-Raphaelite art as being ante-Victorian rather than characteristically Victorian, as of course it was. Madox Brown and Holman Hunt were perhaps more "early-Victorian" than Morris and Burne-Jones; but it is absurd nowadays to write as if the distinction between good Victorian art and bad Victorian art (or no art at all) is a distinction between Florentine and twelfth-century art and Victorian art. All this is a survival of the rivalry in public esteem between Morris's furniture and Maple's; and Mr Mackail, at whatever risk of family obloquy, should shake himself loose from it.

For the rest, Mr Mackail shews a nice sense of what we all want to know about William Morris. He gives us the right portraits and pictures, and the right glimpses into his intimate correspondence. His style is easy reading; and he understands the art of softening a touchy point by a stroke of humorous exaggeration. And he has many other merits as a biographer which cannot be acknowledged in this necessarily very hurried notice—merits which make the writer regret that he has been compelled to dwell at such length on the side of Morris's activity with which Mr Mackail is least familiar.

WILLIAM MORRIS AS ACTOR AND PLAYWRIGHT
From The Saturday Review, 10 *October* 1896

AMONG the many articles which have been written about William Morris during the past week, I have seen none which deal with him as dramatist and actor. Yet I have been present at a play by William Morris; and I have seen him act, and act, too, much better than an average professional of the twenty-pound-a-week class. I need therefore make no apology for making him the subject of an article on the theatre.

Morris was a quite unaffected and accessible person. All and sundry were welcome to know him to the full extent of their capacity for such acquaintance (which was usually not saying much) as far as a busy and sensitive man could make himself common property without intolerable boredom and waste of time. Even to the Press, which was generally—bless its innocence!—either ignorantly insolent to him or fatuously patronizing, as if he were some delightful curio, appreciable only by persons of taste and fancy, he was willing to be helpful. Journalist though I am, he put up with me with the friendliest patience, though I am afraid I must sometimes have been a fearful trial to him.

I need hardly say that I have often talked copiously to him on many of his favorite subjects, especially the artistic subjects. What is more to the point, he has occasionally talked to me about them. No art was indifferent to him. He declared that nobody could pass a picture without looking at it—that even a smoky cracked old mezzotint in a pawnbroker's window would stop you for at least a moment. Some idiot, I notice, takes it on himself to assure the world that he had no musical sense. As a matter of fact, he had a perfect ear, a most musical singing voice, and so fine a sense of beauty in sound (as in everything else) that he could not endure the clatter of the pianoforte or the squalling and shouting of the average singer. When I told him that the Amsterdam choir, brought over here by M. de Lange, had discovered the secret of the beauty of medieval music, and sang it with surpassing excellence, he was full of regret for having missed it; and the viol concerts of Mr Dolmetsch pleased him greatly. Indeed once, during his illness, when Mr Dolmetsch played him some really beautiful music on a really beautiful instrument, he was quite overcome by it. I once urged him to revive the manufacture of musical instruments and rescue us from the vulgar handsomeness of the trade articles with which our orchestras are equipped; and he was by no means averse from the idea, having always, he avowed, thought he should like to make a good fiddle. Only neither in music nor in anything else could you engage him in any sort of intellectual dilettantism: he would not waste his time and energy on the curiosities and fashions of art, but went straight to its highest point in the direct and simple production of beauty. He was ultra-modern—not merely up to date, but far ahead of it: his wall papers, his hangings, his tapestries, and his printed books have the twentieth century in every touch of them; whilst as to his prose word-weaving, our worn-out nineteenth-century Macaulayese is rancid by comparison. He started from the thirteenth century simply because he wished to start from the most advanced point instead of from the most backward one—say 1850 or thereabout. When people called him "archaic," he explained, with the indulgence of perfect knowledge, that they were fools, only they did not know it. In short, the man was a complete artist, who became great by a pre-eminent sense of beauty, and practical ability enough (and to spare) to give effect to it.

And yet—and yet—and yet—! I am sorry to have to say it; but I never could induce him to take the smallest interest in the contemporary theatrical routine of the Strand. As far as I am aware, I share with Mr Henry Arthur Jones the distinction of being the only modern dramatist whose plays were witnessed by him (except Charley's Aunt, which bored him); and I greatly fear that neither of us dare claim his visits as a spontaneous act of homage to modern acting and the modern drama. Now, when Morris would not take an interest in anything, and would not talk about it—and his capacity for this sort of resistance, both passive and active, was remarkably obstinate—it generally meant that he had made up his mind, on good grounds, that it was not worth talking about. A man's mouth may be shut and his mind closed much more effectually by his knowing all about a subject than by his knowing nothing about it; and whenever Morris suddenly developed a downright mulishness about anything, it was a sure sign that he knew it through and through and had quarrelled with it. Thus, when an enthusiast for some fashionable movement or reaction in art would force it into the conversation, he would often behave so as to convey an impression of invincible prejudice and intolerant ignorance, and so get rid of it. But later on he would let slip something that showed, in a flash, that he had taken in the whole movement at its very first demonstration, and had neither prejudices nor illusions about it. When you knew the subject yourself, and could see beyond it and around it, putting it in its proper place and accepting its limits, he would talk fast enough about it; but it did not amuse him to allow novices to break a lance with him, because he had no special facility for brilliant critical demonstration, and required too much patience for his work to waste any of it on idle discussions. Consequently there was a certain intellectual roguery about him of which his intimate friends were very well aware; so that if a subject was thrust on him, the aggressor was sure to be ridiculously taken in if he did not calculate on Morris's knowing much more about it than he pretended to.

On the subject of the theatre, an enthusiastic young firstnighter would probably have given Morris up, after the first attempt to gather his opinion of The Second Mrs Tanqueray, as an ordinary citizen who had never formed the habit of playgoing, and neither knew nor cared anything about the theatre except as a treat for children once a year during the pantomime season. But Morris would have written for the stage if there had been

any stage that a poet and artist could write for. When the Socialist League once proposed to raise the wind by a dramatic entertainment, and suggested that he should provide the play, he set
to at once and provided it. And what kind of play was it? Was it
a miracle play on the lines of those scenes in the Towneley mys-
teries between the "shepherds abiding in the field," which he
used to quote with great relish as his idea of a good bit of comedy?
Not at all: it was a topical extravaganza, entitled Nupkins Awak-
ened, the chief "character parts" being Sir Peter Edlin, Tennyson,
and an imaginary Archbishop of Canterbury. Sir Peter owed
the compliment to his activity at that time in sending Socialists
to prison on charges of "obstruction," which was always proved
by getting a policeman to swear that if any passer-by or vehicle
had wished to pass over the particular spot in a thoroughfare on
which the speaker or his audience happened to be standing, their
presence would have obstructed him. This contention, which
was regarded as quite sensible and unanswerable by the newspapers of the day, was put into a nutshell in the course of Sir
Peter's summing-up in the play. "In fact, gentlemen, it is a
matter of grave doubt whether we are not all of us continually
committing this offence from our cradles to our graves." This
speech, which the real Sir Peter of course never made, though he
certainly would have done so had he had wit enough to see the
absurdity of solemnly sending a man to prison for two months
because another man could not walk through him—especially
when it would have been so easy to lock him up for three on
some respectable pretext—will probably keep Sir Peter's memory
green when all his actual judicial utterances are forgotten. As to
Tennyson, Morris took a Socialist who happened to combine
the right sort of beard with a melancholy temperament, and
drilled him in a certain portentous incivility of speech which,
taken with the quality of his remarks, threw a light on Morris's
opinion of Tennyson which was all the more instructive because
he delighted in Tennyson's verse as keenly as Wagner delighted
in the music of Mendelssohn, whose credit for qualities of larger
scope he, nevertheless, wrote down and destroyed. Morris played

the ideal Archbishop himself. He made no attempt to make up the part in the ordinary stage fashion. He always contended that no more was necessary for stage illusion than some distinct conventional symbol, such as a halo for a saint, a crook for a bishop, or, if you liked, a cloak and dagger for the villain, and a red wig for the comedian. A pair of clerical bands and black stockings proclaimed the archbishop: the rest he did by obliterating his humor and intelligence, and presenting his own person to the audience like a lantern with the light blown out, with a dull absorption in his own dignity which several minutes of the wildest screaming laughter at him when he entered could not disturb. I laughed immoderately myself; and I can still see quite clearly the long top floor of that warehouse in the Farringdon Road as I saw it in glimpses between my paroxysms, with Morris gravely on the stage in his bands at one end; Mrs. Stillman, a tall and beautiful figure, rising like a delicate spire above a skyline of city chimney-pots at the other; and a motley sea of rolling, wallowing, guffawing Socialists between. There has been no other such successful first night within living memory, I believe; but I only remember one dramatic critic who took care to be present—Mr William Archer. Morris was so interested by his experiment in this sort of composition that he for some time talked of trying his hand at a serious drama, and would no doubt have done it had there been any practical occasion for it, or any means of consummating it by stage representation under proper conditions without spending more time on the job than it was worth. Later, at one of the annual festivities of the Hammersmith Socialist Society, he played the old gentleman in the bathchair in a short piece called The Duchess of Bayswater (*not* by himself), which once served its turn at the Haymarket as a curtain raiser. It was impossible for such a born teller and devourer of stories as he was to be indifferent to an art which is nothing more than the most vivid and real of all ways of story-telling. No man would more willingly have seen his figures move and heard their voices than he.

Why, then, did he so seldom go to the theatre? Well, come,

gentle reader, why doesnt anybody go to the theatre? Do you
suppose that even I would go to the theatre twice a year except
on business? You would never dream of asking why Morris did
not read penny novelettes, or hang his rooms with Christmas-
number chromolithographs. We have no theatre for men like
Morris; indeed, we have no theatre for quite ordinary cultivated
people. I am a person of fairly catholic interests: it is my privilege
to enjoy the acquaintance of a few representative people in
various vortices of culture. I know some of the most active-
minded and intelligent of the workers in social and political
reform. They read stories with an avidity that amazes me; but
they dont go to the theatre. I know the people who are struggling
for the regeneration of the arts and crafts. They dont go to the
theatre. I know people who amuse their leisure with edition after
edition of the novels of Mrs Humphry Ward, Madame Sarah
Grand, and Mr Harold Frederic, and who could not for their
lives struggle through two chapters of Miss Corelli, Mr Rider
Haggard, or Mr Hall Caine. They dont go to the theatre. I know
the lovers of music who support the Richter and Mottl concerts
and go to Bayreuth if they can afford it. They dont go to the
theatre. I know the staff of this paper. It doesnt go to the theatre—
even the musical critic is an incorrigible shirk when his duties
involve a visit thither. Nobody goes to the theatre except the
people who also go to Madame Tussaud's. Nobody writes for it,
unless he is hopelessly stage struck and cannot help himself.
It has no share in the leadership of thought: it does not even
reflect its current. It does not create beauty: it apes fashion. It
does not produce personal skill: our actors and actresses, with
the exception of a few persons with natural gifts and graces,
mostly miscultivated or half cultivated, are simply the middle-class
section of the residuum. The curt insult with which Matthew
Arnold dismissed it from consideration found it and left it utterly
defenceless. And yet you ask me why Morris did not go to the
theatre. In the name of common sense, why should he have
gone?

When I say these things to stupid people, they have a feeble

way of retorting, "What about the Lyceum?" That is just the
question I have been asking for years; and the reply always is
that the Lyceum is occupied exclusively with the works of a
sixteenth-seventeenth century author, in whose social views no
educated and capable person today has the faintest interest, and
whose art is partly so villainously artificial and foolish as to
produce no effect on a thirteenth-twentieth century artist like
Morris except one of impatience and discomfort, and partly so
fine as to defy satisfactory treatment at a theatre where there are
only two competent performers, who are neither of them in their
proper element in the seventeenth century. Morris was willing
to go to a street corner and tell the people something that they
very badly needed to be told, even when he could depend on
being arrested by a policeman for his trouble; but he drew the
line at fashionably modernized Shakespear. If you had told him
what a pretty fifteenth-century picture Miss Terry makes in her
flower wreath in Cymbeline's garden, you might have induced
him to peep for a moment at that; but the first blast of the queen's
rhetoric would have sent him flying into the fresh air again. You
could not persuade Morris that he was being amused when he
was, as a matter of fact, being bored; and you could not persuade
him that music was harmonious by playing it on vulgar instruments, or that verse was verse when uttered by people with either
no delivery at all or the delivery of an auctioneer or toastmaster.
In short, you could not induce him to accept ugliness as art, no
matter how brilliant, how fashionable, how sentimental, or how
intellectually interesting you might make it. And you certainly
could not palm off a mess of Tappertitian sentiment daubed over
some sham love affair on him as a good story. This, alas! is as
much as to say that you could not induce him to spend his evenings at a modern theatre. And yet he was not in the least an
Impossibilist: he revelled in Dickens and the elder Dumas; he
was enthusiastic about the acting of Robson, and greatly admired
Jefferson; if he had started a Kelmscott Theatre instead of the
Kelmscott Press, I am quite confident that in a few months,
without going half a mile afield for his company, he would have

produced work that would within ten years have affected every theatre in Europe, from London to St Petersburg, and from New York to Alexandria. At all events, I should be glad to hear any gentleman point out an instance in which he undertook to find the way, and did not make us come along with him. We kicked and screamed, it is true: some of us poor obituarists kicked and screamed—even brayed—at his funeral the other day; but we have had to come along. No man was more liberal in his attempts to improve Morris's mind than I was; but I always found that, in so far as I was not making a most horrible idiot of myself out of misknowledge (I could forgive myself for pure ignorance), he could afford to listen to me with the patience of a man who had taught my teachers. There were people whom we tried to run him down with—Tennysons, Swinburnes, and so on; but their opinions about things did not make any difference. Morris's did.

I feel nothing but elation when I think of Morris. My intercourse with him was so satisfying that I should be the most ungrateful of men if I asked for more. You can lose a man like that by your own death, but not by his. And so, until then, let us rejoice in him.

GIVING THE DEVIL HIS DUE

The Works of Friedrich Nietzsche. Vol. I. "A Genealogy of Morals, and Poems." Translated by William Haussmann and John Gray. Vol. II. "Thus spake Zarathustra: a Book for All and None." Translated by Alexander Tille. (London: Fisher Unwin.)

From The Saturday Review, 13 May 1899

A few years ago there existed a London firm of publishers trading under the title of Henry & Co. Their policy, mainly of desperation, included a project for inviting fastidious members of the public to subscribe an annual sum about equal to the rent of a mansion in Grosvenor Square for a journal to be written throughout by a man of genius and delivered on the breakfast-table twice a week. It did not occur to them to ask Lady Randolph Churchill to edit it; but they invited me to write the first number. I promised, but never rose to the occasion; and the firm meanwhile amused itself by undertaking an English edition of the works of Friedrich Nietzsche, as being, on the whole, the next rashest thing available. I do not myself believe that there ever were any such persons as Henry & Co. The firm was but an avatar of Mr. John T. Grein, the reckless founder of the Independent Theatre, who had begun his career by exploding a performance of Ibsen's Ghosts on an unprepared London, and could hardly have hit on a better man than Nietzsche to repeat the effect with. Two volumes of the translation appeared before the firm paid the penalty of its Impossibilism by decently settling its accounts, selling its remainders, and vanishing from the world of publishers.

It is remarkable, and yet not unusual, that the two Utopian schemes of Henry & Co. should live after them, whilst their more businesslike operations are interréd with their bones. The audaciously expensive periodical which is to stamp its subscriber as an intellectual aristocrat is on the brink of publication. And the Nietzsche translation has resumed its subversive course in the respectable hands of Mr Fisher Unwin.

Nietzsche is a Devil's Advocate of the modern type. Formerly, when there was question of canonizing a pious person, the devil was allowed an advocate to support his claims to the pious person's soul. But nobody ever dreamt of openly defending the devil himself as a much misunderstood and fundamentally rightminded regenerator of the race until the nineteenth century, when William Blake boldly went over to the other side and started a devil's party. Fortunately for himself, he was a poet, and so passed as a paradoxical madman instead of a blasphemer. For a long time the party made little direct progress, the nation being occupied with the passing of its religion through the purifying fire of a criticism which did at last smelt some of the grosser African elements out of it, but which also exalted duty, morality, law, and altruism above faith; reared Ethical Societies; and left my poor old friend the devil (for I, too, was a Diabolonian born) worse off than ever. Mr. Swinburne explained Blake, and even went so far as to exclaim " Come down and redeem us from virtue"; but the pious influences of Putney reclaimed him, and he is now a respectable, Shakespear-fearing man. Mark Twain emitted some Diabolonian sparks, only to succumb to the overwhelming American atmosphere of chivalry, duty, and gentility. A miserable spurious Satanism, founded on the essentially pious dogma that the Prince of Darkness is no gentleman, sprang up in Paris, to the heavy discredit of the true cult of the Son of the Morning. All seemed lost when suddenly the cause found its dramatist in Ibsen, the first leader who really dragged duty, unselfishness, idealism, sacrifice, and the rest of the antidiabolic scheme to the bar at which it had indicted so many excellent Diabolonians. The outrageous assumption that a good man may do anything he thinks right (which in the case of a *naturally* good man means, by definition, anything he likes) without regard to the interests of bad men or of the community at large, was put on its defence; and the party became influential at last.

After the dramatist came the philosopher. In England, G. B. S.: in Germany, Nietzsche. Nietzsche had sat at the feet of Wagner, whose hero, Siegfried, was also a good Diabolonian. Unfortunately, after working himself up to the wildest enthusiasm about Wagner's music, Nietzsche rashly went to Bayreuth and heard it: a frightful disillusion for a man barely capable of Carmen. He threw down his idol, and having thus tasted the joys of iconoclasm (perhaps the one pursuit that is as useful as it is amusing) became an epigrammatic Diabolonian; took his stand "on the other side of good and evil"; "transvalued" our moral valuations; and generally strove to rescue mankind from rulers who are utterly without conscience in their pursuit of righteousness.

The volume just issued by Mr. Fisher Unwin contains A Genealogy of Morals, translated by Mr William Haussmann, with the rhymed maxims and epigrams, and the Dionysos-Dithyrambs, more than cleverly done into English by Mr John

Gray. Thus spake Zarathustra, a diffusion of Diabolonian wisdom in the guise of a concentration of it, has been reissued as a companion volume.

EDGAR ALLAN POE

From The Nation, 16 January 1909

THERE was a time when America, the Land of the Free, and the birthplace of Washington, seemed a natural fatherland for Edgar Allan Poe. Nowadays the thing has become inconceivable: no young man can read Poe's works without asking incredulously what the devil he is doing in *that* galley. America has been found out; and Poe has not; that is the situation. How did he live there, this finest of fine artists, this born aristocrat of letters? Alas! he did not live there: he died there, and was duly explained away as a drunkard and a failure, though it remains an open question whether he really drank as much in his whole lifetime as a modern successful American drinks, without comment, in six months.

If the Judgment Day were fixed for the centenary of Poe's birth, there are among the dead only two men born since the Declaration of Independence whose plea for mercy could avert a prompt sentence of damnation on the entire nation; and it is extremely doubtful whether those two could be persuaded to pervert eternal justice by uttering it. The two are, of course, Poe and Whitman; and there is between them the remarkable difference that Whitman is still credibly an American, whereas even the Americans themselves, though rather short of men of genius, omit Poe's name from their Pantheon, either from a sense that it is hopeless for them to claim so foreign a figure, or from simple Monroeism. One asks, has the America of Poe's day passed away, or did it ever exist?

Probably it never existed. It was an illusion, like the respectable Whig Victorian England of Macaulay. Karl Marx stripped the whitewash from that sepulchre; and we have ever since been struggling with a conviction of social sin which makes every country in which industrial capitalism is rampant a hell to us.

EDGAR ALLAN POE

For let no American fear that America, on that hypothetic Judgment Day, would perish alone. America would be damned in very good European company, and would feel proud and happy, and contemptuous of the saved. She would not even plead the influence of the mother from whom she has inherited all her worst vices. If the American stands today in scandalous pre-eminence as an anarchist and a ruffian, a liar and a braggart, an idolater and a sensualist, that is only because he has thrown off the disguises of Catholicism and feudalism which still give Europe an air of decency, and sins openly, impudently, and consciously, instead of furtively, hypocritically, and muddle-headedly, as we do. Not until he acquires European manners does the American anarchist become the gentleman who assures you that people cannot be made moral by Act of Parliament (the truth being that it is only by Acts of Parliament that men in large communities can be made moral, even when they want to); or the American ruffian hand over his revolver and bowie knife to be used for him by a policeman or soldier; or the American liar and braggart adopt the tone of the newspaper, the pulpit, and the platform; or the American idolater write authorized biographies of millionaires; or the American sensualist secure the patronage of all the Muses for his pornography.

Howbeit, Poe remains homeless. There is nothing at all like him in America: nothing, at all events, visible across the Atlantic. At that distance we can see Whistler plainly enough, and Mark Twain. But Whistler was very American in some ways: so American that nobody but another American could possibly have written his adventures and gloried in them without reserve. Mark Twain, resembling Dickens in his combination of public spirit and irresistible literary power with a congenital incapacity for lying and bragging, and a congenital hatred of waste and cruelty, remains American by the local color of his stories. There is a further difference. Both Mark Twain and Whistler are as Philistine as Dickens and Thackeray. The appalling thing about Dickens, the greatest of the Victorians, is that in his novels there is nothing personal to live for except eating, drinking, and pre-

221

tending to be happily married. For him the great synthetic ideals do not exist, any more than the great preludes and toccatas of Bach, the symphonies of Beethoven, the paintings of Giotto and Mantegna, Velasquez and Rembrandt. Instead of being heir to all the ages, he came into a comparatively small and smutty literary property bequeathed by Smollett and Fielding. His criticism of Fechter's Hamlet, and his use of a speech of Macbeth's to illustrate the character of Mrs. Macstinger, shew how little Shakespear meant to him. Thackeray is even worse: the notions of painting he picked up at Heatherley's school were further from the mark than Dickens's ignorance; he is equally in the dark as to music; and though he did not, when he wished to be enormously pleasant and jolly, begin, like Dickens, to describe the gorgings and guzzlings which make Christmas our annual national disgrace, that is rather because he never does want to be enormously pleasant and jolly than because he has any higher notions of personal enjoyment. The truth is that neither Dickens nor Thackeray would be tolerable were it not that life is an end in itself and a means to nothing but its own perfection; consequently any man who describes life vividly will entertain us, however uncultivated the life he describes may be. Mark Twain has lived long enough to become a much better philosopher than either Dickens or Thackeray: for instance, when he immortalized General Funston by scalping him, he did it scientifically, knowing exactly what he meant right down to the foundation in the natural history of human character. Also, he got from the Mississippi something that Dickens could not get from Chatham and Pentonville. But he wrote A Yankee at the Court of King Arthur just as Dickens wrote A Child's History of England. For the ideal of Catholic chivalry he had nothing but derision; and he exhibited it, not in conflict with reality, as Cervantes did, but in conflict with the prejudices of a Philistine compared to whom Sancho Panza is an Admirable Crichton, an Abelard, even a Plato. Also, he described Lohengrin as "a shivaree," though he liked the wedding chorus; and this shews that Mark, like Dickens, was not properly educated; for Wagner would have been just the man for him if he had been trained to understand and use music as Mr Rockefeller was trained to understand and use money. America did not teach him the language of the great ideals, just as England did not teach it to Dickens and Thackeray. Consequently, though nobody can suspect Dickens or Mark Twain of lacking the qualities and impulses that are the soul of such grotesque makeshift bodies as Church and State, Chivalry, Classicism, Art, Gentility, and the Holy Roman Empire; and nobody blames them for seeing that these bodies were mostly so decomposed as to have become intolerable nuisances, you have only to compare them with Carlyle and Ruskin, or with Euripides and Aristophanes, to see how, for want of a language of art and a body of philosophy, they were so much more interested in the fun and pathos of personal adventure than in the comedy and tragedy of human destiny.

Whistler was a Philistine, too. Outside the corner of art in which he was a virtuoso and a propagandist, he was a Man of Derision. Important as his propaganda was, and admired as his work was, no society could assimilate him. He could not even induce a British jury to award him substantial damages against a rich critic who had "done him out of his job"; and this is certainly the climax of social failure in England.

Edgar Allan Poe was not in the least a Philistine. He wrote always as if his native Boston was Athens, his Charlottesville University Plato's Academy, and his cottage the crown of the heights of Fiesole. He was the greatest journalistic critic of his time, placing good European work at sight when the European critics were waiting for somebody to tell them what to say. His poetry is so exquisitely refined that posterity will refuse to believe that it belongs to the same civilization as the glory of Mrs Julia Ward Howe's lilies or the honest doggerel of Whittier. Tennyson, who was nothing if not a virtuoso, never produced a success that will bear reading after Poe's failures. Poe constantly and inevitably produced magic where his greatest contemporaries produced only beauty. Tennyson's popular pieces, The May Queen and The Charge of the Six Hundred, cannot stand hackneying: they become positively nauseous after a time. The Raven, The Bells, and Annabel Lee are as fascinating at the thousandth repetition as at the first.

Poe's supremacy in this respect has cost him his reputation. This is a phenomenon which occurs when an artist achieves such perfection as to place himself *hors concours*. The greatest painter England ever produced is Hogarth, a miraculous draughtsman and an exquisite and poetic colorist. But he is never mentioned by critics. They talk copiously about Romney, the Gibson of his day; freely about Reynolds; nervously about the great Gainsborough; and not at all about Rowlandson and Hogarth, missing the inextinguishable grace of Rowlandson because they assume that all caricatures of his period are ugly, and avoiding Hogarth instinctively as critically unmanageable. In the same way, we have given up mentioning Poe: that is why the Americans forgot him when they posted up the names of their great in their Pantheon. Yet his is the first—almost the only name that the real connoisseur looks for.

But Poe, for all his virtuosity, is always a poet, and never a mere virtuoso. Poe put forward his Eureka, the formulation of his philosophy, as the most important thing he had done. His poems always have the universe as their background. So have the figures in his stories. Even in his tales of humor, which we shake our heads at as mistakes, they have this elemental quality. Toby Dammit himself, though his very name turns up the nose of the cultured critic, is more impressive and his end more tragic than the serious inventions of most story-tellers. The shortsighted gentleman who married his grandmother is no common butt of a common purveyor of the facetious: the grandmother has the elegance and free mind of Ninon de l'Enclos, the grandson the *tenue* of a marquis. This story was sent by Poe to Horne, whose Orion he had reviewed as poetry ought to be reviewed, with a request that it might be sold to an English magazine. The English magazine regretted that the deplorable immorality of the story made it for ever impossible in England!

In his stories of mystery and imagination Poe created a world-record for the English language: perhaps for all the languages. The story of the Lady Ligeia is not merely one of the wonders of literature: it is unparalleled and unapproached. There is really nothing to be said about it: we others simply take off our hats and let Mr Poe go first. It is interesting to compare Poe's stories with William Morris's. Both are not merely stories: they are complete works of art, like prayer carpets; and they are, in Poe's phrase, stories of imagination. They are masterpieces of style: what people call Macaulay's style is by comparison a mere method. But they are more different than it seems possible for two art works in the same kind to be. Morris will have nothing to do with mystery. "Ghost stories," he used to say, "have all the same explanation: the people are telling lies." His Sigurd has the beauty of mystery as it has every other sort of beauty, being, as it is, incomparably the greatest English epic; but his stories are in the open from end to end, whilst in Poe's stories the sun never shines.

Poe's limitation was his aloofness from the common people. Grotesques, negroes, madmen with delirium tremens, even gorillas, take the place of ordinary peasants and courtiers, citizens and soldiers, in his theatre. His houses are haunted houses, his woods enchanted woods; and he makes them so real that reality itself cannot sustain the comparison. His kingdom is not of this world.

Above all, Poe is great because he is independent of cheap attractions, independent of sex, of patriotism, of fighting, of sentimentality, snobbery, gluttony, and all the rest of the vulgar stock-in-trade of his profession. This is what gives him his superb distinction. One vulgarized thing, the pathos of dying children, he touched in Annabel Lee, and devulgarized it at once. He could not even amuse himself with detective stories without purifying the atmosphere of them until they became more edifying than most of Hymns, Ancient and Modern. His verse sometimes alarms and puzzles the reader by fainting with its own beauty; but the beauty is never the beauty of the flesh. You never say to him as you have to say uneasily to so many modern artists: "Yes, my friend, but these are things that men and women should *live* and not write about. Literature is not a keyhole for people with starved affections to peep through at the banquets of the body." It never became one in Poe's hands. Life cannot give you what he gives you except through fine art; and it was his instinctive observance of this distinction, and the fact that it did not beggar him, as it would beggar most writers, that makes him the most legitimate, the most classical, of modern writers.

It also explains why America does not care much for him, and why he has hardly been mentioned in England these many years. America and England are wallowing in the sensuality which their immense increase of riches has placed within their reach. I do not blame them: sensuality is a very necessary and healthy and educative element in life. Unfortunately, it is ill distributed; and our reading masses are looking on at it and thinking about it and longing for it, and having precarious little holiday treats of it, instead of sharing it temperately and continuously, and ceasing to be preoccupied with it. When the distribution is better adjusted and the preoccupation ceases, there will be a noble reaction in favor of the great writers like Poe, who begin just where the world, the flesh, and the devil leave off.

RODIN

From The Nation, 9 November 1912 and 24 November 1917

IN the year 1906 it was proposed to furnish the world with an authentic portrait-bust of me before I had left the prime of life too far behind. The question then arose: Could Rodin be induced to undertake the work? On no other condition would I sit, because it was clear to me that Rodin was not only the greatest sculptor then living, but the greatest sculptor of his epoch: one of those extraordinary persons who, like Michael Angelo, or Phidias, or Praxiteles, dominate whole ages as fashionable favorites dominate a single London season. I saw, therefore, that any man who, being a contemporary of Rodin, deliberately allowed his bust to be made by anybody else, must go down to posterity (if he went down at all) as a stupendous nincompoop.

Also, I wanted a portrait of myself by an artist capable of seeing me. Many clever portraits of my reputation were in existence; but I have never been taken in by my reputation, having manufactured it myself. A reputation is a mask which a man has to wear just as he has to wear a coat and trousers: it is a disguise we insist on as a point of decency. The result is that we have hardly any portraits of men and women. We have no portraits of their legs and shoulders; only of their skirts and trousers and blouses and coats. Nobody knows what Dickens was like, or what Queen Victoria was like, though their wardrobes are on record. Many people fancy they know their faces; but they are deceived: we know only the fashionable mask of the distinguished novelist and of the queen. And the mask defies the camera. When Mr Alvin Langdon Coburn wanted to exhibit a full-length photographic portrait of me, I secured a faithful representation up to the neck by the trite expedient of sitting to him one morning as I got out of my bath. The portrait was duly hung before a stupefied public as a first step towards the realization of Carlyle's antidote to political idolatry: a naked parliament. But though the body was my body, the face was the face of my reputation. So much so, in fact, that the critics concluded that Mr Coburn had faked his photograph, and stuck my head on somebody else's shoulders. For, as I have said, the mask cannot be penetrated by the camera. It is transparent only to the eye of a veritably god-like artist.

Rodin tells us that his wonderful portrait-busts seldom please the sitters. I can go further, and say that they often puzzle and disappoint the sitters' friends. The busts are of real men, not of the reputations of celebrated persons. Look at my bust, and you will not find it a bit like that brilliant fiction known as G. B. S. or Bernard Shaw. But it is most frightfully like me. It is what is really there, not what you think is there. The same with Puvis de Chavannes and the rest of them. Puvis de Chavannes protested, as one gathers—pointed to his mirror and to his photographs to prove that he was not like his bust. But I am convinced that he was not only like his bust, but that the bust actually was himself as distinct from his collars and his public manners. Puvis, though an artist of great merit, could not see himself. Rodin could. He saw me. Nobody else has done that yet.

Troubetskoi once made a most fascinating Shavian bust of me. He did it in about five hours, in Sargent's studio. It was a delightful and wonderful performance. He worked convulsively, giving birth to the thing in agonies, hurling lumps of clay about with groans, and making strange, dumb movements with his tongue, like a wordless prophet. He covered himself with plaster. He covered Sargent's carpets and curtains and pictures with plaster. He covered me with plaster. And, finally, he covered the block he was working on with plaster to such purpose that, at the end of the second sitting, lo! there stood Sargent's studio in ruins, buried like Pompeii under the scoriæ of a volcano, and in the midst a spirited bust of one of my reputations, a little idealized (quite the gentleman, in fact) but recognizable a mile off as the sardonic author of Man and Superman, with a dash of Offenbach, a touch of Mephistopheles, and a certain aristocratic delicacy and distinction that came from Troubetskoi himself, he being a prince. I should like to have that bust; but the truth is, my wife cannot stand Offenbach-Mephistopheles; and I was not allowed to have the bust any more than I was allowed to have that other witty jibe at my poses, Neville Lytton's portrait of me as Velasquez's Pope Innocent.

Rodin worked very differently. He plodded along exactly as if he were a river-god doing a job of wall-building in a garden for three or four francs a day. When he was in doubt he measured me with an old iron dividers, and then measured the bust. If the bust's nose was too long, he sliced a bit out of it, and jammed the tip of it up to close the gap, with no more emotion or affectation than a glazier putting in a window pane. If the ear was in the wrong place, he cut it off and slapped it into its right place, excusing these ruthless mutilations to my wife (who half expected to see the already terribly animated clay bleed) by re-

228

marking that it was shorter than to make a new ear. Yet a
succession of miracles took place as he worked. In the first
fifteen minutes, in merely giving a suggestion of human shape
to the lump of clay, he produced so spirited a thumbnail bust of
me that I wanted to take it away and relieve him from further
labor. It reminded me of a highly finished bust by Sarah Bern-
hardt, who is very clever with her fingers. But that phase vanished
like a summer cloud as the bust evolved. I say evolved advisedly;
for it passed through every stage in the evolution of art before
my eyes in the course of a month. After that first fifteen minutes
it sobered down into a careful representation of my features in
their exact living dimensions. Then this representation mysteri-
ously went back to the cradle of Christian art, at which point I
again wanted to say: "For Heaven's sake, stop and give me that:
it is a Byzantine masterpiece." Then it began to look as if Bernini
had meddled with it. Then, to my horror, it smoothed out into
a plausible, rather elegant piece of eighteenth-century work,
almost as if Houdon had touched up a head by Canova or
Thorwaldsen, or as if Leighton had tried his hand at eclecticism
in bust-making. At this point Troubetskoi would have broken
it with a hammer, or given it up with a wail of despair. Rodin
contemplated it with an air of callous patience, and went on with
his job, more like a river-god turned plasterer than ever. Then
another century passed in a single night; and the bust became a
Rodin bust, and was the living head of which I carried the model
on my shoulders. It was a process for the embryologist to study,
not the æsthete. Rodin's hand worked, not as a sculptor's hand
works, but as the Life Force works. What is more, I found that
he was aware of it, quite simply. I no more think of Rodin as
a celebrated sculptor than I think of Elijah as a well-known
littérateur and forcible after-dinner speaker. His "Main de Dieu"
is his own hand. That is why all the stuff written about him by
professional art-critics is such ludicrous cackle and piffle. I have
been a professional art-critic myself, and perhaps not much of
one at that (though I fully admit that I touched nothing I did not
adorn), but at least I knew how to take off my hat and hold my

tongue when my cacklings and pifflings would have been impertinences.

Rodin took the conceit out of me most horribly. Once he shewed me a torso of a female figure; an antique. It was a beauty; and I swallowed it whole. He waited rather wistfully for a moment, to see whether I really knew chalk from cheese, and then pointed out to me that the upper half of the figure was curiously inferior to the lower half, as if the sculptor had taught himself as he went along. The difference, which I had been blind to a moment before, was so obvious when he pointed it out, that I have despised myself ever since for not seeing it. There never was such an eye for carved stone as Rodin's. To the average critic or connoisseur half the treasures he collects seem nothing but a heap of old paving-stones. But they all have somewhere a scrap of modelled surface, perhaps half the size of a postage stamp, that makes gems of them. In his own work he shews a strong feeling for the beauty of marble. He gave me three busts of myself: one in bronze, one in plaster, one in marble. The bronze is me (growing younger now). The plaster is me. But the marble has quite another sort of life: it glows; and light flows over it. It does not look solid: it looks luminous; and this curious glowing and flowing keeps people's fingers off it; for you feel as if you could not catch hold of it. People say that all modern sculpture is done by the Italian artizans who mechanically reproduce the sculptor's plaster model in the stone. Rodin himself says so. But the peculiar qualities that Rodin gets in his marbles are not in the clay models. What is more, other sculptors can hire artizans, including those who have worked for Rodin. Yet no other sculptor produces such marbles as Rodin. One day Rodin told me that all modern sculpture is imposture; that neither he nor any of the others can use a chisel. A few days later he let slip the remark: "Handling the chisel is very interesting." Yet when he models a portrait-bust, his method is neither that of Michael Angelo with his chisel nor of a modeller in the round, but that of a draughtsman outlining in clay the thousand profiles which your head would present if it were sliced a thousand times through the centre at different angles.

Rodin, like all great workmen who can express themselves in words, was very straight and simple, and disposed to be useful to those who listened to him, and not to waste their time. He knew what is important and what is not, and what can be taught and what cannot. After all, apart from the acquired skill of his hands, which he shared with any stone-mason, he had only two qualifications to make him the divinest workman of his day. One was a profounder and more accurate vision than anyone else's. The other was an incorruptible veracity. That was all, ladies and gentlemen. Now I have told you his secret, you can all become great sculptors. It is as easy as any other sort of manual labor, and much pleasanter—if you can pick up those two simple qualifications.

THE ARTSTRUCK ENGLISHMAN

MEN OF LETTERS. By Dixon Scott. With an Introduction by Max Beerbohm. (Hodder & Stoughton.)

From The Nation, 17 February 1917

To an Irishman there is always something indecent in the way an Englishman takes to art, when he does take to it. He worships it; exalts its artifices above its inspirations; makes gods of its frail and ridiculous human instruments; pontificates and persecutes in its name; and ends in delirium and drunkenness, which seem to him the raptures of a saint's vigil. Swinburne's article on Victor Hugo in the Encyclopædia Britannica is quite a mild example, though it repeats the word "deathless" as often as a Jingo war editor repeats the word "unflinching." The idolatry of the Bible, which has played such a curious part in British history, is really a worship of literary art: no other nation speaks of "The Book of Books" as if the phrase were in the Athanasian Creed, just as no other nation stands up in the concert room when the Hallelujah chorus is sung. There are moments when a sober man wants to shake the idolater and talk to him like a Dutch uncle, or like Lady Macbeth when she said to her blithering, ghostridden spouse: "When all's said, you look but on a stool."

I am myself a literary artist, and have made larger claims for literature—or, at any rate, put them forward more explicitly—than any writer of my generation as far as I know, claiming a continuous inspiration for modern literature of precisely the same character as that conceded to the ancient Hebrew Scriptures, and maintaining that the man of letters, when he is more than a mere confectioner, is a prophet or nothing. But to listen for a writer's message, even when the fellow is a fool, is one thing: to worship his tools and his tricks, his pose and his style, is an abomination. Admire them by all means, just as you admire the craft of the masons and the carpenters and sculptors who built your cathedral; but dont go inside and sing Te Deums to them.

Dixon Scott was an exceedingly clever young man, with a most remarkable specific literary talent. Reading his criticisms is like watching revolver practice by a crack shot: the explosiveness of the style and the swiftness of the devastation hide the monotony of the mood and method. His longest and most deeply felt effort was an essay on William Morris; his most elaborate, an essay on me. When it first appeared in The Bookman, I read it with the chuckle of the old hand whose professional tricks have landed a young one in a transport of innocent enthusiasm. But I was finally shocked by his preposterous reversal of the natural relative importance of manner and matter. He quoted a long sentence of mine, which derived a certain cumulative intensity from the fact that it was an indictment of civilization, as a specimen of style, and then, with an amazingly callous indifference to the fact that he, like the rest of us, was guilty on all its counts, simply asked, with eager curiosity, and a joyous sense of being the very man to answer the question, "Now what pose is this?" It was very much as if I had told him the house was on fire, and he had said, "How admirably monosyllabic!" and left the nursery stairs burning unheeded. My impulse was to exclaim, "Do you suppose, you conceited young whelp, that I have taken all that trouble and developed all that literary craft to gratify your appetite for style? Get up at once and fetch a bucket of water; or, at least, raise an alarm, unless you wish me to take you by the scruff of the neck and make you do it. You call yourself a critic: you are a mere fancier."

This, I think, is what, in Touchstone's phrase, obliges me to disable Scott's judgment. It comes out extravagantly in his essay on Morris, which is a long and sincerely felt protest against the author of The Defence of Guinevere maturing into the author of Sigurd, of A Dream of John Ball, and of News from Nowhere. It is like a man complaining that his wife does not remain a girl: a sort of *lèse humanité* against which human honor revolts. The excuse is, of course, the writer's youth.

That maturity involves quite poignant losses to set against its consummations is only too true. Mozart's Abduction from the Seraglio is monotonous and resourceless compared to his Don Juan; but it has a charm and freshness that Mozart could not recapture, young as he was when he died. To ask Morris to give Sigurd the charm of Guinevere—a charm of helplessness, weakness, innocence, boyish romance—was like asking any poet of fifty to give us an Alastor: he could not if he would, and what is perhaps more to the point, he would not if he could, because no man will go back on a good bargain merely because one of the coins he had to pay away was a sixpence he had once tried to break with a girl sweetheart. We must put up with these inevitables; and Dixon Scott's complaint that Morris did not spend his whole life in defending Guinevere is no more sensible than a complaint that General Douglas Haig can no longer cut a figure as a sprinter. But when the youth takes it so seriously that he must needs set up the most laboriously ingenious explanations of why Morris and the rest of us deliberately stifled our instincts; corrupted our natures; and perverted our talents instead of going on writing Guineveres and Alastors for him: in short, of why we grew up expressly to spite him, he goes over the edge of silly cleverness into the abyss of folly. One has a startled sense of the artist conceived as a pet lap dog for the *dilettanti*, having his growth stunted by a diet of gin that he may be a more amusing monster than Nature made him.

I should not quarrel with this folly if it were recognized as such; for a good deal of new country is discovered by simply going astray. The straight and narrow path has been so often explored that we all go a little way down the paths of danger and destruction merely to see what they are like; and even the paths of tomfoolery may lead to a view or two. Dixon Scott had qualifications for such ramblings which made him a very agreeable critic, and sometimes a very useful one. Chief among these was his knowledge of the natural history of the artist, which preserved him from many current journalistic sillinesses. To take a personal example, the fact that I am an Irish Protestant, and that I published a volume called Three Plays for Puritans, has created a legend about the gloomy, sour, Sabbath-ridden, Ulster-Covenanting home in which I was brought up, and in which my remarkable resemblance to St Paul, St Anthony, and John Knox was stamped on me. To Dixon Scott this was as patently absurd as an assumption that the polar bear owes its black fur to its negro parents. He at once picked out the truth and packed it into the statement that I am the son of Donizetti's Lucrezia Borgia (as a matter of fact I was brought up in an atmosphere of which two of the main constituents were Italian opera and complete freedom of thought; and my attitude to conventional British life ever since has been that of a missionary striving to understand the superstitions of the natives in order to make himself intelligible to them). All through this book, in dealing with me, with Wells, with Kipling, with Houghton, he is saved again and again by his knowledge of the sort of animal the artist is in his nonage. Unfortunately his knowledge stops there. He does not understand the artist's manhood; protests with all his soul against the inevitable development; and always, however ridiculously, sets up the same theory that the shy romantic dreamer has put on a mask, which, as he wittily says, gets so hard pressed upon his face by popular applause that it moulds his very features to its shape. Shaw, Kipling, Wells, and Co. are timid children desperately playing at being strong but by no means silent men; and he

tries to strip our masks off, and shew our real faces, which, however, are all the same face, and a very obvious doll's face at that.
His mistake is in taking the method of nature, which is a dramatic
method, for a theatrical pose. No doubt every man has a shy
child in him, artist or no artist. But every man whose business it
is to work directly upon other men, whether as artist, politician,
advocate, propagandist, organizer, teacher, or what not, must
dramatize himself and play his part. To the laborer who merely
digs and vegetates, to the squire who merely hunts and eats, to
the mathematician and physicist, the men of the orchestra and the
tribune may seem affected and theatrical; but when they themselves desire to impress their needs or views on their fellows they
find that they, too, must find a pose or else remain paralyzed and
dumb. In short, what is called a pose is simply a technical condition of certain activities. It is offensive only when out of place:
he who brings his public pose to the dinner table is like the
general who brings his sword there, or the dentist who puts his
forceps beside his plate, just to shew that he has one. He cannot,
however, always leave it behind him. Queen Victoria complained
that Gladstone talked to her as if she were a public meeting; but
surely that is the way in which a Prime Minister should address
a queen when affairs of State are on the carpet. Lord Melbourne's
pose may have been more genial and human; but so it was when
he addressed a public meeting. Dixon Scott takes this very simple
natural phenomenon, and, guessing at once that he can be very
clever about it if he begins by being very stupid, pays the price
for being clever. It is monstrously stupid to try to foist Morris,
Wells, and Kipling (to say nothing of myself) on the reader as
creatures with guilty secrets, all their secrets being the same
secret: to wit, that they are not Morris, Wells, and Kipling at all,
but sensitive plants of quite another species. Still, on that stupid
assumption he writes very cleverly, sometimes with penetrating
subtlety. But as he remains the Fancier, he is never sound, and
is only quite satisfactory when dealing with pure virtuosity,
which he finds only in Max Beerbohm's Zuleika. And then he
has to leave you in ignorance of the fact that Max is the most

savage Radical caricaturist since Gillray, and that Zuleika is only his play, not his work.

It was a kind and devoted act of Mr St John Adcock to collect and edit these reviews, and very modest of him to allow Max to take the stage as their introducer. They are the best monument the untimely slain author could have desired. I have no space here to do more than point out the limitations of Dixon Scott's view of art, and how the young literary voluptuary flourished at the expense of the critic of life. But I can guarantee the book as being not only frightfully smart in the wrong places, but, in the best of the right ones, as good as it is in the nature of the best journalistic criticism to be.

SHAMING THE DEVIL ABOUT SHELLEY

From The Albemarle Review, September 1892

WHEN I first saw the proposal that Shelley's native county should celebrate the centenary of his birth by founding a Shelley Library and Museum at Horsham, I laughed: not publicly, because that would have been the act of a spoil-sport, but in my sleeve. The native county in question was Sussex, which had just distinguished itself at the General Election by a gloriously solid Conservative vote which had sent to Parliament a lord (son of a duke), an admiral, two baronets (one of them ex-Groom-in-Waiting to the Queen, and the other an ex-Dragoon officer), and two distinguished commoners (one of them son to a lord and the other to a Canon, once Her Majesty's chaplain): all of them high Tories. Now the difficulty of inducing so true-blue a corner of England to express any feeling towards Shelley but one of indignant abhorrence, can only be appreciated by those who are in possession of a complete and unexpurgated statement of what Shelley taught. Let me, therefore, draw up such a statement, as compendiously as may be.

In politics Shelley was a Republican, a Leveller, a Radical of the most extreme type. He was even an Anarchist of the old-fashioned Godwinian school, up to the point at which he per-

236

ceived Anarchism to be impracticable. He publicly ranged himself with demagogues and gaol-birds like Cobbett and Henry
Hunt (the original "Man in the White Hat"), and not only
advocated the Plan of Radical Reform which was afterwards
embodied in the proposals of the Chartists, but denounced the
rent-roll of the landed aristocracy as the true pension list, thereby
classing himself as what we now call a Land Nationalizer. He
echoed Cobbett's attacks on the National Debt and the Fund-
ing System in such a manner as to leave no reasonable doubt that
if he had been born half a century later he would have been advocating Social-Democracy with a view to its development into
the most democratic form of Communism practically attainable
and maintainable. At the late election he would certainly have
vehemently urged the agricultural laborers of Sussex to procure
a candidate of the type of John Burns and to vote for him against
the admiral, the lord, the two baronets, and against Messrs
Gathorne Hardy and Brookfield.

In religion, Shelley was an Atheist. There is nothing uncommon in that; but he actually called himself one, and urged
others to follow his example. He never trifled with the word
God: he knew that it meant a personal First Cause, Almighty
Creator, and Supreme Judge and Ruler of the Universe, and that
it did not mean anything else, never had meant anything else,
and never whilst the English language lasted would mean anything else. Knowing perfectly well that there was no such person,
he did not pretend that the question was an open one, or imply,
by calling himself an Agnostic, that there might be such a person
for all he knew to the contrary. He did know to the contrary;
and he said so. Further, though there never was a man with so
abiding and full a consciousness of the omnipresence of a living
force, manifesting itself here in the germination and growth of a
tree, there in the organization of a poet's brain, and elsewhere in
the putrefaction of a dead dog, he never condescended to beg
off being an Atheist by calling this omnipresent energy God, or
even Pan. He lived and died professedly, almost boastfully, godless. In his time, however, as at present, God was little more than

a word to the English people. What they really worshipped was the Bible; and our modern Church movement to get away from Bible fetishism and back to some presentable sort of Christianity (*vide* Mr Horton's speech at Grindelwald the other day, for example) had not then come to the surface. The preliminary pick-axing work of Bible smashing had yet to be done; and Shelley, who found the moral atmosphere of the Old Testament murderous and abominable, and the asceticism of the New suicidal and pessimistic, smashed away at the Bible with all his might and main.

But all this, horrifying as it is from the Sussex point of view, was mere eccentricity compared to Shelley's teaching on the subject of the family. He would not draw any distinction between the privilege of the king or priest and that of the father. He pushed to its extremest consequences his denial that blood relationship altered by one jot or tittle the relations which should exist between human beings. One of his most popular performances at Eton and Oxford was an elaborate curse on his own father, who had thwarted and oppressed him: and the entirely serious intention of Shelley's curses may be seen in his solemn imprecation against Lord Eldon, ending with the words:

"I curse thee, though I hate thee not."

His determination to impress on us that our fathers should be no more and no less to us than other men, is evident in every allusion of his to the subject, from the school curse to The Cenci, which to this day is refused a licence for performance on the stage.

But Shelley was not the man to claim freedom of enmity, and say nothing about freedom of love. If father and son are to be as free in their relation to one another as hundredth cousins are, so must sister and brother. The freedom to curse a tyrannical father is not more sacred than the freedom to love an amiable sister. In a word, if filial duty is no duty, then incest is no crime. This sounds startling even now, disillusioned as we are by Herbert Spencer, Elie Reclus, and other writers as to there being anything "natural" in our code of prohibited degrees; but in Shelley's time it seemed the summit of impious vice, just as it would to the Sussexers to-day, if they only knew. Nevertheless, he did not shrink from it in the least: the hero and heroine of Laon and Cythna are brother and sister; and the notion that the bowdlerization of this great poem as The Revolt of Islam represents any repentance or withdrawal on Shelley's part, cannot be sustained for a moment in the face of the facts. No person who is well acquainted with Shelley's work can suppose that he would have thought any the worse of Byron if he had known and believed everything that Mrs Beecher Stowe alleged concerning him. And no one who has ever reasoned out the consequences of such views can doubt for a moment that Shelley regarded the family, in its legal aspect, as a doomed institution.

So much for the opinions which Shelley held and sedulously propagated. Could Sussex be reconciled to them on the ground that they were mere "views" which did not affect his conduct? Not a bit of it. Although Shelley was the son of a prosperous country gentleman, his life was consistently disreputable except at one fatal moment of his boyhood, when he chivalrously married a girl who had run away from school and thrown herself on his protection. At this time he had been expelled from Oxford for writing and circulating a tract called The Necessity of Atheism. His marriage, as might have been expected, was a hopeless failure; and when this fact was fully established the two parted; and Shelley was fallen in love with by the daughter of Mary Wollstonecraft and Godwin. Shelley took young Mary Godwin abroad, and started housekeeping with her without the least scruple; and he suggested that his wife should come and make one of the household, a notion which did not recommend itself to either of the ladies. The courts then deprived him of the custody of his children, on the ground that he was unfit to have charge of them; and his wife eventually committed suicide. Shelley then married Mary Godwin, solely, as he explained, because the law forced him to do so in the interest of his son. The rest of his life was quite consistent with the beginning of it; and it is not improbable that he would have separated from his second wife as from his first, if he had not been drowned when he was twenty-nine.

It only remains to point out that Shelley was not a hot-headed nor an unpractical person. All his writings, whether in prose or verse, have a peculiarly deliberate quality. His political pamphlets are unique in their freedom from all appeal to the destructive passions; there is neither anger, sarcasm, nor frivolity in them; and in this respect his poems exactly resemble his political pamphlets. Other poets, from Shakespear to Tennyson, have let the tiger in them loose under pretext of patriotism, righteous indignation, or what not: he never did. His horror of violence, cruelty, injustice, and bravery was proof against their infection. Hence it cannot for a moment be argued that his opinions and his conduct were merely his wild oats. His seriousness, his anxious carefulness, are just as obvious in the writings which still expose their publishers to the possibility of a prosecution for sedition or blasphemy as in his writings on Catholic Emancipation, the propriety and practical sagacity of which are not now disputed. And he did not go back upon his opinions in the least as he grew older. By the time he had begun The Triumph of Life, he had naturally come to think Queen Mab a boyish piece of work, not that what it affirmed seemed false to him or what it denied true, but because it did not affirm and deny enough. Thus there is no excuse for Shelley on the ground of his youth or rashness. If he was a sinner, he was a hardened sinner and a deliberate one.

The delicate position of the gentlemen who invited Sussex to honor Shelley on the 4th of last month will now be apparent, especially when it is added that the facts are undeniable, accessible to all inquirers, and familiar to most fanciers of fine literature. The success of the celebration evidently depended wholly on the chances of inducing the aforesaid fanciers to wink and say nothing in as many words as possible. A conspiracy to keep an open secret of so scandalous a character seems extravagant; and yet it almost succeeded. The practical question was not whether Shelley could be shewn to be infamous, but whether anyone wished to undertake that demonstration. In Shelley's case it appeared that everybody—that is, everybody whose desire weighed two straws with the public—was anxious to make Shelley a saint. Mr Cordy Jeaffreson's attempt to prove him the meanest of sinners had been taken in such uncommonly bad part that no literary man with any regard for his own popularity cared to follow up Mr Jeaffreson's line. The feeblest excuses for Shelley had been allowed to pass. Matthew Arnold had explained how poor Percy had the misfortune to live in a low set, as if he had not been more free to choose his own set than most other men in England. Others had pleaded that he was young; that he was a poet; that you would find his works full of true piety if you only read them in a proper spirit; and—most exquisite of all—that the people who persisted in raking up the story of Harriet must be low-minded gossips, to allude to so improper a story. On all sides there went up the cry, "We want our great Shelley, our darling Shelley, our best, noblest, highest of poets. We will not have it said that he was a Leveller, an Atheist, a foe to marriage, an advocate of incest. He was a little unfortunate in his first marriage; and we pity him for it. He was a little eccentric in his vegetarianism; but we are not ashamed of that; we glory in the humanity of it [with morsels of beefsteak, fresh from the slaughter house, sticking between our teeth]. We ask the public to be generous—to read his really great works, such as the Ode to a Skylark, and not to gloat over those boyish indiscretions known as Laon and Cythna, Prometheus, Rosalind and Helen, The Cenci, The Masque of Anarchy, etc., etc. Take no notice of the Church papers; for our Shelley was a true Christian at heart. Away with Jeaffreson; for our Shelley was a gentleman if ever there was one. If you doubt it, ask—"

That was just the difficulty: who were we to ask when the Centenary came round? On reflection, the Horsham Committee decided that we had better ask Mr Gosse. It was a wise choice. The job was one which required a certain gift of what is popularly called cheek; and Mr Gosse's cheek is beyond that of any man of my acquaintance. I went down to Horsham expressly to hear him; and I can certify that he surpassed himself. I confess I thought he was going to overdo it, when, extolling the poet's patriotism in selecting England for his birth-place, he applied to Shelley a brilliant paraphrase of Mr Gilbert's

"For he might have been a Rooshan," etc.,

but no: it came off perfectly. A subsequent fearless assertion that there was surprisingly little slime—he said slime—on Shelley's reputation, and that the "sordid" details of his career were really not so very numerous after all, hit off to a nicety the requirements of the occasion; and when he handsomely remarked that for his part he thought that far too much talk had already been made about Harriet, we all felt that a gentleman could say no less. It was a happy thought also to chaff Shelley as an eater of buns and raisins, the satirist being no doubt stoked up for the occasion with gobbets of cow or sheep, and perhaps a slice or two of pig. But what fairly banged everything in his address was his demonstration that Shelley was so fragile, so irresponsible, so ethereally tender, so passionate a creature that the wonder was that he was not a much greater rascal. The dodge of making allowances for a great man's differences with small men on the plea of his being a privileged weakling is one which I have of course often seen worked; but I never saw it brought to such perfection as by Mr Gosse at Horsham. It was a triumph not only of audacity but of platform manner. At the stiffest parts of the game Mr Gosse contrived to get on a sort of infatuated pomposity which is quite indescribable. Whilst it completely imposed on the innocents, there was yet lurking behind it a sly relish for the fun of the situation which disarmed those out-and-out Shelleyans who half expected to see Mr Gosse struck by lightning for his presumption. For my own part, I have seldom been worse misunderstood than by the gentleman who wrote to a daily paper alleging, in proof of my sympathy with his own outraged feelings, that I walked out of the room in disgust. I protest I only went to catch the 5.17 train to London, where I had to act as the best available substitute for Mr Gosse at the proletarian celebration of Shelley in the easterly parish of St Luke's.

In a rougher, homelier, style, the chairman, Mr Hurst, Justice of the Peace and Deputy Lieutenant for the county, gave Mr Gosse an admirable lead. The judicious way in which he dwelt on the central fact that Shelley had been born in the neighbourhood; his remarks on the intellectual value of a free public library to the working classes, and his declaration that if Shelley were alive he would be the first to support a free library; his happy comparison of Horsham to Stratford-on-Avon (which brought the house down at once); his deprecation of the harshness of Oxford University in expelling Shelley for a "mere dialectical view" (meaning The Necessity of Atheism); and his genial peroration on the theme of "boys will be boys," pitched so as to half confess that he himself had held quite desperate views when he was young and foolish; all this was so ingenious that when I described it in the evening at the Hall of Science it established my reputation in St Luke's as a platform humorist of the first order. But his point about the free library was really the essential one. It was for the sake of the library that I refused to blow the gaff by speaking at Horsham when Mr Stanley Little, with characteristic intrepidity, invited me to do so. It was presumably for the sake of the library that Mr Hurst, Mr Gosse, and Mr Frederic Harrison deliberately talked bogus Shelleyism to the reporters. Miss Alma Murray and Mr Herbert Sims Reeves may have recited and sung for the sake of the real Shelley; and Professor Nicholl, as I gather, shewed an alarming disposition to let the cat out of the bag in moving a vote of thanks to the chair; but the rest were solid for the library, even if the front were to be decorated with a relief representing Shelley in a tall hat, Bible in hand, leading his children on Sunday morning to the church of his native parish.

Of the meeting in the evening at the Hall of Science I need say but little. It consisted for the most part of working men who took Shelley quite seriously, and were much more conscious of his opinions and of his spirit than of his dexterity as a versifier. It was summoned without the intervention of any committee by Mr G. W. Foote, the President of the National Secular Society, who, by his own personal announcement and a few handbills, got a meeting which beat Horsham hollow. The task of the speakers was so easy that Mr Gosse and Mr Frederic Harrison might well have envied us. Mr Foote, a militant Atheist like Shelley himself, and one who has suffered imprisonment under the outrageous Blasphemy Laws which some people suppose to be obsolete, was able to speak with all the freedom and force of a man who not only talks Shelley but lives him. Dr Furnivall, incorrigible in the matter of speaking his mind, frankly stated how far he went with Shelley, which was far enough to explain why he was not one of the Horsham orators. As for me, my quotations from the Horsham proceedings came off so immensely that I could not but feel jealous of Mr Hurst. For the rest, I had nothing to do but give a faithful account of Shelley's real opinions, with every one of which I unreservedly agree. Finally Mr Foote recited Men of England, which brought the meeting to an end amid thunders of applause. What would have happened had anyone recited it at Horsham is more than I can guess. Possibly the police would have been sent for.

Mr Foote's meeting, which was as spontaneous as the absence of committee and advertisement could make it, was composed for the most part of people whose lives had been considerably influenced by Shelley. Some time ago Mr H. S. Salt, in the course of a lecture on Shelley, mentioned on the authority of Mrs Marx Aveling, who had it from her father, Karl Marx, that Shelley had inspired a good deal of that huge but badly managed popular effort called the Chartist movement. An old Chartist who was present, and who seemed at first much surprised by this statement, rose to confess that, "now he came to think of it" (apparently for the first time), it was through reading Shelley that he got the ideas that led him to join the Chartists. A little further inquiry elicited that Queen Mab was known as The Chartists' Bible; and Mr Buxton Forman's collection of small, cheap copies, blackened with the finger-marks of many heavy-handed trades, are the proofs that Shelley became a power—a power that is still growing. He made and is still making men and women join political societies, Secular societies, Vegetarian societies, societies for the loosening of the marriage contract, and Humanitarian societies of all sorts. There is at every election a Shelleyan vote, though there is no means of counting it. The discussion of his life, which makes our literary *dilettanti* so horribly uneasy, cannot be checked, no matter how exquisitely they protest. He is still forcing us to make up our minds whether the conventional judgment of his life as that of a scoundrel is the truth or only a *reductio ad absurdum* of the conventional morality. That is a vital question; and it is pitifully useless for the exponents of the fashionable culture to deprecate it as "chatter about Harriet," when no sensible man can hear any chattering except that of their own teeth at the prospect of having to face Shelley's ideas seriously.

Without any ill-conditioned desire to rub the situation into those who have offered Shelley a carnival of humbug as a centenary offering, I think no reasonable man can deny the right of those who appreciate the scope and importance of Shelley's views to refuse to allow the present occasion to be monopolized by triflers to whom he was nothing more than a word-jeweller. Besides, the Horsham affair has been a failure: nobody has been taken in by it. Mr Foote scores heavily; and Mr Gosse and Mr Frederic Harrison are left sitting down, rather pensively, even though no newspaper except the Pall Mall Gazette and the Daily Chronicle dared to prick the bubble. I now venture to suggest that in future the bogus Shelley be buried and done with. I make all allowances for the fact that we are passing through an epidemic of cowardice on the part of literary men and politicians which will certainly make us appear to the historians of 1992 the most dastardly crew that has ever disgraced the platform and the press. It seems that as the march of liberty removes concrete terrors from our path, we become the prey of abstract fear, and are more and more persuaded that society is only held together by the closest trade unionism in senseless lying and make-believe. But it is vain to lie about Shelley: it is clear as day that if he were nothing more than what we try to make him out, his Centenary would be as little remembered as that of Southey. Why not be content to say, "I abhor Shelley's opinions; but my abhorrence is overwhelmed by my admiration of the exquisite artistic quality of his work," or "I am neither an Atheist nor a believer in Equality nor a Free Lover; and yet I am willing to celebrate Shelley because I feel that he was somehow a good sort," or even "I think Shelley's poetry slovenly and unsubstantial, and his ideas simply rot; but I will celebrate him because he said what he thought, and not what he was expected to say he thought." Instead of this, each of us gets up and says, "I am forced for the sake of my wife and family and social position to be a piffler and a trimmer; and as all you fellows are in the same predicament, I ask you to back me up in trying to make out that Shelley was a piffler and a trimmer too." As one of the literary brotherhood myself, I hope I am clubbable enough to stand in with any reasonable movement in my trade; but this is altogether too hollow. It will not do: the meanest Shelley reader knows better. If it were only to keep ourselves from premature putrefaction, we must tell the truth about somebody; and I submit that Shelley has pre-eminent claims to be that somebody. Hence this article.

HAS HERBERT SPENCER REALLY TRIUMPHED?

HERBERT SPENCER. By Hugh Elliot. (Constable.)

From The Nation, 17 *March* 1917

IN a way, Mr Havelock Ellis's celebration of The Triumph of Herbert Spencer is very pleasant to me. As a Socialist, I have been in full reaction against Herbert Spencer's senile politics (not those of his prime) for nearly forty years; and I see in the experience of the war, not their triumph, but the *coup de grâce* that puts them out of their lingering pain. But I have always been revolted by that mean belittlement of the hero which in our unmannerly community is the received method of questioning his influence. Herbert Spencer quite naturally and unaffectedly lived the life of a great man, and played the great game all through; and whoever does not see this and take off his hat to him, does not know a gentleman when he meets one. When Mr Havelock Ellis faces an ungrateful and ungenerous posterity, and calls for three cheers for Herbert Spencer, I cannot believe that any decent soul will refuse to hail his name with three times three if he really knows what Spencer did and how much the world owed to it in his time. Even those who take no interest in his philosophy will feel a quaint affection for the man who, when he was not faithfully straightening out the tangled thought of his century, was inspiring himself with Meyerbeer's music; giving up his horse because, on its discovery of his intense dislike to coerce any living creature, it went slower than he walked, and finally grazed by the roadside without respect for the philosopher's pressing appointments; refusing the proffered affection of George Eliot because she was not as beautiful as the Venus of Milo; and, when his landlady objected to his describing her in the census paper as "the lady with whom Mr Herbert Spencer lives," pondered on her unaccountable recalcitrance for an hour, and then altered the entry to "the lady who lives with Mr Herbert Spencer." Speculative criticism may yet conjecture that he must have been the original of Wagner's Parsifal, "*der reine Thor durch Mitleid wissend.*" All the horses in paradise are probably now struggling for the honor of carrying him at full gallop to whatever destination he may be seeking uncoercively.

Mr Havelock Ellis inevitably salutes him as "the essential Englishman, pure and unmitigated, the complete middle-class Englishman of the straitest sect, the naked, typical Englishman." That is what we always say of a man who disagrees with his contemporaries on every subject on which it is possible for a man to disagree with the majority without being stark mad, and who would have been lynched if the common Englishman of his day had been intelligent or erudite enough to find out what he really believed and disbelieved—especially what he disbelieved. It is like saying that St Sophia's is a typical church. Mr Havelock Ellis offers as evidence the fact that Spencer was a member of the committee of the Athenæum Club, which is hardly a general

English characteristic, and that he did not know German, in which respect he might be described as a typical Chinaman. I am afraid the statement that Spencer was a typical Englishman will not wash. But it may be said fairly and significantly that he was one of those men of whom Englishmen say that he was typically English: a thing they never say of Shelley. And when the proposition is narrowed down to his being a typical middle-class Englishman, it may be interpreted as meaning that as he had never been broken in to communal life either by slavery, by graduation at a university, by State service, or by belonging to a social circle so exclusive that everybody in it is supposed to know everybody else, he was an inveterate anarchist. Being also a man of vigorous mind, a freethinker in the best sense, he was, within the limits imposed by his humanity and common sense, a great Anti, or Conscientious Objector.

Mr Havelock Ellis says that "the war has put the final seal on Herbert Spencerism." But I have heard another man say that the war has put the kybosh on Herbert Spencer. I cannot find the word "kybosh" in the dictionary: it may be Hebrew for the final seal, for all I know. Perhaps the editor will invite philologers to open a correspondence on the subject. But I think the gentleman I have just quoted meant that the war had made Spencer's Unsocialism ridiculous. And the only demurrer that can be put in is that war is not a fair test of anything. You cannot reasonably say that war has put the kybosh on domestic architecture or on cities that do not see the sky through steel nets, merely because our houses will not resist the impact of nine-inch shells, and the atmosphere is not proof against the droppings from Zeppelins. I should admit that if Spencerism had made good in peace, it could not be discredited because it had broken down with a crash in war. But the truth is that Spencerism was such a disastrous failure in peace that war actually produced comparative prosperity and social sanity by a better distribution of wealth and a more patriotic employment of men. The fact that the evils of Unsocialism had created vested interests in waste, in poverty, in dishonesty, in drunkenness, in prostitution, in incompetence, snobbery, and imposture, so huge that they resisted everything short of Armageddon, may be the explanation of Armageddon; but it is no justification of Unsocialism, and no triumph for the philosopher who opposed both Socialism and Militarism.

The mischief of the present situation is that we have been too lazy to accept the teachings either of the Socialists or of Herbert Spencer and his disciple, Hilaire Belloc. From Turgot and Adam Smith to Cobden, Bastiat, and Herbert Spencer, economists and philosophers have preached freedom of contract and of everything else; and from Robert Owen and Fourier to Morris and the Sidney Webbs, they have preached the common rule, the collective bargain, the communal life, and the doctrine that Robinson Crusoe, monarch of all he surveys, is far more a slave than the man who carries the weight of a thousand laws and works for something bigger than himself. But, bless you! the British people have not taken the slightest notice of these intellectual and imaginative exercises. When the slaughter of children's bodies and souls in the cotton factories became unbearable, they drifted into sham factory legislation for fifty years, and then, all the shams being exposed, made the legislation real. They drifted into Free Trade because there was money in it; and when, later on, the Midlands concluded that there was money for them in Protection and tried to revive it under the title of Tariff Reform, the ensuing debates proved nothing except that our political Free Traders did not know the A B C of Free Trade. We have drifted down stream in the current, and up stream in the eddy, without the least notion whither we are going. No statesman has lost a vote by talking the crassest Little Englandism to the working classes, and the crudest bellicose Imperialism to the non-working classes, in the same breath.

Things came to a pitch at last at which the governing classes found the British people out as the helpless drudges they are, and the British people found the governing classes out as the voluptuous and amiably incapable ignoramuses *they* are. What is more, both sides found themselves out at the same moment. Thus, bereft of the reciprocal idolatry which both of them once tried to live up to, they fell into mere cynical opportunism, neither knowing nor caring whether the particular measure at which they happened to be snatching or railing was Socialism or Unsocialism, or what deluge it might bring down or stave off next year. In those days statesmen committed themselves to gigantic wars, and lied about them instead of preparing for them, lest they should split their half-Pacifist party. When the war came, they amused the people by discussing the colossal indemnities they intended to exact from the Powers before whose troops their own were in headlong flight; and these same Powers, who had been terrifying the world (to their own undoing) for years by their boasts of an irresistibly perfect military organization and devotion to the State, were unable to follow up their outnumbered and half-equipped foes because their military nonpareils proved to be tacticians of the school of Offenbach's General Boum, and tried to reduce fortresses without siege guns, and to dash to Paris without provisions. The really big part of the business of government, both in Germany and England, has been too silly for words. To suggest, even in an epithalamium, that the crash in which it has ended has any reference to political science or philosophy, or can be either a triumph or a defeat for anybody who ever gave five minutes' thought to its problems, is to become an accomplice in the welter of humbug and intellectual confusion in which great names are current only as advertisements for the party intrigues of commonplace men.

The mess we are in just now is due to the fact that, though war on the present scale promptly reduces private capitalism and *laisser-faire* to absurdity, it cannot improvise the trained public service required by Socialism. Mr Lloyd George's attempt to repeat Cromwell's Reign of the Saints with a Reign of Practical Business Men provokes Mr Gilbert Chesterton's scepticism as to its underlying theory that, as he concisely puts it, "every man who desires to make a great deal out of the community will also ardently desire the community to make a great deal out of him." Mr Chesterton might have gone further, and pointed out that even if the war has saved the souls of the great exploiters, and made them genuinely anxious to do the very reverse of what they have made their fortunes by doing, they are still much less qualified to begin than the novices who have nothing to unlearn, or even than the old bureaucracy, which has, at least, the tradition of public service. What has already actually happened is that they have begun doing the thing they are accustomed to do and know how to do, like the acrobat who became a monk, and, finding himself too illiterate to pray to the Blessed Virgin, turned double somersaults on the steps of her altar. Our Lady, no doubt, took the will for the deed, being in no very pressing need of a few extra prayers; but we shall not beat the Germans on the strength of the well-intended somersaults of our ex-provision merchants, railway directors, and family solicitors. Cromwell's experiment ended in a dictatorship and government by major-generals. Fortunately for himself, Cromwell was equal to the job, which was then a comparatively small one. It is now enormously bigger and more complex. Thus, Mr Lloyd George has, in fact, backed himself to have an enormously bigger and more complex brain than Cromwell.

Also, it is to be observed that the powers he wields are stupendously more dangerous and destructive than any within Cromwell's reach. Shakespear warned us that

"Could great men thunder
As Jove himself does, Jove would ne'er be quiet;
For every pelting petty officer
Would use his heaven for thunder, nothing but thunder."

Well, Mr Lloyd George, like the Kaiser, can thunder, and worse. No calamity yet attributed to God has laid the earth waste, and strewn it with mangled and poisoned and strangled men, as the policies of modern statesmen have laid waste our battle fronts. No natural famine and pestilence in civilized Europe has left behind it a region as vast as Poland drily reporting that in all its borders no child under seven is left alive. Lucky had it been for the inhabitants of these desolate places had our pelting petty officers wielded "nothing but thunder." Heroic, indeed, must be the confidence of Mr Lloyd George and Lord Northcliffe and the Practical Men of Business, who are prepared to handle these plagues and save their country and everybody else's country, without knowing what Herbert Spencer knew, by their mother wit alone. And they had better be as good as their word; for such is the nature of these plagues that if you do not handle them pretty masterfully, they tear you to pieces. Any fool can set them raging; but it takes a very considerable statesman to control and finally stop them.

The Ottoman Empire, in the days of its glory, recognized this, and did not trust to casual commercialists turning their hands to keeping an empire on the strength of having spent their prime in keeping a shop. It deliberately selected the most promising Christian children, and educated and trained them as a governing caste. Thereby it procured an Imperial service which enabled it for centuries to walk over its less thoughtful neighbors as a tank walks over a machine gun. There was no resisting it until this Imperial service, corrupted by its own power, connived at its own corruption, and became the sham that made Turkey the Sick Man of Europe. It is the inevitability of this corruption, in civilizations otherwise commercial, that has produced democracy, which begins as a sham, and ends (let us hope) as a reality, instead of beginning, like the Ottoman Empire and the feudal system, as a reality, and ending as a sham.

The peril of the present juncture is that we are at the sham end of feudalism and the sham beginning of democracy, each baffling and muddling the other, and neither having any real grasp of the situation. The Kaiser's nobles have no more real statesmanship than our own upstarts. They are all empirics attacking symptoms, and incapable of discovering or contriving causes. A statesman should be able to produce a result at ten removes: the rulers of Europe cannot do it at one, and are tumbling back helplessly into every exploded crudity, like mutineers who throw the captain overboard, because they think that the art of navigation is only his tyranny.

Just as literature is produced by teaching everyone to read and write, and letting who can produce Hamlet and Prometheus Unbound, so democracy must be produced by giving everyone a careful political education, and letting who can govern by consent. At present our most carefully educated people know the difference (until they forget it) between a spondee and a dactyl, and do not know the difference between a trade unionist and a Thug. We cover up the deplorable result by an idolatry of the voter more impudent than any idolatry of kings and icons has ever been, and call it democracy. We cling to property and Unsocialism until nine-tenths of the people have no property and are not "in Society"; and when we try Socialism, we are so ignorant of how to do it that we throw our liberties after our property, guaranteeing the dividends of our remaining proprietors, and making ourselves the slaves of their agents, the employers. Naturally, the ghost of Herbert Spencer rises and points to the title of his old pamphlet on The Coming Slavery; and Mr Belloc says, "I told you so."

But that does not help very much. We have held it happier to be thriftless and imprudent, and to enjoy ourselves with the Bing Boys. And, whatever the British journalists and tub-thumpers who have never been in Germany may pretend, the Germans have been more thoroughly, scientifically, and beerily pleasure-loving and Bing-boyish than we. So let us drop all this nonsense about the triumph of the philosophers, and set to work cheerfully to muddle out as we muddled in, like jolly Britons with an ingrained contempt for spoil-sports like Herbert Spencer. We have chucked Mr Asquith and Viscount Grey because, having got us into this mess, it became clear that they could not get us out of it. And as it is thus made sufficiently probable that Mr Lloyd George will be chucked also if *he* cannot get us out of it, we may as well give him a sporting chance, and let him rip. I use the language appropriate to the nature of the case.

TOLSTOY ON ART

WHAT IS ART? By Leo Tolstoy. Translation from the Russian original by Aylmer Maude, embodying the Author's last alterations and revisions. (London: The Brotherhood Publishing Co.)

From The Daily Chronicle, 10 *September* 1898

LIKE all Tolstoy's didactic writings, this book is a most effective booby-trap. It is written with so utter a contempt for the objections which the routine critic is sure to allege against it, that many a dilettantist reviewer has already accepted it as a butt set up by Providence to shew off his own brilliant marksmanship. It seems so easy to dispose of a naïf who moralizes on the Trojan war as if it were a historical event!

Yet Tolstoy will be better understood in this volume than in his Christian epistles, because art is at present a more fashionable subject than Christianity. Most people have a loose impression that Tolstoy as a Christian represents Evangelicalism gone mad. As a matter of fact, Tolstoy's position, as explained by himself, is, from the Evangelical point of view, as novel as it is blasphemous. What Evangelicalism calls revelation, vouchsafed to man's incapacity by Divine wisdom, Tolstoy declares to be a piece of common sense so obvious as to make its statement in the gospels superfluous. "I will go further," he says. "This truth [resist not evil] appears to me so simple and so clear that I am persuaded I should have found it out by myself, even if Christ and His doctrine had never existed." Blasphemy can go no further than this from the point of view of the Bible-worshipper. Again he says, "I beg you, in the name of the God of truth whom you adore, not to fly out at me, nor to begin looking for arguments to oppose me with, before you have meditated, not on what I am going to write to you, but on the gospel; and not on the gospel as the word of God or of Christ, but on the gospel considered as the neatest, simplest, most comprehensible and most practical doctrine on the way in which men ought to live."

What makes this attitude of Tolstoy's so formidable to Christians who feel that it condemns their own systematic resistance to evil, is the fact that he is a man with a long, varied, and by no means exclusively pious experience of worldly life. In vain do we spend hours in a highly superior manner in proving that Tolstoy's notions are unpractical, visionary: in short, cranky; we cannot get the sting and the startle out of his flat challenge as to how much we have done and where we have landed ourselves by the opposite policy. No doubt the challenge does not make all of us uneasy. But may not that be because he sees the world from behind the scenes of politics and society, whilst most of us are sitting to be gulled in the pit? For, alas! nothing is plainer to the dupe of all the illusions of civilization than the folly of the seer who penetrates them.

If Tolstoy has made himself so very disquieting by criticizing the world as a man of the world, he has hardly made himself more agreeable by criticizing art as an artist of the first rank. Among the minor gods of the amateur he kindles a devastating fire. Naturally, the very extensive literary output of delirium tremens in our century receives no quarter from him: he has no patience with nonsense, especially drunken nonsense, however laboriously or lusciously it may be rhymed or alliterated. But he spares nobody wholly, dealing unmercifully with himself, sweeping away Mr Rudyard Kipling with the French decadents, and heaping derision on Wagner. Clearly, this book of his will not be valued for its specific criticisms, some of which, if the truth must be told, represent nothing but the inevitable obsolescence of an old man's taste in art. To justify them, Tolstoy applies a test highly characteristic of the Russian aristocrat. A true work of art, he maintains, will always be recognized by the unsophisticated perception of the peasant folk. Hence, Beethoven's Ninth Symphony, not being popular among the Russian peasantry, is not a true work of art!

Leaving the Ninth Symphony to take care of itself, one cannot help being struck by the fact that Russian revolutionists of noble birth invariably display what appears to us a boundless credulity concerning the virtues of the poor. No English county magnate has any doubt as to which way an English agricultural laborer would choose between Tolstoy's favorite Chopin nocturne (admitted by him to be true art) and the latest music-hall tune. We know perfectly well that the simplicity of our peasants' lives is forced on them by their poverty, and could be dispelled at any moment by a sufficient legacy. We know that the equality which seems to the rich man to be accepted among laborers (because he himself makes no distinction among them) is an illusion, and that social distinctions are more pitifully cherished by our poor than by any other class until we get down to the residuum which has not self-respect enough even for snobbery. Now, whether it is that the Russian peasantry, being illiterate and outlandish, has never been absorbed by European civilization as ours has been, or else that the distance between peasant and noble in Russia is so great that the two classes do not know one another, and fill up the void in their knowledge by millennial romancing, certain it is that the Russian nobles Kropotkin and Tolstoy, who have come into our counsels on the side of the people, seem to assume that the laboring classes have entirely escaped the class vices, follies, and prejudices of the bourgeoisie.

If it were not for this unmistakeable error in Tolstoy's premisses, it would be very difficult to dissent from any of his judgments on works of art without feeling in danger of merely providing him with an additional example of the corruption of taste which he deplores. But when his objection to a masterpiece is based solely on the incapacity of a peasant to enjoy it or understand it, the misgiving vanishes. Everything that he says in condemnation of modern society is richly deserved by it; but if it were true that the working classes, numbering, say, four-fifths of the population, had entirely escaped the penalties of civilization, and were in a state so wholesomely natural and benevolent that Beethoven must stand condemned by their coldness towards his symphonies, then his whole case against civilization must fall to the ground, since such a majority for good would justify any social system. In England, at least, one cannot help believing that if Tolstoy were reincarnated as a peasant he would find that the proletarian morality in which he has so much faith is nothing but the morality of his own class, modified, mostly for the worse, by ignorance, drudgery, insufficient food, and bad sanitary conditions of all kinds. It is true that the absolutely idle class has a peculiar and exasperating nonentity and futility, and that this class wastes a great deal of money in false art; but it is not numerically a very large class. The demand of the professional and mercantile classes is quite sufficient to maintain a considerable body of art, the defects of which cannot be ascribed to the idleness of its patrons.

If due allowance be made for these considerations, which, remember, weaken society's defence and not Tolstoy's attack, this book will be found extraordinarily interesting and enlightening. We must agree with him when he says, "To thoughtful and sincere people there can be no doubt that the art of the upper classes can never be the art of the whole people." Only, we must make the same reservation with regard to the art of the lower classes. And we must not forget that there is nothing whatever to choose between the average country gentleman and his gamekeeper in respect of distaste for the Ninth Symphony.

Tolstoy's main point, however, is the establishment of his definition of art. It is, he says, "an activity by means of which one man, having experienced a feeling, intentionally transmits it to others." This is the simple truth: the moment it is uttered, whoever is really conversant with art recognizes in it the voice of the master. None the less is Tolstoy perfectly aware that this is not the usual definition of art, which amateurs delight to hear described as that which produces beauty. Tolstoy's own Christian view of how he should treat the professors of this or any other heresy is clearly laid down in those articles of faith, already quoted above, which conclude his Plaisirs Cruels. "To dispute with those who are in error is to waste labor and spoil our exposition of the truth. It provokes us to say things that we do not mean, to formulate paradoxes, to exaggerate our thought, and, leaving on one side the essential part of our doctrine, play off tricks of logic on the slips which have provoked us." Fortunately for the entertainment of the readers of What is Art? Tolstoy does not carry out his own precepts in it. Backsliding without the slightest compunction into the character of a first-rate fighting man, he challenges all the authorities, great and small, who have committed themselves to the beauty theory, and never quits them till he has left them for dead. There is always something specially exhilarating in the spectacle of a Quaker fighting; and Tolstoy's performance in this kind will not soon be forgotten. Our generation has not seen a heartier bout of literary fisticuffs, or one in which the challenger has been more brilliantly victorious.

Since no man, however indefatigable a reader he may be, can make himself acquainted with all that Europe has to say on any subject of general interest, it seldom happens that any great champion meets the opponent we would most like to see him join issue with. For this reason we hear nothing from Tolstoy of William Morris's definition of art as the expression of pleasure in work. This is not exactly the beauty doctrine: it recognizes, as Tolstoy's definition does, that art is the expression of feeling; but it covers a good deal of art work which, whilst proving the artist's need for expression, does not convince us that the artist wanted to convey his feeling to others. There have been many artists who have taken great pains to express themselves to themselves in works of art, but whose action, as regards the circulation of those works, has very evidently been dictated by love of fame or money rather than by any yearning for emotional intercourse with their fellow-creatures. It is, of course, easy to say that the works of such men are not true art; but if they convey feeling to others, sometimes more successfully and keenly than some of the works which fall within Tolstoy's definition, the distinction is clearly not a practical one. The truth is that definitions which are applied on the principle that whatever is not white is black never are quite practical. The only safe plan is to ascertain the opposite extremes of artistic motive, determine which end of the scale between them is the higher and which the lower, and place each work in question in its right position on the scale.

There are plenty of passages in this very book of Tolstoy's—itself a work of art according to its own definition—which have quite clearly been written to relieve the craving for expression of the author's own combativeness, or fun, or devotion, or even cleverness, and would probably have been written equally had he been the most sardonic pessimist that ever regarded his fellow-creatures as beyond redemption.

Tolstoy's justification in ignoring these obvious objections to the accuracy and universality of his treatise is plain enough. Art is socially important—that is, worth writing a book about—only in so far as it wields that power of propagating feeling which he adopts as his criterion of true art. It is hard to knock this truth into the heads of the English nation. We admit the importance of public opinion, which, in a country without intellectual habits (our own, for example), depends altogether on public feeling. Yet, instead of perceiving the gigantic importance which this gives to the theatre, the concert room, and the bookshop as forcing houses of feeling, we slight them as mere places of amusement, and blunder along upon the assumption that the House of Commons, and the platitudes of a few old-fashioned leader writers, are the chief fountains of English sentiment. Tolstoy knows better than that.

Look carefully [he says] into the causes of the ignorance of the masses, and you may see that the chief cause does not at all lie in the lack of schools and libraries, as we are accustomed to suppose, but in those superstitions, both ecclesiastical and patriotic, with which the people are saturated, and which are unceasingly generated by all the methods of art. Church superstitions are supported and produced by the poetry of prayers, hymns, painting; by the sculpture of images and of statues; by singing, by organs, by music, by architecture, and even by dramatic art in religious ceremonies. Patriotic superstitions are supported and produced by verses and stories, which are supplied even in schools; by music, by songs, by triumphal processions, by royal meetings, by martial pictures, and by monuments. Were it not for this continual activity in all departments of art, perpetuating the ecclesiastical and patriotic intoxication and embitterment of the people, the masses would long ere this have attained to true enlightenment.

It does not at all detract from the value of Tolstoy's thesis that what he denounces as superstitions may appear to many to be wholesome enthusiasms and fruitful convictions. Still less does it matter that his opinions of individual artists are often those of a rather petulant veteran who neither knows nor wants to know much of works that are too new to please him. The valid point is that our artistic institutions are vital social organs, and that the advance of civilization tends constantly to make them, especially in the presence of democratic institutions and compulsory schooling, more important than the political and ecclesiastical institutions whose traditional prestige is so much greater. We are too stupid to learn from epigrams; otherwise Fletcher of Saltoun's offer to let whoever wished make the laws of the nation provided he made its songs, would have saved Tolstoy the trouble of telling us the same thing in twenty chapters. At all events, we cannot now complain of want of instruction. With Mr Ashton Ellis's translation of Wagner's Prose Works to put on the shelves of our libraries beside the works of Ruskin, and this pregnant and trenchant little volume of Tolstoy's to drive the moral home, we shall have ourselves to thank if we do not take greater care of our art in the future than of any other psychological factor in the destiny of the nation.

TOLSTOY: TRAGEDIAN OR COMEDIAN?

Copyright. International Magazine Co. New York. 1921.

Substance of an extemporized speech made at the Tolstoy Commemoration at Kingsway Hall in London on November 30, 1921.

WAS Tolstoy tragedian or comedian? The popular definition of tragedy is heavy drama in which everyone is killed in the last act, comedy being light drama in which everyone is married in the last act. The classical definition is, of tragedy, drama that purges the soul by pity and terror, and, of comedy, drama that chastens morals by ridicule. These classical definitions, illustrated by Eschylus-Sophocles-Euripides *versus* Aristophanes in the ancient Greek theatre, and Corneille-Racine *versus* Molière in the French theatre, are still much the best the critic can work with. But the British school has always scandalized classic scholarship and French taste by defying them: nothing will prevent the English playwright from mixing comedy, and even tomfoolery, with tragedy. Lear may pass for pure tragedy; for even the fool in Lear is tragic; but Shakespear could not keep the porter out of Macbeth nor the clown out of Antony and Cleopatra. We are incorrigible in this respect, and may as well make a merit of it.

We must therefore recognize and examine a third variety of drama. It begins as tragedy with scraps of fun in it, like Macbeth, and ends as comedy without mirth in it, the place of mirth being taken by a more or less bitter and critical irony. We do not call the result melodrama, because that term has come to mean drama in which crude emotions are helped to expression by musical accompaniment. Besides, there is at first no true new species: the incongruous elements do not combine: there is simply frank juxtaposition of fun with terror in tragedy and of gravity with levity in comedy. You have Macbeth; and you have Le Misanthrope, Le Festin de Pierre, All's Well That Ends Well, Troilus and Cressida: all of them, from the Aristotelian and Voltairean point of view, neither fish, fowl, nor good red herring.

When the censorship killed serious drama in England, and the dramatists had to express themselves in novels, the mixture became more lawless than ever: it was practised by Fielding and culminated in Dickens, whose extravagances would have been severely curbed if he had had to submit his Micawbers and Mrs Wilfers to the test of representation on the stage, when it would have been discovered at once that their parts are mere repetitions of the same joke, and have none of that faculty of developing and advancing matters which constitutes stage action. Dickens would have been forced to make something better than Aunt Sallies of them. Since Dickens one can think of no great writer who has produced the same salad of comedy and tragedy except Anatole France. He remains incorrigible: even in his most earnest attempts to observe the modesties of nature and the proprieties of art in his autobiographical Le Petit Pierre he breaks down and launches into chapters of wild harlequinade (think of the servant Radegond and the Chaplinesque invention of Simon of Nantua and the *papegai*) and then returns ashamed and sobered to the true story of his life, knowing that he has lost every right to appear before the Judgment Seat with Le Petit Pierre in his hand as the truth, the whole truth, and nothing but the truth, so help him Rousseau. On his comic side Anatole France is Dickens's French double, disguised by culture. In one of his earliest stories, Jocaste, the heroine's father is a more perfect Dickens comic personage than Dickens himself ever succeeded in putting on paper.

After Dickens, Comedy completed its development into the new species, which has been called tragi-comedy when any attempt has been made to define it. Tragedy itself never developed: it was simple, sublime, and overwhelming from the first: it either failed and was not tragedy at all or else it got there so utterly that no need was felt for going any further. The only need felt was for relief; and therefore, though tragedy remains unchanged from Eschylus to Richard Wagner (Europe's last great tragic poet), the reaction to a moment of fun which we associate with Shakespear got the upper hand even of Eschylus, and produced his comic sentinels who, afraid to go to the rescue of Agamemnon, pretend that nothing is happening, just as it got the better of Victor Hugo, with his Don Cæsar de Bazan tumbling down the chimney, and his Rustighello playing Wamba to the Duke of Ferrara's Cedric the Saxon. But in the main Tragedy remained on its summit, simple, unmixed, and heroic, from Sophocles to Verdi.

Not so Comedy. When the Merry Wives of Windsor gave way to Marriage à la Mode, Romeo to Hamlet, Punch to Don Juan, Petruchio to Almaviva, and, generally, horseplay and fun for fun's sake to serious chastening of morals less and less by ridicule and more and more by irony, the comic poet becoming less and less a fellow of infinite jest and more and more a satirical rogue and a discloser of essentially tragic ironies, the road was open to a sort of comedy as much more tragic than a catastrophic tragedy as an unhappy marriage, or even a happy one, is more tragic than a railway accident. Shakespear's bitter play with a bitter title, All's Well That Ends Well, anticipates Ibsen: the happy ending at which the title sneers is less comforting than the end of Romeo and Juliet. And Ibsen was the dramatic poet who firmly established tragi-comedy as a much deeper and grimmer entertainment than tragedy. His heroes dying without hope or honor, his dead, forgotten, superseded men walking and talking with the ghosts of the past, are all heroes of comedy: their existence and their downfall are not soul-purifying convulsions of pity and horror, but reproaches, challenges, criticisms addressed to society and to the spectator as a voting constituent of society. They are miserable and yet not hopeless; for they are mostly criticisms of false intellectual positions which, being intellectual, are remediable by better thinking.

Thus Comedy has become the higher form. The element of accident in Tragedy has always been its weak spot; for though an accident may be sensational, nothing can make it interesting or save it from being irritating. Othello is spoilt by a handkerchief, as Shakespear found out afterwards when he wrote A Winter's Tale. The curtain falls on The School for Scandal just when the relations between the dishonorable Joseph Surface and the much more dishonorable Lady Teazle have become interesting for the first moment in the play. In its tragedy and comedy alike, the modern tragi-comedy begins where the old tragedies and comedies left off; and we have actually had plays made and produced dealing with what happened to Ibsen's *dramatis personae* before the first act began.

Tolstoy is now easily classed as a tragi-comedian, pending the invention of a better term. Of all the dramatic poets he has the most withering touch when he wants to destroy. His novels shew this over and over again. A man enters a house where someone lies dead. There is no moralizing, no overt irony: Tolstoy, with the simplicity he affects so well, just tells you that the undertaker has left the coffin lid propped against the wall in the entrance hall, and that the visitor goes into the drawing room and sits down on a *pouf.* Instantly the mockery and folly of our funeral pomps and cemetery sentimentalities laugh in our faces. A judge goes into court to set himself up as divine justice and send his fellow-creatures to the gallows. Tolstoy does not improve the occasion or allow his brow to contract or his eye to twinkle; but he mentions that before the judge leaves his room he goes through a few gymnastic exercises. Instantly that judge is in the mud with his ermine and scarlet making him and all judges unspeakably ridiculous. Dickens makes us laugh by describing how the handle of the Orfling's corkscrew comes off and hits her on the chin. We applaud the wanton humorist; but the Orfling is none the worse five minutes later. Tolstoy could slay a soul with a corkscrew without letting you know either that he was a humorist or that you are laughing.

This terrible but essentially comedic method is the method of all Tolstoy's plays except the first, The Powers of Darkness, which is, on the whole, a true tragedy. His Fruits of Culture, coming long before Granville-Barker's Marrying of Ann Leete or the plays of Tchekov, is the first of the Heartbreak Houses, and the most blighting. He touches with his pen the drawing room, the kitchen, the doormat in the entrance hall, and the toilet tables upstairs. They wither like the garden of Klingsor at the sign of Parsifal. The Living Corpse is as alive as most fine gentlemen are. But gentry as an institution crumble to dust at his casual remark that unless a gentleman gets a berth under Government as soldier or diplomatist, there is nothing left for him to do but to kill himself with wine and women. It is a case of "God damn you, merry gentlemen: let all things you dismay."

But Tolstoy's masterpiece is his Light Shining Through Darkness. In it he turns his deadly touch suicidally on himself. The blight falls on him ruthlessly. That the hero of Sevastopol becomes a second-rate dug-out is nothing. That the Levine of

Anna Karenina becomes a common domestic quarreller is hardly noticed. It is the transfiguration of the great prophet into a clumsy mischievous cruel fool that makes the tragi-comedy. Mr Aylmer Maude, in his biography of Tolstoy, holds the scales very fairly between husband and wife, and gives no quarter to the notion that a great man can do no wrong; but where he is respectfully critical Tolstoy himself is derisively merciless. He does not even pay himself the compliment of finishing the play. He left the last act unwritten, but with precise instructions as to how he was to be shot in it like a mad dog by the mother of the young man he had ruined by his teaching as he ruined everyone else who listened to him.

Nevertheless Tolstoy does not really give the verdict against himself: he only shews that he was quite aware of the disastrousness of his negative anarchistic doctrine, and was prepared to face that disastrousness sooner than accept and support robbery and violence merely because the robbers and militarists had acquired political power enough to legalize them. It must be assumed that if everyone refused compliance, the necessities of the case would compel social reconstruction on honest and peaceful lines. His own notions of such reconstruction did not go apparently beyond an uncritical acceptance of Henry George's demonstration of the need for land nationalization; and he does not seem to have foreseen that any reconstruction whatever must involve more State compulsion of the individual than the present system, which relies for its unofficial but omnipresent compulsion on the pressure of circumstances brought about by the destitution of the proletariat. Tolstoy, like the rather spoiled aristocrat, natural and artificial, that he was, could not stand compulsion, and instinctively refused to give his mind to the practical problem of social reconstruction on his principles: that is, how to organize the equitable sharing among us of the burden of that irreducible minimum of exertion without which we must perish: a matter involving, as Lenin has discovered, a considerable shooting up of the recalcitrant. Like many other prophets, he preached the will without finding the way. Therefore his influence was extremely dangerous to individual fools (he included himself among the number in Light Shining Through Darkness); but he is a great Social Solvent, revealing to us, as a master of tragi-comic drama, the misery and absurdity of the idle proud life for which we sacrifice our own honor and the happiness of our neighbors.

BEERBOHM TREE

Contributed to Max Beerbohm's collection of memoirs of his brother

A TRIBUTE to Tree from the playwright's point of view is a duty of such delicacy that it is quite impossible to be delicate about it at all: one must confess bluntly at the outset that Tree was the despair of authors. His attitude towards a play was one of whole-hearted anxiety to solve the problem of how to make it please and interest the audience.

Now this is the author's business, not the actor's. The function of the actor is to make the audience imagine for the moment that real things are happening to real people. It is for the author to make the result interesting. If he fails, the actor cannot save the play unless it is so flimsy a thing that the actor can force upon it some figure of his own fancy and play the author off the stage. This has been done successfully in several well-known, though very uncommon cases. Robert Macaire and Lord Dundreary were imposed by their actors on plays which did not really contain them. Grimaldi's clown was his own invention. These figures died with their creators, though their ghosts still linger on the stage. Irving's Shylock was a creation which he thrust successfully upon Shakespear's play; indeed, all Irving's impersonations were changelings. His Hamlet and his Lear were to many people more interesting than Shakespear's Hamlet and Lear; but the two pairs were hardly even related. To the author, Irving was not an actor: he was either a rival or a collaborator who did all the real work. Therefore, he was anathema to master authors, and a godsend to journeymen authors, with the result that he had to confine himself to the works of dead authors who could not interfere with him, and, very occasionally, live authors who were under his thumb because they were unable to command production of their works in other quarters.

Into this tradition of creative acting came Tree as Irving's rival and successor; and he also, with his restless imagination, felt that he needed nothing from an author but a literary scaffold on which to exhibit his own creations. He, too, turned to Shakespear as to a forest out of which such scaffolding could be hewn without remonstrance from the landlord, and to foreign authors who could not interfere with him, their interests being in the hands of adapters who could not stand up against his supremacy in his own theatre. As far as I could discover, the notion that a play could succeed without any further help from the actor than a simple impersonation of his part never occurred to Tree. The author, whether Shakespear or Shaw, was a lame dog to be helped over the stile by the ingenuity and inventiveness of the actor-producer. How to add and subtract, to interpolate and prune, until an effective result was arrived at, was the problem of production as he saw it. Of living authors of eminence the two he came into personal contact with were Brieux and Henry Arthur Jones; and I have reason to believe that their experience of him in no way contradicts my own. With contemporary masters of the stage like Pinero and Carton, in whose works the stage business is an integral part of the play, and the producer, when he is not the author in person, is an executant and not an inventor, Tree had never worked; and when he at last came upon the species in me, and found that, instead of having to discover how to make an effective histrionic entertainment on the basis of such scraps of my dialogue as might prove useful, he had only to fit himself into a jig-saw puzzle cut out by me, and just to act his part as well as he could, he could neither grasp the situation nor resist the impersonal compulsion of arrangements which he had not made, and was driven to accept only by the fact that they were the only ones which would work. But to the very end they bewildered him; and he had to go to the box office to assure himself that the omission of his customary care had not produced disastrous results.

Just before the production of my play we lunched together at the Royal Automobile Club. I said to him: "Have you noticed during the rehearsals that though you and I are no longer young, and have achieved all the success possible in our respective professions, we have been treating one another throughout as beginners?" To this, on reflection, he had to assent, because we actually were, relatively to one another, beginners. I had never had to deal with him professionally before, nor he with me; and he was quite unaccustomed to double harness, whilst I was so accustomed to every extremity of multiple harness, both in politics and in the theatre, that I had been trained to foresee everything and consider everybody. Now if I were to say that Tree foresaw nothing and considered nobody, I should suggest that he was a much less amiable man than he was. Let me therefore say that he never foresaw anything or considered anybody in cold blood. Of the foresight which foresees and faces entirely uninteresting facts, and the consideration which considers entirely uninteresting persons, he had as little as a man can have without being run over in the street. When his feelings were engaged, he was human and even shrewd and tenacious. But you really could not lodge an indifferent fact in his mind. This disability of his was carried to such a degree that he could not remember the passages in a play which did not belong to or bear directly upon his own conception of his own part: even the longest run did not mitigate his surprise when they recurred. Thus he never fell into that commonest fault of the actor: the betrayal to the audience that he knows what his interlocutor is going to say, and is waiting wearily for his cue instead of conversing with him. Tree always seemed to have heard the lines of the other performers for the first time, and even to be a little taken aback by them.

Let me give an extreme instance of this. In Pygmalion the heroine, in a rage, throws the hero's slippers in his face. When we rehearsed this for the first time, I had taken care to have a very soft pair of velvet slippers provided; for I knew that Mrs Patrick Campbell was very dexterous, very strong, and a dead shot.

And, sure enough, when we reached this passage, Tree got the slippers well and truly delivered with unerring aim bang in his face. The effect was appalling. He had totally forgotten that there was any such incident in the play; and it seemed to him that Mrs Campbell, suddenly giving way to an impulse of diabolical wrath and hatred, had committed an unprovoked and brutal assault on him. The physical impact was nothing; but the wound to his feelings was terrible. He collapsed on the nearest chair, and left me staring in amazement, whilst the entire personnel of the theatre crowded solicitously round him, explaining that the incident was part of the play, and even exhibiting the prompt-book to prove their words. But his *moral* was so shattered that it took quite a long time, and a good deal of skilful rallying and coaxing from Mrs Campbell, before he was in a condition to resume the rehearsal. The worst of it was that as it was quite evident that he would be just as surprised and wounded next time, Mrs Campbell took care that the slippers should never hit him again, and the incident was consequently one of the least convincing in the performance.

This, and many similar scenes that are told of Tree, will not be believed by experienced men of business. They will say curtly that it is no use trying to stuff them with stories like that: that running a theatre like His Majesty's must have been a big business, and that no man could possibly have done it for so long without being too capable and wide-awake to forget everything that did not amuse or interest him. But they will be quite wrong. Theatrical business is not like other business. A man may enter on the management of a theatre without business habits or knowledge, and at the end of forty years of it know less about business than when he began. The explanation is that a London West-End theatre is always either making such an enormous profit that the utmost waste caused by unbusinesslike management is not worth considering, or else losing so much that the strictest economy cannot arrest the process by a halfpenny in the pound. In an industrial concern the addition of a penny to the piecework rate or the hourly time rate of wages, the slowing of a steam engine by a few revolutions, the retention of a machine two years out-of-date, or the loss of fifteen minutes' work in the day by unpunctuality, may make all the difference between profit and bankruptcy. The employer is held to rigid conditions by a stringent factory code enforced by a Government inspector on the one hand and by a jealous trade union on the other. He is the creature of circumstance and the slave of law, with so little liberty for sentiment and caprice that he very soon loses not only the habit of indulging them but even the sense of possessing them. Not so the manager of a theatre. Tree was accustomed to make two hundred per cent profit every day when he was in luck. With such a margin to play with, it was no more worth his while to economize or remember uninteresting things than it was to walk when there was a taxi at his beck. When his theatre was built for him, the equipment of its stage, apart from the electric lighting instalment, was exactly what it would have been a hundred years before, except that there were no grooves for side wings. If every employee on the premises had come an hour late every day and had received double wages, the difference in profit would have been hardly worth noticing. A theatre is a maddening place to a thrifty man of business, and an economic paradise to an artist, because there is practically no limit to the waste of time and money that may go on, provided the doors are open every night and the curtain up half an hour later. But for this necessity, and a few County Council by-laws, an actor-manager would be as unbridled as Nero, without even the Neronian check of a Prætorian Guard to kill him if he went beyond all bearing.

There is no denying that such conditions put a strain on human character that it can seldom sustain without injury. If Tree's caprices, and his likes and dislikes, had not been on the whole amiable, the irresponsibility and power of his position would have made a fiend of him. As it was, they produced the oddest results. He was always attended in the theatre by a retinue of persons with no defined business there, who were yet on the salary list. There was one capable gentleman who could get things done; and I decided to treat him as the stage manager; but until I saw his name in the bill under that heading I never felt sure that he was not some casual acquaintance whom Tree had met in the club or in the street and invited to come in and make himself at home. Tree did not know what a stage manager was, just as he did not know what an author was. He had not even made up his mind any too definitely what an actor was. One moment he would surprise and delight his courtiers (for that is the nearest word I can find for his staff and entourage) by some stroke of kindness and friendliness. The next he would commit some appalling breach of etiquet by utterly ignoring their functions and privileges, when they had any. It was amiable and modest in him not to know his own place, since it was the highest in the theatre; but it was exasperating in him not to know anyone else's. I very soon gave up all expectation of being treated otherwise than as a friend who had dropped in; so, finding myself as free to interfere in the proceedings as anyone else who dropped in would apparently have been, I interfered not only in my proper department but in every other as well; and nobody gainsaid me. One day I interfered to such an extent that Tree was moved to a mildly sarcastic remonstrance. "I seem to have heard or read somewhere," he said, "that plays have actually been produced, and performances given, in this theatre, under its present management, before you came. According to you, that couldnt have happened. How do you account for it?" "I cant account for it," I replied, with the blunt good faith of a desperate man. "I suppose you put a notice in the papers that a performance will take place at half-past eight, and take the money at the doors. Then you *have* to do the play somehow. There is no other way of accounting for it." On two such occasions it seemed so brutal to worry him, and so hopeless to advance matters beyond the preliminary arrangement of the stage business (which I had already done), that I told him quite cordially to put the play through in his own way, and shook the dust of the theatre from my feet. On both occasions I had to yield to urgent appeals from other members of the cast to return and extricate them from a hopeless mess; and on both occasions Tree took leave of me as if it had been very kind of me to look in as I was passing to see his rehearsals, and received me on my return as if it were still more friendly of me to come back and see how he was getting on. I tried once or twice to believe that he was only pulling my leg; but that was incredible: his sincerity and insensibility were only too obvious. Finally, I had to fight my way through to a sort of production in the face of an unresisting, amusing, friendly, but heart-breakingly obstructive principal.

We finally agreed that I should have been an actor and he an author; and he always sent me his books afterwards. As a matter of fact, he had a very marked literary talent, and, even as an amateur, achieved a finish of style and sureness of execution that was not always evident in his acting, especially when, as in the case of Pygmalion, he had to impersonate a sort of man he had never met and of whom he had no conception. He tried hard to induce me to let him play the dustman instead of the Miltonic professor of phonetics; and when he resigned himself to his unnatural task, he set to work to make this disagreeable and incredible person sympathetic in the character of a lover, for which I had left so little room that he was quite baffled until he lit on the happy thought of throwing flowers to Eliza in the very brief interval between the end of the play and the fall of the curtain. If he had not been so amusing, so ingenious, and so entirely well-intentioned he would have driven me crazy. As it was, he made me feel like his grandfather. I should add that he never bore the slightest malice for my air of making the best of a bad job. A few days before his death, when he was incredibly young and sanguine, and made me feel hopelessly old and grumpy, he was discussing a revival of Pygmalion as if it promised to be a renewal of the most delightful experience of our lives. The only reproach he ever addressed to me was for not coming to Pygmalion every night, which he thought the natural duty of an author. I promised to come on the hundredth night, adding rather unkindly that this was equivalent to not coming at all. The hundredth night, however, was reached and survived; and I redeemed my promise, only to find that he had contributed to my second act a stroke of comic business so outrageously irrelevant that I solemnly cursed the whole enterprise, and bade the delinquents farewell for ever.

The fact that Tree could do and be done by thus without bloodshed, although he had all the sensitiveness of his profession, and all the unrestrained impulsiveness of a man who had succeeded in placing himself above discipline from the beginning of his adult life, shews that he was never quite unpardonable; and though this, to the world that knows nothing of the theatre, may seem more of an apology than a tribute, those who know the theatre best will understand its value. It has to be considered, too, that the statement that he did nothing unpardonable does not imply that he did nothing irreparable. Almost all the wrongs and errors of the West-End London theatre are like the wrongs and errors of the battlefield: they cannot be undone. If an actor's or an author's chance is spoilt, it is spoilt for years and perhaps for ever: neither play nor part gets a second chance. I doubt whether there is an actor-manager living who has not done both these wrongs more than once. Tree was no exception; but as the result, like that of the elephant sitting on the hen's eggs, was never intended, it was impossible to bear malice for long. I have seen him try to help a very able Shakespearean actor, and, incidentally, to help Shakespear, through what he thought a tedious scene, by pretending to catch flies, with ruinous consequences to both player and Bard. He put a new complexion on Brieux's La Foi, with effects on the feelings of that illustrious author which I shall not attempt to describe. He meant equally well on both occasions.

And here I come to a source of friction between authors and actor-managers which is worth explaining with some care, as it bears on the general need in England for a school of physical training for the arts of public life as distinguished from the sports. An author who understands acting, and writes for the actor as a composer writes for an instrument, giving it the material suitable to its range, tone, character, agility and mechanism, necessarily assumes a certain technical accomplishment

273

common to all actors; and this requires the existence of a school of acting, or at least a tradition. Now we had no such provision in the days of Tree's novitiate. He had not inherited the tradition handed down at rehearsal by Phelps to Forbes Robertson; nor was there any academic institution with authority enough to impress a novice of his calibre. To save others from this disadvantage he later on founded the Academy of Dramatic Art in Gower Street, which now supplies the want as far as an unendowed institution can. But he had to do without teaching himself. Like Irving, he had to make a style and technique out of his own personality: that is, out of his peculiar weaknesses as well as his peculiar powers. And here he sowed dragons' teeth between himself and the authors. For no uncommissioned author can write for an idiosyncratic style and technique: he knows only the classical one. He must, like Shakespear, assume an executant who can perform and sustain certain physical feats of deportment, and build up vocal climaxes with his voice through a long crescendo of rhetoric. Further, he assumes the possession of an English voice and an English feeling for splendor of language and rhythm of verse. Such professional skill and national gift are not accidents of personality: they are more or less within every Englishman's capacity. By themselves they will no more make an actor than grammar and spelling will make an author, or fingering and blowing a bandsman; but one expects every actor to possess them, just as one expects every author to parse and spell correctly and every bandsman to finger and blow properly.

Tree, like so many of our actors who have picked up their profession on the stage without systematic training, found that he could not produce these stock effects. When they were demanded by the author, he had to find a way round them, and, if possible, an interesting way. Thus he had not only to struggle against his handicap, but to triumph over it by turning it into an advantage. And his handicap was not a light one. Instead of that neutral figure which an actor can turn into anything he pleases, he was tall, and built like nobody else on earth. His Dutch extraction gave him an un-English voice, which, again, was like nobody else's voice and could not be disguised. His feeling for verbal music was entirely non-Miltonic: he had a music of his own; but it was not the music characteristic of English rhetoric; and blank verse, as such, had no charm for him; nor, I suspect, did he credit it with charm for anyone else.

The results were most marked in his Shakespearean work, and would certainly have produced curious scenes at rehearsal had the author been present. No doubt it is an exaggeration to say that the only unforgettable passages in his Shakespearean acting are those of which Tree and not Shakespear was the author. His Wolsey, which was a "straight" performance of high merit and dignity, could be cited to the contrary. But take, for examples, his Richard II and his Malvolio. One of the most moving points in his Richard was made with the assistance of a dog who does not appear among Shakespear's *dramatis personae*. When the dog—Richard's pet dog—turned to Bolingbroke and licked his hand, Richard's heart broke; and he left the stage with a sob. Next to this came his treatment of the entry of Bolingbroke and the deposed Richard into London. Shakespear makes the Duke of York describe it. Nothing could be easier with a well-trained actor at hand. And nothing could be more difficult and inconvenient than to bring horses on the stage and represent it in action. But this is just what Tree did. One still remembers that great white horse, and the look of hunted terror with which Richard turned his head as the crowd hooted him. It passed in a moment; and it flatly contradicted Shakespear's description of the saint-like patience of Richard; but the effect was intense: no one but Chaliapine has since done so much by a single look and an appearance for an instant on horseback. Again, one remembers how Richard walked out of Westminister Hall after his abdication.

Turn now to the scenes in which Shakespear has given the actor a profusion of rhetoric to declaim. Take the famous "For God's sake let us sit upon the ground, and tell sad stories of the death of kings." My sole recollection of that scene is that when I was sitting in the stalls listening to it, a paper was passed to me.

I opened it and read: "If you will rise and move a resolution, I will second it.—Murray Carson." The late Murray Carson was, above all things, an elocutionist; and the scene was going for nothing. Tree was giving Shakespear, at immense trouble and expense, and with extraordinary executive cunning, a great deal that Shakespear had not asked for, and denying him something much simpler that he did ask for, and set great store by.

As Malvolio, Tree was inspired to provide himself with four smaller Malvolios, who aped the great chamberlain in dress, in manners, in deportment. He had a magnificent flight of stairs on the stage; and when he was descending it majestically, he slipped and fell with a crash sitting. Mere clowning, you will say; but no: the fall was not the point. Tree, without betraying the smallest discomfiture, raised his eyeglass and surveyed the landscape as if he had sat down on purpose. This, like the four satellite Malvolios, was not only funny but subtle. But when he came to speak those lines with which any old Shakespearean hand can draw a laugh by a simple trick of the voice, Tree made nothing of them, not knowing a game which he had never studied.

Even if our actors came to the stage with complete executive mastery of all the traditions and all the conventions, there would still be a conflict between the actor's tendency to adapt the play to his own personality and the author's desire to adapt the actor's personality to the play. But this would not make any serious trouble between them; for a good part can be played a dozen different ways by a dozen different actors and be none the worse: no author worth his salt attaches a definite and invariable physiognomy to each variety of human character. Every actor must be allowed to apply his own methods to his own playing. But if, as under our system, an actor, instead of laying the foundation of a general technique of speech and action, is driven, by the absence of any school in which he can acquire such a technique, to develop his own personality, and acquire a technique of exploiting that personality which is not applicable to any other purpose, then there will be friction at rehearsals if the author produces his own play, as all authors should. For the actor will inevitably try to force a changeling on the author. He will say, in effect: "I will not play this part that you have written; but I will substitute one of my own which is ever so much better." And it will be useless for the author to assert himself, and say: "You *shall* play the part as I have written it." If he knows his business, he will see that the "will not" of the actor really means "cannot," because the author has written for a classical technique which the actor does not possess and cannot learn in three weeks, or even three years. It is better to let the actor do what he can: indeed, there is no alternative.

What Tree could do was always entertaining in some way or other. But, for better for worse, it was hardly ever what the author meant him to do. His parts were his avatars; and the play had to stand the descent of the deity into it as best it could. Sometimes, as in my case, the author understood the situation and made the best of it. Sometimes, no doubt, the author either did not understand the situation or would not make the best of it. But Tree could not act otherwise than as he did; and his productions represented an output of invention on his part that may have supplied many deficiencies in the plays.

One of his ambitions was to create a Tree Don Quixote. He used to discuss this with me eagerly as a project we might carry out together. "What I see," he said, "is a room full of men in evening dress smoking. Somebody mentions the Don. They begin talking about him. They wonder what he would make of our modern civilization. The back wall vanishes; and there is Piccadilly, with all the buses and cabs coming towards you in a stream of traffic; and with them, in the middle, the long tall figure in armor on the lean horse, amazing, foreign, incongruous, and yet impressive, right in the centre of the picture." "That is really a very good idea," I would say. "I must certainly carry it out. But how could we manage the buses and things?" "Yes," he would go on, not listening to me after my first words of approval: "there you see him going down the mountain-side in Spain just after dawn, through the mist, you know, on the horse, and—"

"And Calvert as Sancho Panza on the ass," I would say. That always surprised him. "Yes," he would say slowly. "Yes. Sancho, of course. Oh, yes." Though he had quite forgotten Sancho, yet, switching instantly over to his Falstaff line, he would begin to consider whether he could not double the two parts, as he doubled Micawber and Peggotty. For your true actor is still what he was in the days of Bottom: he wants to play every part in the comedy.

But the heart of the matter (which I have been coming to slowly all this time) is that the cure for the disease of actor-managership (every author must take that pathological view of it) is actor-author-managership: the cure of Molière, who acted his plays as well as wrote them, and managed his theatre into the bargain. And yet he lasted fifty-one years. Richard Wagner was author-composer-conductor-manager at Bayreuth: a much more arduous combination. Tree should have written his own plays. He could have done so. He had actually begun to do it as Shakespear and Molière began, by tinkering other men's plays. The conflict that raged between him and me at the rehearsals in his theatre would then have taken place in his own bosom. He would have taken a parental pride in other parts beside his own. He would have come to care for a play as a play, and to understand that it has powers over the audience even when it is read by people sitting round a table or performed by wooden marionettes. It would have developed that talent of his that wasted itself in *jeux d'esprit* and epigrams. And it would have given him what he was always craving from authors, and in the nature of the case could never get from them: a perfect projection of the great Tree personality. What did he care for Higgins or Hamlet? His real objective was his amazing self. That also was Shakespear's objective in Hamlet; but Shakespear was not Tree, and therefore Hamlet could never be to Tree what Hamlet was to Shakespear. For with all his cleverness in the disguises of the actor's dressing room, Tree was no mere character actor. The character actor never dares to appear frankly in his own person: he is the victim of a mortal shyness that agonizes and paralyzes him when his mask is stripped off and his cothurnus snatched from beneath his feet. Tree, on the contrary, broke through all his stage disguises: they were his robes of state; and he was never happier than when he stepped in front of the curtain and spoke in his own immensity to the audience, if not as deep calling unto deep (for the audience could not play up to him as splendidly as that), at least as a monarch to his courtiers.

I trust that in the volume of memoirs collected by his equally famous brother Max, who has asked me to contribute this pen-and-ink sketch, he may find his bard, as Elliston found Charles Lamb. It is my misfortune that I cannot do him justice, because, as author and actor, we two were rivals who regarded one another as usurpers. Happily, no bones were broken in the encounter; and if there is any malice in my description of it, I hope I have explained sufficiently to enable the reader to make the necessary allowance and correction.

H. G. WELLS ON THE REST OF US
From The Christian Commonwealth, 19 May 1909

BEFORE everybody breaks out into wrathful denunciation of Wells as being very far from the nice, cheerful, friendly soul they took him to be from his writings, let me complete his lively series of sketches of our friends by adding one of himself.

Wells is a spoiled child. His life has been one long promotion. He was born cleverer than anybody within hail of him. You can see from his pleasant figure that he was never awkward or uncouth or clumsy-footed or heavy-handed as so many quite personable men have been when they were mere cubs. He was probably stuffed with sweets and smothered with kisses until he grew too big to stand it. When they put him to business, he broke away and began teaching other people. He won scholarships, and had hardly turned his success over under his tongue to get the full taste of it when he tried his hand at literature, and immediately succeeded. The world that other men of genius had to struggle with, and which sometimes starved them dead, came to him and licked his boots. He did what he liked; and when he did not like what he had done, he threw it aside and tried something else, unhindered, unchecked, unpunished, apparently even undisliked. In course of time he took to Socialism and joined the Fabian Society, where he was received with a distinguished consideration never accorded by that irreverent body to any mortal before or since. He insulted it freely and proceeded to rearrange it according to his own taste. No pen can describe his conduct during this process. Take all the sins he ascribes to his colleagues: the touchiness of Hyndman, the dogmatism of Quelch, Blatchford's preoccupation with his own methods, Grayson's irresponsibility; add every other petulance of which a spoiled child or a successful operatic tenor is capable; multiply the total by ten; square the result; cube it; raise it to the millionth power and square it again; and you will still fall short of the truth about Wells. Yet, the worse he behaved the more he was indulged; and the more he was indulged the worse he behaved. He literally cost me personally over a thousand pounds hard cash by wasting my time; for it fell to my lot to undo the mischief he did daily. At last he demanded: first, that the order of public meeting should be abolished, and he himself made both chairman and speaker when he addressed the public; and, second, that the Fabian Society should pass a vote, not merely of censure, but of contempt, on its executive committee, in order that its old leaders should be compelled to resign and leave him sole Fabian Emperor. At this point any other man would have been hurled out of the society by bodily violence with heated objurgation. Wells was humbly requested to withdraw his demand, as it was not convenient just then to serve him up Sidney Webb's head on a charger. As a reward for his condescension in complying he was elected to the executive committee nearly at the top of the poll; and I, because I had been the spokesman of our deprecation of the vote of contempt (selected for that job because it was known that I liked him and would let him down easily), was reproached for my brutality to the society's darling. He repaid these acts of faith by refusing to attend committees or do any routine work whatever, and presently resigned, writing a letter for publication at the same time to explain that he had done so because we were a parcel of sweeps.

I never met such a chap. I could not survive meeting such another. I pause to read over this description of him, and am discouraged by its tame inadequacy—its failure to grapple with the outrageous truth.

My consolation is that it does not matter in the least. You can trump up these moral indictments against anybody. I do it only to shew Wells how easy it is. Blatchford, says Wells, is vain. Well, why shouldnt he be? He has done plenty to be vain of. He is a lion who can roar, says Wells; and he wants to roar. I daresay he does. Most men want to do the thing they can do well. If you come to that, Wells wants to write books. Hyndman is spiteful, says Wells. In other words, "this animal is wicked; when he is teased he bites." Grayson, says Wells, is not to be trusted with a horse. Neither were Macaulay and Herbert Spencer. Who wants to trust Grayson with a horse? Wells reminds me of the man who said that farming is impossible in this country because bulls are short-tempered and the weather very changeable. His letter reminds me of a Georgian tract entitled An Examination of the Character of Bonaparte, by a Country Clergyman. The question is, not whether our prominent Socialists are angels or not, but whether they are good enough for a reasonable man to work with. With the single exception of myself, none of us can be described as perfect; and even with me Wells could not work. As to his objection to work with Quelch, that does not matter, as Quelch would not work with him, Quelch's requirements being even sterner than H. G.'s. However, Wells admits that there are three men in the movement of whom he unreservedly approves: Keir Hardie, Ramsay MacDonald, and Philip Snowden. This is a proud day for the three; but let them not be too conceited about it. They have never tried working with Wells; I have. When they do try it, the verdict of the coroner's jury will be justifiable homicide, or else Keir and Mac will be hanged, and Snowden will see nothing but Wells's ghost, with two dirks sticking in it, for the rest of his life. I fancy I see Hodge and

Shackleton—but enough. It is time to draw the moral and conclude.

Nine-tenths of the difficulties that obstruct Socialism and every other advance that requires organization and co-operation consist in the propensity of Englishmen to contradict, insult, and quarrel with one another, and then trump up moral indictments to excuse their manners. Now, there is a point at which a moral indictment may arise to the level of genuine criticism. If Wells feels that he really must point out our faults, let him fire away by all means, provided he takes the work seriously. It is no use telling us that So-and-so is unfit to be a leader because he is spiteful. Napoleon was so spiteful that he kicked Volney in the stomach for saying that France wanted the Bourbons back again; but nobody supposes that Napoleon was an incapable leader on that account. It is no use telling us that Blatchford is vain; he is not half so vain as Julius Cæsar, who nevertheless had some qualifications as a political organizer. All that is like Henley telling us that Stevenson never passed a looking-glass without a glance into it, and that he thought twice before spending sixpence; statements that are true of every man that has lived since looking-glasses and sixpences were invented. It may be necessary to say that a woman is a murderess or a thief; it can never be necessary to call her a female. You may call a man anything except a fellow. The reason is that whereas the question whether a woman is a murderess or not may be of the greatest importance to a movement with which her name is publicly identified, the fact that she is a female is so obvious that it can be expressly stated for no other purpose than to insult her. Similarly, if you call me a liar I may argue the point; but if you call me a creature or a thing, I must either pocket an intentional slight or smite you on the nose. It is like saying that a woman is no better than she ought to be, which is perfectly true of even the best woman in the world, and is for that very reason entirely senseless except as a deliberate insult. Granted that all Wells's rude remarks are true, what then? He might as well say, "There are milestones on the Dover Road; therefore I will go by Folkestone-Boulogne," as say "Hyndman is spiteful; Blatchford is vain; therefore I will go home and write novels and not speak to any of them any more." We are all vain; we are all spiteful. To complain of such things is to complain that the leaves are green and the sky blue.

OSCAR WILDE

A Letter to Frank Harris, published by him in his Life of Wilde, 1918

My Dear Harris:—

Why was Wilde so good a subject for a biography that none of the previous attempts which you have just wiped out are bad? Just because his stupendous laziness simplified his life almost as if he knew instinctively that there must be no episodes to spoil the great situation at the end of the last act but one. It was a well-made life in the Scribe sense. It was as simple as the life of Des Grieux, Manon Lescaut's lover; and it beat that by omitting Manon and making Des Grieux his own lover and his own hero.

Des Grieux was a worthless rascal by all conventional standards; and we forgive him everything. We think we forgive him because he was unselfish and loved greatly. Oscar seems to have said: "I will love nobody: I will be utterly selfish; and I will be not merely a rascal but a monster; and you shall forgive me everything. In other words, I will reduce your standards to absurdity, not by writing them down, though I could do that so well—in fact, *have* done it—but by actually living them down and dying them down."

However, I mustnt start writing a book to you about Wilde: I must just tumble a few things together and tell you them. To take things in the order of your book, I can remember only one occasion on which I saw Sir William Wilde, who, by the way, operated on my father to correct a squint, and overdid the correction so much that my father squinted the other way all the rest of his life. To this day I never notice a squint: it is as normal to me as a nose or a tall hat.

I was a boy at a concert in the Antient Concert Rooms in

Brunswick Street in Dublin. Everybody was in evening dress; and—unless I am mixing up this concert with another (in which case I doubt if the Wildes would have been present)—the Lord-Lieutenant was there with his courtiers in blue facings. Wilde was dressed in snuffy brown; and as he had the sort of skin that never looks clean, he produced a dramatic effect beside Lady Wilde (in full fig) of being, like Frederick the Great, Beyond Soap and Water, as his Nietzschean son was beyond Good and Evil. He was currently reported to have a family in every farmhouse; and the wonder was that Lady Wilde didnt mind—evidently a tradition from the Travers case, which I did not know about until I read your account, as I was only eight in 1864.

Lady Wilde was nice to me in London during the desperate days between my arrival in 1876 and my first earning of an income by my pen in 1885, or rather until, a few years earlier, I threw myself into Socialism and cut myself contemptuously loose from everything of which her at-homes—themselves desperate affairs enough, as you saw for yourself—were part. I was at two or three of them; and I once dined with her in company with an ex-tragedy queen named Miss Glynn, who, having no visible external ears, reared a head like a turnip. Lady Wilde talked about Schopenhauer; and Miss Glynn told me that Gladstone formed his oratorical style on Charles Kean.

I ask myself where and how I came across Lady Wilde; for we had no social relations in the Dublin days. The explanation must be that my sister, then a very attractive girl who sang beautifully, had met and made some sort of innocent conquest of both Oscar and Willie. I met Oscar once at one of the at-homes; and he came and spoke to me with an evident intention of being specially kind to me. We put each other out frightfully; and this odd difficulty persisted between us to the very last, even when we were no longer mere boyish novices and had become men of the world with plenty of skill in social intercourse. I saw him very seldom, as I avoided literary and artistic coteries like the plague, and refused the few invitations I received to go into society with burlesque ferocity, so as to keep out of it without offending people past their willingness to indulge me as a privileged lunatic.

The last time I saw him was at that tragic luncheon of yours at the Café Royal; and I am quite sure our total of meetings from first to last did not exceed twelve, and may not have exceeded six.

I definitely recollect six: (1) At the at-home aforesaid. (2) At Macmurdo's house in Fitzroy Street in the days of the Century Guild and its paper The Hobby Horse. (3) At a meeting somewhere in Westminster at which I delivered an address on Socialism, and at which Oscar turned up and spoke. Robert Ross surprised me greatly by telling me, long after Oscar's death, that it was this address of mine that moved Oscar to try his hand at a similar feat by writing The Soul of Man Under Socialism. (4) A chance meeting near the stage door of the Haymarket Theatre, at which our queer shyness of one another made our resolutely cordial and appreciative conversation so difficult that our final laugh and shakehands was almost a reciprocal confession. (5) A really pleasant afternoon we spent together on catching one another in a place where our presence was an absurdity. It was some exhibition in Chelsea: a naval commemoration, where there was a replica of Nelson's Victory and a set of P. & O. cabins which made one seasick by mere association of ideas. I dont know why I went or why Wilde went; but we did; and the question what the devil we were doing in that galley tickled us both. It was my sole experience of Oscar's wonderful gift as a raconteur. I remember particularly an amazingly elaborate story which you have no doubt heard from him: an example of the cumulation of a single effect, as in Mark Twain's story of the man who was persuaded to put lightning conductor after lightning conductor at every possible point on his roof until a thunderstorm came and all the lightning in the heavens went for his house and wiped it out.

Oscar's much more carefully and elegantly worked out story was of a young man who invented a theatre stall which economized space by ingenious contrivances which were all described.

A friend of his invited twenty millionaires to meet him at dinner so that he might interest them in the invention. The young man convinced them completely by his demonstration of the saving in a theatre holding, in ordinary seats, six hundred people, leaving them eager and ready to make his fortune. Unfortunately he went on to calculate the annual saving in all the theatres of the world; then in all the churches of the world; then in all the legislatures; estimating finally the incidental and moral and religious effects of the invention until at the end of an hour he had estimated a profit of several thousand millions: the climax of course being that the millionaires folded their tents and silently stole away, leaving the ruined inventor a marked man for life.

Wilde and I got on extraordinarily well on this occasion. I had not to talk myself, but to listen to a man telling me stories better than I could have told them. We did not refer to Art, about which, excluding literature from the definition, he knew only what could be picked up by reading about it. He was in a tweed suit and low hat like myself, and had been detected and had detected me in the act of clandestinely spending a happy day at Rosherville Gardens instead of pontificating in his frock-coat and so forth. And he had an audience on whom not one of his subtlest effects was lost. And so for once our meeting was a success; and I understood why Morris, when he was dying slowly, enjoyed a visit from Wilde more than from anybody else, as I understand why you say in your book that you would rather have Wilde back than any friend you have ever talked to, even though he was incapable of friendship, though not of the most touching kindness on occasion.

Our sixth meeting, the only other one I can remember, was the one at the Café Royal. On that occasion he was not too preoccupied with his danger to be disgusted with me because I, who had praised his first plays, handsomely, had turned traitor over The Importance of Being Earnest. Clever as it was, it was his first really heartless play. In the others the chivalry of the eighteenth-century Irishman and the romance of the disciple of Théophile Gautier (Oscar was old-fashioned in the Irish way, except as a critic of morals) not only gave a certain kindness and gallantry to the serious passages and to the handling of the women, but provided that proximity of emotion without which laughter, however irresistible, is destructive and sinister. In The Import-ance of Being Earnest this had vanished; and the play, though extremely funny, was essentially hateful. I had no idea that Oscar was going to the dogs, and that this represented a real degeneracy produced by his debaucheries. I thought he was still developing; and I hazarded the unhappy guess that The Importance of Being Earnest was in idea a young work written or projected long before under the influence of Gilbert and furbished up for Alexander as a potboiler. At the Café Royal that day I calmly asked him whether I was not right. He indignantly repudiated my guess, and said loftily (the only time he ever tried on me the attitude he took to John Gray and his more abject disciples) that he was disappointed in me. I suppose I said, "Then what on earth has happened to you?" but I recollect nothing more on that subject except that we did not quarrel over it.

When he was sentenced I spent a railway journey on a Socialist lecturing excursion to the North drafting a petition for his release. After that I met Willie Wilde at a theatre which I think must have been the Duke of York's, because I connect it vaguely with St Martin's Lane. I spoke to him about the petition, asking him whether anything of the sort was being done, and warning him that though I and Stewart Headlam would sign it, that would be no use, as we were two notorious cranks, and our names would by themselves reduce the petition to absurdity and do Oscar more harm than good. Willie cordially agreed, and added, with maudlin pathos and an inconceivable want of tact: "Oscar was NOT a man of bad character: you could have trusted him with a woman anywhere." He convinced me, as you discovered later, that signatures would not be obtainable; so the petition project dropped; and I dont know what became of my draft.

When Wilde was in Paris during his last phase I made a point of sending him inscribed copies of all my books as they came out; and he did the same to me.

In writing about Wilde and Whistler, in the days when they were treated as witty triflers, and called Oscar and Jimmy in print, I always made a point of taking them seriously and with scrupulous good manners. Wilde on his part also made a point of recognizing me as a man of distinction by his manner, and repudiating the current estimate of me as a mere jester. This was not the usual reciprocal-admiration trick: I believe he was sincere, and felt indignant at what he thought was a vulgar underestimate of me; and I had the same feeling about him. My impulse to rally to him in his misfortune, and my disgust at "the man Wilde" scurrilities of the newspapers, was irresistible: I dont quite know why; for my charity to his perversion, and my recognition of the fact that it does not imply any general depravity or coarseness of character, came to me through reading and observation, not through sympathy. I have all the normal violent repugnance to homosexuality—if it be really normal, which nowadays one is sometimes provoked to doubt.

Also, I was in no way predisposed to like him: he was my fellow-townsman, and a very prime specimen of the sort of fellow-townsman I most loathed: to wit, the Dublin snob. His Irish charm, potent with Englishmen, did not exist for me; and on the whole it may be claimed for him that he got no regard from me that he did not earn.

What first established a friendly feeling in me was, unexpectedly enough, the affair of the Chicago anarchists, whose Homer you constituted yourself by your story called The Bomb, I tried to get some literary men in London, all heroic rebels and sceptics on paper, to sign a memorial asking for the reprieve of these unfortunate men. The only signature I got was Oscar's. It was a completely disinterested act on his part; and it secured my distinguished consideration for him for the rest of his life.

To return for a moment to Lady Wilde. You know that there is a disease called giantism, caused by "a certain morbid process in the sphenoid bone of the skull—viz., an excessive development of the anterior lobe of the pituitary body" (this is from the nearest encyclopedia). "When this condition does not become active until after the age of twenty-five, by which time the long bones are consolidated, the result is acromegaly, which chiefly manifests itself in an enlargement of the hands and feet." I never saw Lady Wilde's feet; but her hands were enormous, and never went straight to their aim when they grasped anything, but minced about, feeling for it. And the gigantic splaying of her palm was reproduced in her lumbar region.

Now Oscar was an overgrown man, with something not quite normal about his bigness: something that made Lady Colin Campbell, who hated him, describe him as "that great white caterpillar." You yourself describe the disagreeable impression he made on you physically, in spite of his fine eyes and style. Well, I have always maintained that Oscar was a giant in the pathological sense, and that this explains a good deal of his weakness.

I think you have affectionately underrated his snobbery, mentioning only the pardonable and indeed justifiable side of it; the love of fine names and distinguished associations and luxury and good manners. You say repeatedly, and *on certain planes*, truly, that he was not bitter and did not use his tongue to wound people. But this is not true on the snobbish plane. On one occasion he wrote about T. P. O'Connor with deliberate, studied, wounding insolence, with his Merrion Square Protestant pretentiousness in full cry against the Catholic. He repeatedly declaimed against the vulgarity of the British journalist, not as you or I might, but as an expression of the odious class feeling that is itself the vilest vulgarity. He made the mistake of not knowing his place. He objected to be addressed as Wilde, declaring that he was Oscar to his intimates and Mr Wilde to others, quite unconscious of the fact that he was imposing on the men with whom, as a critic and journalist, he had to live and work, the alternative of granting him an intimacy he had no right to ask or a deference to which he had no claim. The vulgar hated him for snubbing them; and the valiant men damned his impudence and cut him. Thus he was left with a band of devoted satellites on the one hand, and a dining-out connection on the other, with here and there a man of talent and personality enough to command his respect, but utterly without that fortifying body of acquaintance among plain men in which a man must move as himself a plain man, and be Smith and Jones and Wilde and Shaw and Harris instead of Bosie and Robbie and Oscar and Mister. This is the sort of folly that does not last forever in a man of Wilde's ability; but it lasted long enough to prevent Oscar laying any solid social foundations.

Another difficulty I have already hinted at. Wilde started as an apostle of Art; and in that capacity he was a humbug. The notion that a Portora boy, passed on to T.C.D. and thence to Oxford and spending his vacations in Dublin, could without special circumstances have any genuine intimacy with music and painting, is to me ridiculous. When Wilde was at Portora, I was at home in a house where important musical works, including several typical masterpieces, were being rehearsed from the point of blank amateur ignorance up to fitness for public performance. I could whistle them from the first bar to the last as a butcher's boy whistles music-hall songs, before I was twelve. The toleration of popular music—Strauss's waltzes, for instance—was to me positively a painful acquirement, a sort of republican duty.

I was so fascinated by painting that I haunted the National Gallery, which Doyle had made perhaps the finest collection of its size in the world; and I longed for money to buy painting materials with. This afterwards saved me from starving: it was as a critic of music and painting in The World that I won through my ten years of journalism before I finished up with you on The Saturday Review. I could make deaf stockbrokers read my two pages on music, the alleged joke being that I knew nothing about it. The real joke was that I knew all about it.

Now it was quite evident to me, as it was to Whistler and Beardsley, that Oscar knew no more about pictures than anyone of his general culture and with his opportunities can pick up as he goes along. He could be witty about Art, as I could be witty about engineering; but that is no use when you have to seize and hold the attention and interest of people who really love music and painting. Therefore, Oscar was handicapped by a false start, and got a reputation for shallowness and insincerity which he never retrieved until too late.

Comedy: the criticism of morals and manners *viva voce*, was his real forte. When he settled down to that he was great. But, as you found when you approached Meredith about him, his initial mistake had produced that "rather low opinion of Wilde's capacities," that "deep-rooted contempt for the showman in him," which persisted as a first impression and will persist until the last man who remembers his æsthetic period has perished. The world has been in some ways so unjust to him that one must be careful not to be unjust to the world.

In the preface on education, called Parents and Children, to my volume of plays beginning with Misalliance, there is a section headed Artist Idolatry, which is really about Wilde. Dealing with "the powers enjoyed by brilliant persons who are also connoisseurs in art," I say, "the influence they can exercise on young people who have been brought up in the darkness and wretchedness of a home without art, and in whom a natural bent towards art has always been baffled and snubbed, is incredible to those who have not witnessed and understood it. He (or she) who reveals the world of art to them opens heaven to them. They become satellites, disciples, worshippers of the apostle. Now the apostle may be a voluptuary without much conscience. Nature may have given him enough virtue to suffice in a reasonable environment. But this allowance may not be enough to defend him against the temptation and demoralization of finding himself a little god on the strength of what ought to be a quite ordinary culture. He may find adorers in all directions in our uncultivated society among people of stronger character than himself, not one of whom, if they had been artistically educated, would have had anything to learn from him, or regarded him as in any way extraordinary apart from his actual achievements as an artist. Tartufe is not always a priest. Indeed, he is not always a rascal: he is often a weak man absurdly credited with omniscience and perfection, and taking unfair advantages only because they are offered to him and he is too weak to refuse. Give everyone his culture, and no one will offer him more than his due."

That paragraph was the outcome of a walk and talk I had one afternoon at Chartres with Robert Ross.

You reveal Wilde as a weaker man than I thought him: I still believe that his fierce Irish pride had something to do with his refusal to run away from the trial. But in the main your evidence is conclusive. It was part of his tragedy that people asked more moral strength from him than he could bear the burden of, because they made the very common mistake—of which actors get the benefit—of regarding style as evidence of strength, just as in the case of women they are apt to regard paint as evidence of beauty. Now Wilde was so in love with style that he never realized the danger of biting off more than he could chew: in other words, of putting up more style than his matter would carry. Wise kings wear shabby clothes, and leave the gold lace to the drum major.

I was at your Saturday Review lunch at the Café Royal when Wilde came in just before the trial. He said he had come to ask you to go into the witness box next day and testify that Dorian Gray was a highly moral work. Your answer was something like this: "For God's sake, man, put everything on that plane out of your head. You dont realize what is going to happen to you. It is not going to be a matter of clever talk about your books. They are going to bring up a string of witnesses that will put art and literature out of the question. Clarke will throw up his brief. He will carry the case to a certain point; and then, when he sees the avalanche coming, he will back out and leave you in the dock. What you have to do is to cross to France tonight. Leave a letter saying that you cannot face the squalor and horror of a law case; that you are an artist and unfitted for such things. Dont stay here clutching at straws like testimonials to Dorian Gray. *I tell you I know.* I know what is going to happen. I know Clarke's sort. I know what evidence they have got. You must go."

It was no use. Wilde was in a curious double temper. He made no pretence either of innocence or of questioning the folly of his proceedings against Queensberry. But he had an infatuate haughtiness as to the impossibility of his retreating, and as to his right to dictate your course. Oscar finally rose with a mixture of impatience and his grand air, and walked out with the remark that he had now found out who were his real friends.

What your book needs to complete it is a portrait of yourself as good as your portrait of Wilde. Oscar was not combative, though he was supercilious in his early pose. When his snobbery was not in action, he liked to make people devoted to him and to flatter them exquisitely with that end. Mrs Calvert, whose great final period as a stage old woman began with her appearance in my Arms and the Man, told me one day, when apologizing for being, as she thought, a bad rehearser, that no author had ever been so nice to her except Mr Wilde.

Pugnacious people, if they did not actually terrify Oscar, were at least the sort of people he could not control, and whom he feared as possibly able to coerce him. You suggest that the Queensberry pugnacity was something that Oscar could not deal with successfully. But how in that case could Oscar have felt quite safe with you? You were more pugnacious than six Queensberrys rolled into one. When people asked, "What has Frank Harris been?" the usual reply was, "Obviously a pirate from the Spanish Main."

Oscar, from the moment he gained your attachment, could never have been afraid of what you might do to him, as he was sufficient of a connoisseur in Blut Bruderschaft to appreciate yours; but he must always have been mortally afraid of what you might do or say to his friends.

You had quite an infernal scorn for nineteen out of twenty of the men and women you met in the circles he most wished to propitiate; and nothing could induce you to keep your knife in its sheath when they jarred on you. The Spanish Main itself would have blushed rosy red at your language when classical invective did not suffice to express your feelings.

It may be that if, say, Edmund Gosse had come to Oscar when

he was out on bail, with a couple of first-class tickets in his pocket, and gently suggested a mild trip to Folkestone, or the Channel Islands, Oscar might have let himself be coaxed away. But to be called on to gallop *ventre à terre* to Erith—it might have been Deal—and hoist the Jolly Roger on board your lugger, was like casting a light comedian and first lover for Richard III. Oscar could not see himself in the part.

I must not press the point too far; but it illustrates, I think, what does not come out at all in your book: that you were a very different person from the submissive and sympathetic disciples to whom he was accustomed. There are things more terrifying to a soul like Oscar's than an as yet unrealized possibility of a sentence of hard labor. A voyage with Captain Kidd may have been one of them. Wilde was a conventional man: his unconventionality was the very pedantry of convention: never was there a man less an outlaw than he. You were a born outlaw, and will never be anything else.

That is why, in his relations with you, he appears as a man always shirking action—more of a coward (all men are cowards more or less) than so proud a man can have been. Still this does not affect the truth and power of your portrait. Wilde's memory will have to stand or fall by it.

You will be blamed, I imagine, because you have not written a lying epitaph instead of a faithful chronicle and study of him; but you will not lose your sleep over that. As a matter of fact, you could not have carried kindness further without sentimental folly. I should have made a far sterner summing up. I am sure Oscar has not found the gates of heaven shut against him: he is too good company to be excluded; but he can hardly have been greeted as "Thou good and faithful servant." The first thing we ask a servant for is a testimonial to honesty, sobriety, and industry; for we soon find out that these are the scarce things, and that geniuses and clever people are as common as rats. Well, Oscar was not sober, not honest, not industrious. Society praised him for being idle, and persecuted him savagely for an aberration which it had better have left unadvertized, thereby making a hero of him; for it is in the nature of people to worship those who have been made to suffer horribly: indeed I have often said that if the Crucifixion could be proved a myth, and Jesus convicted of dying of old age in comfortable circumstances, Christianity would lose ninety-nine per cent of its devotees.

We must try to imagine what judgment we should have passed on Oscar if he had been a normal man, and had dug his grave with his teeth in the ordinary respectable fashion, as his brother Willie did. This brother, by the way, gives us some cue; for Willie, who had exactly the same education and the same chances, must be ruthlessly set aside by literary history as a vulgar journalist of no account. Well, suppose Oscar and Willie had both died the day before Queensberry left that card at the Club! Oscar would still have been remembered as a wit and a dandy, and would have had a niche beside Congreve in the drama. A volume of his aphorisms would have stood creditably on the library shelf with La Rochefoucauld's Maxims. We should have missed the Ballad of Reading Gaol and De Profundis; but he would still have cut a considerable figure in the Dictionary of National Biography, and been read and quoted outside the British Museum reading room.

As to the Ballad and De Profundis, I think it is greatly to Oscar's credit that, whilst he was sincere and deeply moved when he was protesting against the cruelty of our present system to children and to prisoners generally, he could not write about his own individual share in that suffering with any conviction or sympathy. Except for the passage where he describes his exposure at Clapham Junction, there is hardly a line in De Profundis that he might not have written as a literary feat five years earlier. But in the Ballad, even in borrowing form and melody from Coleridge, he shews that he could pity others when he could not seriously pity himself. And this, I think, may be pleaded against the reproach that he was selfish. Externally, in the ordinary action of life as distinguished from the literary action proper to his genius, he was no doubt sluggish and weak because of his giantism. He ended as an unproductive drunkard and swindler;

for his repeated sales of the Daventry plot, in so far as they imposed on the buyers and were not transparent excuses for begging, were undeniably swindles. For all that, he does not appear in his writings a selfish or base-minded man. He is at his worst and weakest in the suppressed part of De Profundis; but in my opinion it had better be published, for several reasons. It explains some of his personal weakness by the stifling narrowness of his daily round, ruinous to a man whose proper place was in a large public life. And its concealment is mischievous because, first, it leads people to imagine all sorts of horrors in a document which contains nothing worse than any record of the squabbles of two touchy men on a holiday; and, second, it is clearly a monstrous thing that one of them should have a torpedo launched at him and timed to explode after his death.

Now that you have written the best life of Oscar Wilde, let us have the best life of Frank Harris. Otherwise the man behind your works will go down to posterity as the hero of my very inadequate preface to The Dark Lady of the Sonnets.

INDEX

INDEX

INDEX

INDEX

Tobacco smoking, 103
Tolstoy, Leo, 23, 254-60; trage-
dian or comedian?, 260-66; his
plays, 264-5
Trade unionism, 132
Trafalgar Square, battle of, 204
Tragedy, 261-3
Tragi-comedy, 262-4
Tree, Sir H. Beerbohm, 266-79
Treitschke, Heinrich von, 66
Trevelyan, George, 28
Trotsky, Leo Davidovich, 137
Troubetskoi, 228, 229
Truth, 142; the press and, 35-9
Twain, Mark, 219, 221, 222, 223,
285
Tyler, Thomas, 121

Ugliness, 68
Unitarianism, 148

Vaccination, 99
VIKINGS IN HELGELAND, 170
Volition, 68-9
Volney, Comte de, 282
Voltaire, François M. A. de, 59
Voter, idolatry of the, 253

Wage, a minimum, 150
Wages Fund, 155
Wagner, Richard, 61, 62, 109,
128, 213, 219, 222, 255, 262,
278
Walker, Emery, 55, 172
——, John, 4-6
Walkley, A. B., 146
Walpole, Sir Robert, 93
War, 190

War of 1914-1918, 111-14, 173,
250-52
WAY OF ALL FLESH, 53, 58
Wealth, distribution of, 102
Webb, Philip, 207
——, Sidney, 80, 81, 103, 104,
128, 131, 132, 156, 202, 207,
280
Weismann, August, 70
Wells, H. G., 71, 72, 77, 78, 80,
81, 130, 131, 135, 147, 234, 235;
his Outline of History, 133;
Henry Arthur Jones's book
on, 171-6, 179; his connection
with the Fabian Society, 279-83
WHAT IS ART?, 254
Whistler, James A. M., 221, 223,
288, 290
Whitman, Walt, 220
Whittier, John Greenleaf, 223
Wilde, Lady, 284, 288, 289
——, Oscar, 66, 86, 124, 283-96
——, Sir William, 283
——, Willie, 284, 287, 295
Will, 88; freedom of the, 192
William III, 93
Williams, John, 205
Women, 282
Woodroffe, Sir John, 28
Wordsworth, William, 184
Work craze, 80
WORLD, THE, 29
World, end of the, 156
Wrangel, Peter N., 137, 188

Yellow Press, 73-4

Zola, Émile, 19

THE END